Born in Saskatoon, Saskatchewan, Canada, Allan Moffat won the Australian Touring Car Championship four times, the Sandown 500 six times and the Bathurst 500/1000 four times. He is one of only two drivers to have won The Great Race at Bathurst in both formats—500 miles and 1000 kilometres. He was inducted into the V8 Supercars Hall of Fame in 1999, and became an Australian citizen in 2004. After he retired from racing he became an expert commentator on motor-sport telecasts for Channel Seven, Channel 9 and the ABC.

John Smailes is a journalist, motor-sport commentator, publicist and, until recently, the proprietor of a specialised communications agency. He was co-commentator with Will Hagon on the ABC's national coverage of the Australian Touring Car Championship at the combative height of the Ford versus Holden wars. He is the author of a history of the Confederation of Australian Motor Sport.

CLIMBING THE MOUNTAIN

ALLAN MOFFAT
WITH JOHN SMAILES

ALLEN&UNWIN
SYDNEY • MELBOURNE • AUCKLAND • LONDON

This edition published in 2018
First published in 2017

Allen & Unwin
83 Alexander Street
Crows Nest NSW 2065
Australia
Phone: (61 2) 8425 0100
Email: info@allenandunwin.com
Web: www.allenandunwin.com

A catalogue record for this book is available from the National Library of Australia

ISBN 978 1 76052 819 5

Set in 12.5/18.5 pt Adobe Garamond Pro by Bookhouse, Sydney
Printed and bound in Australia by Griffin Press

10 9 8 7 6 5 4 3 2 1

I would like to dedicate this book to all my fans and all the people who have supported my racing career for so many years.

CONTENTS

1	The Greatest Form 1–2 Ever	1
2	On the Road	19
3	Changing Up	43
4	Allan Moffat Racing	65
5	Hand to Mouth	89
6	The Greatest Trans Am of All	107
7	Ho Ho Ho	137
8	Ford Finale	171
9	Friends and Foes	197
10	Project B52 and Project Phoenix	219
11	Mazda Man	247
12	Brock	281
13	ANZ: Banking on Success	309
14	Gun for Hire	341
15	Obsession and Success	371
16	Rear Vision	395
Acknowledgements		419
Index		422

1

THE GREATEST
FORM 1–2 EVER

THIS IS GOING TO BE MY GREATEST WIN EVER.

Bathurst 1977 and my Falcon coupe is humming like a Pan Am 747 at cruise altitude.

We are 925 kilometres into Australia's 1000-kilometre Great Race, and only my car and its sibling are on the same lead lap.

Peter Brock, my nemesis, fiercest competitor and later to be saviour, is three laps down and charging up through the pack after an uncharacteristic spin and unscheduled pit stops, but with twelve laps to go he isn't going to catch us.

Nothing is going to stop us.

I am the easiest of people on the car. I squeeze the brakes, I stroke the wheel. I'm never aggressive with it. That's how you win Bathurst.

It's the golden era of touring-car racing in Australia. The Ford-versus-Holden battle is drawing huge crowds and creating massive salesroom response. And I'm on top of my game.

Coming up through the Cutting, the aptly named gash in the hillside that marks the steepest part of the 600-metre vertical ascent to the top of Mount Panorama, I tap the brakes to make sure there's pedal pressure for the rush over Skyline and down to Conrod Straight. The next really hard braking point is Forrest's Elbow and, although it's half a circuit away, you need the reassurance.

All okay.

But when I get to the corner—dropping away, downhill—there's nothing.

The pedal goes to the floor.

Smoke pours out of the front right-wheel arch. It's not tyre smoke, because the wheels haven't locked up. It's the brakes quitting.

I have my big moment, use the gearbox, in itself fragile, to slow the car just sufficiently for the corner and then I floor it down Conrod Straight. All these years later I don't recall having a moment of panic or of disappointment. This is time for calculation, for situation assessment.

Pull to the pits? They're at the bottom of the straight, one corner away. Although the crew won't be ready, there's the possibility they can fix it; a brake-pad change takes at least two minutes, a rotor change—that's the whole brake assembly—is longer. That's if everything goes well. I'll lose the lead to my teammates Colin Bond and Alan Hamilton and I'll possibly fall into the clutches of the lead Holden of Peter Janson and Larry Perkins. If things go really badly, maybe even Brock.

Keep going? Twelve laps of Bathurst without brakes. People would say it's impossible. The television commentary is calling: 'The chances of Allan Moffat winning Bathurst are negated. No way Moffat can go on like that.'

That wasn't going to happen.

I lost my first Bathurst in 1969 because the Ford team called me to the pits for an unnecessary tyre change. I won in 1971 because I ignored their call to come to the pits to have track debris removed from my radiator when the team thought it 'might' cause the car to overheat. In both cases I was at the wheel, in control, the only one who really knew what was going on and the only person truly qualified to make a decision.

By the time I reach the drive-in movie theatre, halfway down the country road called Conrod Straight on the way to Murray's Corner, I've made a captain's call.

Coming in is bad. Staying out is good.

The decision has taken less than ten seconds and it's been necessary to make it that fast. Without brakes, from a speed of 250 km/h, I've got to back off half a kilometre earlier for the 90-degree left-hander that leads onto pit straight. The drive-in movie gates will become my new braking marker for the rest of the race.

This Bathurst race was my biggest ever assault on the mountain.

It's my team, supported by Ford, ostensibly through its dealers, but the entire rig—lock, stock and mortgage—is mine. Everything I have in the world is riding on this one race. It's not the first time in my life that's been the case, but this is the big investment, the make-or-break moment. It won't be the end of my motor-racing career if I fail. There are always drives to be had as a gun for hire. But that's not my ambition. I've always wanted more. To be master of my own destiny—and that means you put everything on the line, every time.

I had stolen Colin Bond from the Holden Dealer Team to be my teammate in 1977, a massive coup, earth-shattering to the fans and the two factories, and between us we had swept the floor with the Holden opposition, winning the Australian Touring Car Championship.

I'd secured the services of the US team-management guru Carroll Smith. The man who literally wrote the textbooks on team and race-car preparation had brought his family to Australia on a one-year contract to help turn my already-winning team into a dominant one.

I'd secured the co-driving services of four-times Le Mans 24 Hour winner, Belgium's Jacky Ickx, the best long-distance racer in the world. He had cost me $10,000—in those days, half the price of the house I couldn't afford.

At the last moment, when motorcycle ace Gregg Hansford was injured, I'd drafted Australian Porsche distributor, hill-climb champion and open-wheeler ace Alan Hamilton into the team as Bond's co-driver. A swift and safe pair of hands.

And the cars were sensational. Two brand-new Ford Falcon Superbirds, exquisitely hand-built for the season, fettled by the best and best-drilled team in the business, running on Goodyear rubber brought to Australia by the tyre boss who'd been my guardian angel in motor sport since virtually the outset, Mike Babich.

If ever there was a sweet spot, I'd found it.

I drove to Sydney's Kingsford Smith airport early to pick up Jacky Ickx. Although he was six years younger than me, it was like greeting royalty.

Jacky had won Le Mans four times, the last three years in succession. It wasn't just that he'd won—it was the way he did it. In 1969, his first Le Mans drive and first win in the mighty Ford GT40, he had defied team orders and, instead of participating in the mad run across the track to begin the race, had quietly walked to the car and buckled up properly before starting, dead last, only to go on to win. That year one of the runners was killed on the first lap because he had not done up his belts and was most probably still getting his metabolism under control.

Jacky deserved respect.

He wanted to go straight to Bathurst and we got there before most of the crew.

This would be the first time he'd driven a car like the XC Falcon. He was used to purpose-built, robust race cars that fitted you like a glove and that you could punish to within a lap of their race life. Early in his career, he had raced a Lotus Cortina, just like me, and he had won the Belgian touring-car title in it. But even the Lotus was a thoroughbred compared to the Falcon. As we pulled into the pits at Mount Panorama, I wished I knew the French translation for 'compromise'.

He hated the race seat in our car. It was too broad for his slim racing driver's bum. He tried the seat in the Number Two car and it was just right. I got the crew to swap the seats. It's not something I ever told Colin Bond or Alan Hamilton, who were the drivers of that car. They didn't need to know.

Bathurst is Australia's biggest and most prestigious domestic motor race. That year it attracted a record nineteen international entrants, most of them co-drivers. There were IndyCar winners, touring-car champions from other countries, even our own three-time F1 world champion, Jack Brabham. Holden had launched a new rocket ship: the A9X Torana, the best production car they ever built. It had soundly defeated us on debut at the prelude long-distance race at Melbourne's Sandown Raceway. Despite our runaway success in the touring-car championship sprint races, the A9X was the favourite for Bathurst.

At a motor race, you don't talk to me. I get in a zone. People know that and it's become part of my persona. Some think it's arrogance, others that it's just plain rude. I call it focused.

I like to sit in the race car and think. In the first session of practice on Friday, I had done that so much that my very expensive co-driver was left without a drive. It was frustrating for him, but unnoticed by me. Colin Bond handed over his car so Jacky could get a sighting lap. 'Next time I may as well just come on Saturday,' he said to Colin.

When Jacky finally got in the Number One Falcon, he was back in the pits in a lap.

'Allan,' he said, 'the car has no brakes.'

To say I was alarmed was an understatement. I had him out of the car in an instant and went for my own exploration. A lap later I was back.

'Jacky,' I said, 'the brakes are perfect—the best they've ever been.'

He was quickly coming to terms with compromise.

Unlike the one-lap dash for pole position introduced years later, in 1977 you could qualify for a grid position in any of the Saturday practice sessions. I threw down the gauntlet in the first session, setting a time that stood for pole until the last three laps of the final session. Then Brock, who had been hampered all day by niggling problems, pulled out a blinder and seized pole away. Colin Bond was on track and he responded to take second place on the front row, forcing me one row back.

Brock had this thing called the Brock Crush where he would sprint from the start and establish a gap from which he'd control the race—even in an event as long as Bathurst. It was a mind game. I never believed in it but with Brock you never knew, so, when the flag dropped, I went for the gap between the front-row cars, determined to pass or at least stay with him.

A long-distance race should be run at a long-distance pace but this was a sprint. These days that sort of ten-tenths sprint-race mentality is expected even at Bathurst but, back then, with the cars so fragile, it was rolling the dice. Happily it rolled in Ford's favour.

By lap six, Colin and I were in front: a Ford one–two, both of us former Bathurst winners and understanding what it takes to bring a car home. You should never underestimate the value of race-winning experience. Co-drivers, then, knew the drill. They were unlikely to be asked to equally share the load. If you were a co-driver, you weren't expected to be quite as on the pace. You probably didn't know the car or the track as well as the lead driver. At least one Bathurst race was won by a driver whose partner did just the one obligatory lap required under the rule. Co-drivers could be nine-tenths of effort competitors, not just seat minders, but close, even if your name was Jacky Ickx. It's different now: a co-driver has to be able to pull the same lap times with the same consistency as the lead driver, otherwise the team is just not in the race.

To further reinforce the value of experience, Carroll Smith insisted Colin and I both did double stints. That means when we pulled to the pits for our first stop, after more than 250 kilometres of hard racing, we stayed in the car. Those were the days before cool-suits that pump freezing water through capillaries to keep drivers' body temperatures constant. Cooling air was minimal and at the 1977 race the car-to-pit UHF radios, which had been installed for the very first time for a Bathurst event, universally failed to function, so in the car you were deserted on your own island. It was hot and hard.

Forty laps of leading Bathurst are punishing. Eighty laps are murder. I stayed out to within a minute of the maximum allowable time for one driver without a change and then I handed over to the world's best long-distance driver to do the minimum. My race gloves were shredded and my hands blistered. 'Be careful,' I said to Jacky, 'take it easy on the brakes.'

Colin had handed over to Alan Hamilton three laps earlier, on the same regimen. Each of our co-drivers would do one 40-lap, 250-kilometre stint, then we'd be back in for the finish.

We were looking good. We both kicked back in our caravan and in the spirit of the moment I put a deal to Colin. 'Why don't we swap cars for the last stint? That way we'll be classified as finishers in both cars so we could both win, and we'd spread the odds if something goes wrong.' Colin gave it some thought and then refused. While he was grateful for the offer, he was concerned about the legality.

Drivers, including Brock, had previously been cross-entered in team cars and they had taken the second car when their own had failed. But Colin was unsure if you could do the same swap if both cars were running without problem. It was just the sort of uncertainty that Holden's team manager Harry Firth could protest on, so we stayed where we were.

Out on the track there was a speed disparity between Ickx and Hamilton. Jacky's pace was faster and he was opening a gap on Alan. I guess the term 'go easy' is relative. In Jacky's world, the pace he was running at would have been medium. It was his call. You've got to run at a pace that suits you. Too slow and you lose rhythm. That can be as dangerous as going too fast.

Both Falcons were now two laps ahead of the nearest Holden and things were looking great. We made no attempt to slow Jacky down.

When I took over again with 37 laps, 230 kilometres, to go to the chequered flag the car felt good.

So how, now, was I facing ruin with just a third of that distance to run?

I didn't blame Jacky then and I don't blame him now. In fact I was to have him back as co-driver the following year. But there's no doubt our difference in driving styles and particularly the different way we used the brakes had been contributing factors to the brake wear which now threatened our win.

Controlling the big Falcon without brakes took more than a small amount of finesse. It wasn't so much the braking zones. You can discipline yourself to roll out of the speed earlier and use your gears, sparingly, so that you enter each corner not too fast but not too slow. That's judgement.

Happily, as contradictory as it sounds, the massively fast Bathurst track is not overly taxing on brakes. Going fast for long distances at Mount Panorama is about rhythm and pace, not about hard braking. If this had happened at another track, like Sandown, I couldn't have survived.

The big problem was lapped traffic. Bathurst in 1977 was open to smaller capacity cars with huge speed differentials. If one of the tiddlers got it wrong, they could carry you off. It required immense anticipation, even more so without brakes.

Carroll Smith was on to it. Although we could not communicate by radio, he knew that there was no way I was pitting, but he had the crew on standby.

Colin was closing rapidly on me, making up the ground that Hamilton had lost to Ickx. It was then that Carroll did something that was sensible and in accordance with my obvious wishes. He hung out a pit board that read 'Form 1–2 finish'. Seven years earlier my then Ford teammate Bruce McPhee had received a similar order from team boss Al Turner, dictating that he hold back in second while I took my first Bathurst win. But this was different: the board was calling for 'Formation'.

That had never been done before in Australia.

Ford had tried something similar at Le Mans in 1966 with its GT40s and it had come unstuck. They had dictated their two dominant lead cars to cross the line together, share victory and create a huge publicity coup. But French officials outfoxed them, declaring after the race that the winner would be determined by the distance they had covered—in other words by the few metres that separated the two cars on the starting grid.

So Carroll was being very specific: 'Form 1–2'. I was to win; Colin was to come second.

Can you imagine how Colin felt? I was dropping back to him at a huge rate, running at least ten seconds a lap off the pace. He had won Bathurst on debut for Holden in 1969. I had won it for the first time, for Ford, in 1970, and when you're a racing driver you just want to win again and again. Both of us craved this win and this race was his for the taking.

But we had established precedent all year.

When he joined me, it was for more money than he had ever earned at Holden—the whole house, not just half of it—and we'd done a deal to pool our prize money and then share it, admittedly disproportionately, 70 per cent to me and 30 per cent to him. (I was, after all, taking the financial risk.) The caveat was I was the team owner and leader and, barring stopping, would be the first of us to cross the line.

All season long Colin had stuck with the deal. In the touring-car title, where we dominated, I would take the lead and he'd be my wingman, maybe even dropping back to play with the Toranas before coming back up to me at the finish.

But this was a margin call.

I was obviously wounded. If I had to defend my lead I couldn't do it. But I hadn't stopped and that was the kernel of our deal.

I reversed onto him with three laps to go. He was not pushing to catch me; I was falling back.

And that, to my incredible relief, was where he stayed, right on my flank.

So much was riding on this. The recently knighted Sir Brian Inglis, the president of Ford Australia, was in my pit along with his top brass. The prime minister, Malcolm Fraser, was on the Hardie-Ferodo balcony with the trophy. My wife, Pauline, was perched on the pit wall, on the stop watches, and in charge of the bank account that had been decimated for this moment.

'Down the straight they go,' called Evan Green on the national Channel Seven telecast. 'Cars one and two. A demonstration of the crushing victory to Allan Moffat and the Moffat Ford Dealer Team.'

Into the last corner Colin ranged up alongside—his moment of truth. I looked across at him, telepathically willing him to back off. He was on the inside, perfectly positioned. I just got the car stopped around the outside and then lined up for the chequered flag. It was in that final 100 metres, driving into the setting sun, that I had confirmed what I'd always known: he was a gentleman. The race timing said it all. Moffat/Ickx a race time of 6 hours 59 minutes 0.8 seconds; Bond/Hamilton 6 hours 59 minutes 0.9 seconds.

The formation-finish picture—Car One in the lead, Car Two on its flank—has become one of the iconic images of Bathurst, in fact of all Australian motor sport.

On the podium, the Hardie-Ferodo balcony, the prime minister described it as a 'long and hard race'. He didn't know the half of it. 'Enormous congratulations to Allan Moffat,' he said.

If only it had ended there.

That Bathurst win was to take me to the heights of elation and lead me into the depths of despair.

Connections of Colin Bond were to pursue me for a greater share of the prize money. Although I'd paid out for second place, which was in excess of our pooled prize-money agreement, they felt that Colin's magnanimous gesture was worth more. The argument went on for years and, although Colin got a result, the lawyers took most of it. I'm not sure Colin would have pressed the issue. Much later in our lives we both agreed the 'Form 1–2' was worth more than any money.

'If I'd passed Moffat and taken the win a minute ahead of him, and someone years later had asked, "Who won Bathurst '77?", the first guess would be "Brock—doesn't he always win?"' Colin said with his cackling laugh, long after the dust had settled. 'But the formation finish created a milestone in motor racing. No one will ever forget it, or who came first and second.'

My bigger disappointment was to come two days after the race.

I'd been partying in Sydney, naturally enough, when I got the call to Ford's headquarters in Melbourne for a boardroom lunch. Ford was a different place in 1977 to the one I'd joined in 1969. At the beginning, we were all swamped in the enthusiasm that came right from the top, the charismatic American managing director Bill Bourke, as he strove firstly to save Ford's

Australian outpost from extinction and secondly to drive it to market leadership. The feeling was that money was no object, although clearly it was. But you didn't care. You just powered on against all odds. Testosterone ruled. It wasn't just about motor racing. This was the golden age, where performance cars dictated a car company's reputation. We were all on a mission to make Ford Number One.

After Ford officially withdrew from motor racing in 1974, a result of political pressure and a changing corporate ethic, the company continued to support me through a back door, but it was comparatively hand to mouth and it was a difficult situation for both of us, with factions inside the company forever questioning my value to the corporation.

Surely 1977 would change that. I'd delivered them the Australian Touring Car Championship and the best Bathurst win ever. 'Win on Sunday, sell on Monday' had never been more real.

Sir Brian Inglis was at the head of the table. I was alongside him. His marketing director Max Gransden was on his other side. Sir Brian gently tapped his glass with his knife and called the room to order. He made a wonderful speech about me and about Ford's gratitude. Then he reached into his pocket and pulled out a small sealed envelope, which he handed to me.

I firmly believe there are two voices in my head and, while I've always relied on both of them, I follow the advice of only one. One is the tearaway that says: 'Go for it'. The other is the voice of reason that says: 'Caution'.

This time 'Caution' won. Instead of opening the envelope, I slipped it in my pocket and made an equally gracious speech thanking Ford and its management team for their support. Then as soon as I could I sprinted for the car park and tore it open. I was thinking $50,000, maybe $100,000—something that wouldn't match my outlay but would still be a fitting reward for the best brand awareness and dealer motivation you could deliver. Better still, it would be a harbinger of opportunity, a reinforcement of my future.

The cheque was for $1000.

Ford's Bathurst winning bonus didn't even cover the cost of the after-party.

It was at that moment that I knew my time with this particular branch of the Blue Oval was running out and, as enjoyable as it had been, it would be in my best interests to start looking elsewhere.

2

ON THE ROAD

IT'S THE SUMMER OF 1964, END OF JUNE, AND I'M HANGING OFF THE CHAIN-
wire pit fence at the Watkins Glen motor-race track in New York State. On the other side of the fence is the Team Lotus paddock area, situated directly behind their pit. The works Lotus Cortina saloon-car team is contesting the fifth round of the US Road Racing Championship and I've driven 400 kilometres from my home in Toronto on a mission to stake my claim to a motor-racing career. It's a big ask, because I know absolutely no one, have next-to-no experience and, seriously, have no prospects.

I'm a door-to-door pots-and-pans salesman, 24 pushing 25—which is far too old to start up a race-driving career—and, as the hot summer's day drifts by, you'd forgive me for wondering what the hell I'm doing here. But I don't think that. All my life I've been single-minded, driven by an ambition I just can't explain.

Three weeks before, I'd had a first attempt at making contact. This time I'd driven 800 kilometres to the Indianapolis 500, America's and at the time the world's greatest motor race. It was the first motor race I'd ever attended in the USA and I'd bought a ticket in the grandstand opposite the pits. Just me and

200,000 of my closest friends. But, the night before the big race, I'd used my Australian motor-racing licence to talk my way into the official Gasoline Alley cocktail party. For two hours I worked that room—selling pots and pans makes you resilient—but to no avail. There's not much a Canadian with a handful of Australian races under his wheels can add to a Brickyard conversation. And, besides, Team Lotus wasn't there—at least not that I could see. No Jimmy Clark, no Dan Gurney, no Colin Chapman. They were the faces I'd know from the magazines. Anyone else would have to have been wearing a name badge.

Next day, two laps into the greatest motor-racing spectacle on Earth, Eddie Sachs and Dave MacDonald died in a fiery seven-car crash just 400 metres from my grandstand seat.

MacDonald hit the wall in an ungainly US-built rear-engine car, burst into flames and cannoned into the path of the field. Sachs went for the space between MacDonald and the wall and became a fireball too. Jack Brabham in his Cooper-Offy just blasted through the flame, accelerating strongly so the airflow would extinguish the fire that engulfed him.

I recall the organisers handled the incident politely, covering the scene with tarpaulins.

In the 90-minute break before racing resumed, we heard over the PA: 'It is with deepest regret that we make this announcement. Driver Eddie Sachs was fatally injured in the accident on the main straightaway.' (MacDonald was to die later from his injuries.)

That led to an incredible, impromptu, eulogy by radio network anchor Sid Collins: 'There's not a sound. Men are taking off their hats. People are weeping, over three hundred thousand fans here; not moving, disbelieving. Some men try to conquer life in a number of ways. These days of our outer-space attempts, some men try to conquer the universe. Race drivers are courageous men who try to conquer life and death, and they calculate their risks. And in our talking with them over the years, I think we know their inner thoughts in regards to racing: they take it as part of living. No one is moving on the race track. They're standing silently. A race driver who leaves this Earth mentally when he straps himself into the cockpit to try what for him is the biggest conquest he can make, is aware of the odds; and Eddie Sachs played the odds . . . We're all speeding towards death at the rate of sixty minutes every hour. The only difference is we don't know how to speed faster, and Eddie Sachs did . . . Eddie Sachs exits this Earth in a race car. And knowing Eddie, I assume that's the way he would have wanted it.'

In motor racing, more then than now, accidents happen. Appalling as the sight had been, I didn't know the guys so I was somewhat detached.

My mood wasn't helped by the fact that Scotsman Jim Clark, who'd started from pole position in his rear-engine Lotus 34 Ford, was out after 47 laps, having led fourteen of them. His rear tyre delaminated and that broke his suspension, dropping the little Lotus to the ground like a broken stick insect, with Jimmy working all his magic to keep it under control at upwards of 250 km/h as it danced around with sparks flying from underneath and the wall getting perilously close.

That summer Jim Clark, in motor-racing terms, was almost as big in the USA as the Beatles. The Fab Four had flown into

New York for the first time in February and sung 'I Wanna Hold Your Hand' in front of 73 million viewers on the *Ed Sullivan Show*. Jim had come second at Indy the year before, his race heard by a radio audience almost as big. In 1964 Indy was televised for the first time. It was a closed-circuit broadcast played into cinemas across the land. Jim's irregular appearances in the USA in Indy, sports- and touring-car races electrified motor racing at a time when it was drawing huge and growing crowds. Jim was just three years older than me, and he'd done a lot more in his life. He wasn't exactly a hero; I've never really had those. He was more a benchmark really, an aspiration.

I thought he'd be at Watkins Glen. But Team Lotus, working under contract to Ford's European car division in Detroit, was rotating drivers through a variety of commitments; that weekend the team drivers were Britain's Sir John Whitmore and Mike Spence—who also was to die at Indianapolis, just four years later.

But I was a long way separated from the drivers and they weren't my target anyway. I wanted to meet the mechanics and maybe, if I could, team management. My goal wasn't to present my racing credentials. In fact, I'd resolved not to tell anyone I'd ever raced a car. That's a sure way to be dismissed as a wannabe. My tactic was to simply get a start: to do anything the team asked, in order to get on the inside.

My place on the fence was right next to the water tap. Team Lotus mechanics, dressed in their British racing green overalls, would come and go, cleaning parts or simply freshening up. It was a bit like being at the zoo. People on my side of the fence could peer into the pit to see the cars being worked on and maybe even catch a glimpse of a driver. Spectators, too, would come and go. There's just so much time you can spend watching the same monkeys. But I stayed . . . and stayed. And at 4.30 in the afternoon one of the mechanics took some kind of interest in me. A 'g'day' turned into an invitation to come and have a closer look at the cars at the end of the race meeting.

At that moment my motor-racing career began, and my life changed for ever.

I was born in Saskatoon in the wheat-belt province of Saskatchewan along the Trans-Canada Yellowhead Highway, the first of three sons of Arthur Wilfred and Evelyn Anne Moffat, on 10 November 1939, two months to the day after Canada entered World War II. My grandpa, Dad's father, had emigrated to Canada from Scotland and had decided the only way to make guaranteed money in a gold rush was to sell gold pans. Grandpa opened a machinery shop and built a wheat silo in a whistle-stop town where the trains only came to a halt to receive the grain. Same idea, different gold. But it worked fine.

Dad loved the machinery side of the business, which is why by the time I was born he wasn't working with Grandpa but was already a rising executive with one of Canada's true manufacturing success stories, Massey-Harris. The Massey family made its considerable fortune working the same principle as my grandpa.

In 1847 Daniel Massey began making some of the world's first mechanical threshers. By the 1930s Massey-Harris had become an international conglomerate, responsible among other things for introducing the world's first self-propelled combine harvesters and the world's first four-wheel-drive tractors.

If Canada hadn't already had a royal family, the Masseys would have been it. They pretty much funded all cultural and educational development in Toronto, where we eventually lived after spending several years moving through Massey outposts across Canada. Vincent Massey became Governor General of Canada. The wild child of the family, Raymond, went to Hollywood, played Sherlock Holmes in the first 'talkie' movies and was so cool he had a cocktail named in his honour.

It was natural that Massey-Harris should support the World War II effort, as reluctant as Canada was to enter the conflict. They made tanks and, ironically, tank destroyers, howitzer guns, anti-aircraft guns and tractor-tugs to haul aircraft around. Dad was in the thick of it, prevented from entering active war service because he was an important part of an essential industry.

I was proud of my dad, so much so that, at age five, I decided to visit him at the factory, several suburbs away. The great trek took me across railway lines and through a timber mill where an active buzz saw presented a daunting roadblock until I worked up the courage to jump across it. It was the sound of the buzz saw that scared me: the fearful, flailing noise. I was to hear it once more in my life at a moment that changed the trajectory of my motor-racing career.

The steps of the high-security factory looked like a stairway to heaven and at the top there was Dad, alerted by, I guess, my mother. For them, it was the last straw. I had already escaped from school and been brought back by two senior students, one on each side of me. I was also something of a regular as the tail-gunner of the armed forces groups that marched up our streets. Mum and Dad didn't want to overly curb my spirit but they did want to keep me safe. So they devised a long leash that clipped onto a sort of dragline that was part of our clothes line. I could run up and down, explore in the backyard but no longer could I roam free.

A little later, their concern was brought tragically home. My middle brother Gordon and I were born pretty close to each other, fourteen months apart. Our baby brother Terry came along later. By then I had a paper run: another adventure with 100 papers delivered each morning, even in snow. I used to stack the papers up front of the handlebars for easy throwing and there was room for Terry to sit on a rack on the back. He was a great kid, and he loved being out with his big brother. Our home had one of those typical North American cellars, a door opening from the kitchen down stairs to the furnace and laundry beneath. One day while Gordon and I were at school Terry found the door open and stumbled on the top step. Our mum was below but there was nothing she could do. He died at her feet.

I suppose at the time we were counselled, although I don't recall it and I'm not sure it would have been called that in those days. But afterwards we never spoke of Terry. It was as if he'd just gone away. I can't imagine what his death must have done to my mum, but in our family the concept of support was a relative term, especially from Dad. He was so busy in his job that there wasn't a lot of time for a conventional father–son relationship.

That, along with the constant moves, tended to toughen you up, and also to mould your character.

By the time I was sixteen I'd been to more schools than some kids have had hamburgers. For me there wasn't a lot of socialising. The number of times I went out on a Friday night as a teenager I could count on the fingers of two hands. It wasn't that I was antisocial or on the other hand that I was lonely. I was just who I was—capable of walking a straight line and not too concerned about any distractions.

I wasn't a pushover. At one school three guys decided to straighten out the new kid and started to knock me about. I went at one of them not with a defensive fist but with a deliberately aimed crooked-elbow into his face. He went down hard and the other two ran off. That little act didn't end with a trip to the headmaster. Instead I was promoted to quarterback in the football team. Same with the ice-hockey squad. I was never a star but at least I didn't fall on my behind. I wish I could say the same thing academically. My grades were at best mid-field, partly because my way of doing things didn't suit the schools' way. It may also have had something to do with my eyesight. In my mid-teens I started to wear trifocals to improve short, medium and long vision and they have become something of a trademark in my career. My best subject was geography, which was just as well as the Moffat family entered the next phase of Dad's career.

In 1953 Dad and two or three other Massey heavies flew to London for merger and takeover talks. When they came back, the company was Massey-Harris-Ferguson, soon to be shortened to Massey Ferguson. It was the start of an international acqui-sition program and for Dad the opportunity to become one of the seriously senior people in the colonies. Within months we were heading for South Africa. Dad went first. Mum, Gordon and I followed.

It was my first-ever time on a big plane: no jets, just propellers. We flew from Toronto to London, then south to Rome with a visit to the Vatican, then onto Khartoum for another overnighter before dropping into Johannesburg. Even then it was a big city, but that wasn't our destination. Dad's car and driver picked us up for the 70-kilometre journey south-west to Vereeniging or, more correctly, to our company estate outside the industrial city, where we were greeted by our African maid and two garden boys. It was going to be a different life.

My first car was a 1935 flathead Ford V8—the hot-rodders' special—but my first motorised transport was a two-wheeled two-stroke scooter that I used to ride from home to the General Smuts High School. Under-aged and unlicensed—you could do that in South Africa in those days. I learned to drive in a brand-new Chevy 6 pick-up truck on the nursery farm of a school friend. The flower farm was a big deal, servicing most of Johannesburg, so the driving was serving a real purpose for my schoolmate's family as we moved produce and equipment around the acreage. I never drove it on the highway, never threw it sideways on the dirt roads, never sped. I was there to do a job and my single-mindedness curbed my boyish enthusiasm.

Different thing with the flathead Ford. That became effect-ively my first race car. In the middle of the night we'd line up,

Le Mans-style, and race to the next roundabout. And we were never caught and never hurt.

I bought the Ford for $20 while still at school, hauled it home and spent two years working on it before I got to drive it. It was a 221 Fordor with bench seats, transverse leaf springs—which made things interesting on every corner as it tried to flip on its side—and its side valve V8 engine was the one all hot-rodders craved. For a young man who didn't enjoy reading, I surprised myself by devouring workshop manuals. I read about this thing called a master cylinder and went looking for it. I figured as the 'master' it had to be the most important cylinder of all. But it turned out to be part of the brake system. Go figure.

The whole Ford experience taught me so much about cars and mechanicals, and that really helped my race career. I was never 'just' a driver. My mechanical knowledge and my desire to always make my cars better was my edge. Much later on, some people would comment on my patience—at how long I could spend at a test day chasing a minute advantage that others might make up for with natural driving ability. The inference was that perhaps I wasn't as naturally talented as others, that I had to make up for lack of skill. That's rubbish. I'm not lacking in innate ability but, simply put, if you've maximised the car, then you'll always go faster.

The General Smuts High School was quite an eye-opener. Apartheid, the enforced separation of blacks and whites, had been declared in 1948 by hardline Afrikaners. Prime Minister Jan Smuts had lost the federal election and his leadership by taking a more moderate approach. He died just two years later, while continuing to work for reconciliation. Apartheid was happening all around us, but it just wasn't on a teenager's radar. Just up the road, a manufactured town, Sharpeville, was being promoted as a municipality to provide better housing for Africans. In reality it was a relocation centre to move blacks away from Vereeniging. The conditions were pretty horrible. In 1960 it became the scene of the Sharpeville Massacre when 69 black people were killed and 180 wounded by police during the Pan Africanist Congress protest, in which black Africans burnt the 'passports' that restricted them from going into certain areas.

But I knew nothing of Sharpeville and we had left South Africa by 1960.

Perhaps I could have been more observant, more socially aware, but for me there were only two class distinctions: the English and the Afrikaners. There were no blacks or coloureds at our school and they weren't really part of our lives. Segregation of a sort did exist though. One block of the school was dedicated to English speakers and the other to Afrikaans. We crossed paths only when we attended each other's language sessions, which became my undoing as we approached matriculation. I could speak Afrikaans pretty well but I couldn't write it, and without written ability I wasn't going to graduate.

Outside school, and even in the common areas, the Englishers and Afrikaners got on well. We had one shared headmaster, an Afrikaner, and for some reason, unfathomable, he elected me head prefect. It didn't last long. We were on a school excursion when he came to me in our train carriage, highly agitated and demanding to know if I was aware of what was going on in the carriage behind: 'Some of the girls and boys are kissing,' he spat. 'I'll have to put a stop to it. And by the way you're fired as head prefect.' It had apparently been my job to segregate the sexes and it was downhill from there. Pretty soon I was on watch-list for caning, only two at a time across the backside from a wicked piece of birch, while some of my classmates got six. But it was enough for me to hate that guy. It wasn't just the hurt; it was the humiliation.

My solace was the flathead Ford. It could have been a great father-and-son project but on the weekends Dad would disappear to the golf course. He did surprise me by having an entire workshop bench, complete with a vice, delivered to our estate. I loved working with my hands and I took great delight in it. It wasn't as if he didn't notice and didn't care. There was just this giant disconnect that characterised our entire lives.

As I pulled down the Ford, I struck up a friendship with the local spare-parts shop owner. You wouldn't have called it a speed shop, even though the intention was to go faster. If you worked the 'Flatty' hard, you could get a pretty reliable 80 horsepower. Doesn't sound like much today, but it was something like a 30 per cent leap over standard and it made the thing a rocket. It taught me a big lesson though: it's always best to get the handling and braking right, as well as the horsepower.

The spares-shop bloke knew I was serious, which is why, one day in 1956, he invited me to my first motor-race meeting. It's a stretch to call the now-defunct Grand Central Racetrack, north of Johannesburg, en route to Pretoria, anything more than a club circuit. It was first built in the mid-1930s by a group of wealthy enthusiasts as a combined airfield and race track. We drove up there in my friend's Triumph TR2, resplendent in British racing green, with the ragtop down, of course. For its time, the sports-car version of the Standard Vanguard was pretty advanced, with coil-sprung independent front suspension absolutely hamstrung by its live axle leaf-sprung rear. The back end just wasn't capable of keeping up with the front. Or to put it another way, the tail was always wagging the dog. Still it was good enough in competition form to claim first and second in the 1954 RAC Rally. In all honesty I think I enjoyed the ride up and back more than the race meeting itself.

The track was pretty flat, as you'd expect from an airstrip. It was 3.4 kilometres around with six corners, a lot of run-off areas, and the advantage for spectators like us was that we could get close to the action and into the pits. It was a mixed bag of competition cars. For example, the main race that day was claimed by a home-made Ford Mercury 4200 from a proper D-type Jaguar, which in those days was worth next to nothing at the end of its Continental competition life but which today can fetch up to $20 million. It was the first time I'd seen a D-type but, honestly, the privilege of being that close to a Le Mans winner evaded me. The D-type was white with blue stripes and it was driven by a big man wearing white overalls, a flat cap and a kidney belt. Turns out he was Jimmy de Villiers, the Rhodesian champion. That evaded me too. I came home that night with no particular desire to go motor racing.

Besides, there were more important agenda items. University was the family's expectation of me . . . no excuses. At the General

Smuts High School I'd passed all but one matriculation subject: Afrikaans. So I was put on a plane back to Canada to matriculate. Wrong: language was a requirement there too, and I bombed French. Back to South Africa briefly, on a mission of the heart, but the girl I'd been seeing, Evelyn, same name as my mum, had hooked up with an Afrikaner in my absence, so it was a big fail all round.

And then Dad was transferred to Australia.

In 1955 Massey Ferguson had bought the Australian company Sunshine Harvester. Almost a century before, H.V. McKay had invented the stripper harvester and he built on that breakthrough to create the largest implement factory in the southern hemisphere. In fact it was so big that the residents of Braybrook Junction in Melbourne's west, where the plant was located, voted to change the name of their suburb to Sunshine in honour of the harvester. Throughout World War II, while Massey-Harris was building weapons in Canada, H.V. McKay was making farm machinery to ship to England to help in wartime food production.

Dad took on a massive undertaking as marketing director and, when his family arrived, he already had a plan for his number one son. First stop was school, with intensive coaching in the evenings. Two months later, with no second language requirements, I'd matriculated, finally successful after three attempts in three different continents. Then it was off to work. Yet again Dad had a plan. He'd arranged for me to start a marketing cadetship at Volkswagen Australia with a requirement that I undertake a part-time bachelor's degree at the newly opened

Monash University. Simple. Career settled. Stick with it and 30 years from now you'll end up just like your dad.

In 1959 Australia was becoming a car-making powerhouse. In fact it was making more cars than Japan. It was a Holden-led charge. General Motors was building more than 100,000 FC Holdens a year, with an almost 45 per cent share of the market. Ford was second on 15 per cent. Volkswagen was providing counterpoint, proving through victories in various long-distance motor-sport events that a light car like the Beetle could handle the most punishing of outback roads. VW began local assembly at a purpose-built factory at Clayton, south of the city. By the time I got there, the local state distributors had come to an agreement with VW AG (Germany) to fund full local production with better than 90 per cent local content.

It was a heady place to be. George Reynolds—who'd soon win his class in the Armstrong 500 at Phillip Island with Jim McKeown in a VW 1200, and then two years later win the Bathurst 500 outright in a Ford Cortina GT with Bob Jane—was a regular visitor, courtesy of his Round Australia Trial ties with the factory. But people like him were way above my status. The four members of the first intake of marketing cadets were pen-pushers, occasionally sent to the airport to pick up visiting dealers and to take them on tours of the factory. My closest cadet colleague was Gordon Bingham, who went on to become something of a visionary in the auto industry, heading VW's Porsche Audi Division in the USA and then joining the management team that started BMW of North America. He ended up owning a bank.

Life was good. Spurred by my South African experience and with the grand sum of £18 salary a week in my pocket, I bought a second-hand red Triumph TR3A on the never-never. I was living with my parents in Toorak and it wasn't a hardship. At least not until Dad was posted back to Canada. It was early 1962 and I didn't know how hard it was going to get.

The option was there for me to travel back with them but, for so many reasons, Australia had become my home. I was 22, well capable of looking after myself and I elected to stay on. The family provided me with an emergency airline ticket, just in case.

First thing I did was move into the single-room flat of a nice Yugoslavian landlady, Julie, and her husband Zorro. The next thing I did was give up studying—a big mistake because, when I went into the next exam, there was not a lot on the paper I understood. The repercussions would come later.

I was in the cadet office at VW one day when the door opened and Anne, the secretary for the heavies one floor up, asked if she could see me in the corridor. Anne was way more than just attractive and I was bowled over when she asked me ever so nicely if I'd be kind enough to escort her to a gathering at the local car club that Friday night. 'Put it down to the TR3,' I thought, but it turned out Anne owned an MGA as well as having a boyfriend who couldn't make it that night. The reason she wanted me along was because of the six o'clock swill.

Buying alcohol after 6 p.m. was illegal in those days so the car club boys tended to stash a lot away and then binge drink it, which made for some pretty rough company. At the car club function, two local heroes had already spotted Anne. I got her out of there pretty quickly but not before both she and I had signed up for a track day at the newly opening Calder Raceway, north of the city at Diggers Rest.

Calder had started out as a dirt track carved out of a paddock to let a few local lads let off steam. But in 1961 things got serious, and the first proper race meeting was held on the almost exactly 1.6-kilometre bitumen track in January 1962. It was run by the Australian Motor Sports Club, an organisation founded by members of the 750 cc Car Club to reboot motor racing after World War II. The club was headed by Maurie Monk, who would also become the first president of the Confederation of Australian Motor Sport (CAMS) in 1953.

I turned up for the drive day in the TR, with not a lot of preparation completed: I'd packed the hood away and laid the windscreen flat on the bonnet for better aerodynamics. In those days Calder was two straights joined by a squiggle. What could go wrong?

Into the first corner I braked, turned right, kept winding on steering lock then booted the throttle, unleashing most of the TR's massive 95 hp. Instead of bounding down the back straight as intended, the Triumph kept turning right with the back wheels rapidly overtaking the fronts. I'd spun on my very first corner.

That day I guess I got about a dozen laps in. Not a lot, but then there wasn't a lot of help either. Now, people who attend try-and-drive experiences have instructors, marshals and mentors made up of senior drivers happy to share their knowledge. I can't remember anyone even talking to me.

But somehow or other the lightning came. I don't know how it happened or what it was. I just knew this was what I wanted to do, maybe for the rest of my life.

In March 1962 I went to the very first race meeting at Sandown International Raceway, in the outer Melbourne suburb of Springvale, the 3.1-kilometre motor-racing circuit built around a planned horseracing track that would not be completed for another three years. As much as I would have liked to have gone as a driver, that was beyond me. But I achieved something almost as good. I became a member of Stirling Moss's pit crew.

The feature race was the Craven Filter International Trophy for Formula Libre Cars and the field was full of the world's best: Australia's own world champion Jack Brabham, Jim Clark, Bruce McLaren, the Woolworth's heir Lance Reventlow and Chuck Daigh both in Scarabs, John Surtees and, of course, Stirling, winner of the 1956 Olympic Australian Grand Prix at Albert Park.

Organisers called for volunteers to help time each of the internationals. I leapt at the chance, which is how I came to be perched on the top of Stirling's pit counter in white overalls, clutching a hand-wound stopwatch, watching the best in the world fight it out. Brabham won that day by just 0.8 seconds from Surtees, McLaren and Daigh, with Moss fifth ahead of Jim Clark. The first true local was Bill Patterson, three laps behind Jack.

I never got to talk to Stirling. I do recall him stepping from a white limo in the pits, shirtless as was his wont, accompanied by not one, not two, but three exceptionally attractive girls. That race meeting was just one month before Stirling's near-fatal crash at Goodwood in Britain that ended the motor-racing career of the man dubbed the best never to win the world title.

Sandown excited me beyond my own expectation. The sheer professionalism of those teams, even then, was inspirational. I watched how deliberately the two or three mechanics worked around Stirling's car. He was every bit the well-defined international driver. Nothing happened accidentally.

I entered every race meeting in Victoria I could. I persuaded Julie and Zorro to let me turn their driveway into a workshop, complete with block and tackle, to remove the engine. I worked out cunning ways to disguise the car's road registration because the hire-purchase agreement expressly prohibited motor racing. I developed a pile of excuses for non-payment of the monthly instalments because I was so overcommitted financially that repayments weren't always possible.

And I wasn't even winning.

Nor was I garnering that much attention. Here's a race report from *Racing Car News*, May 1962:

In Event 10 John Skipper won in the Allard from A. Moffat's TR3A. Frank White (MGA Twin Cam) scrambled through the field to pip Anne Bennett's MGA Coupe on the line for third place. Notable drive, her first in competition, from Anne Bennett a young (20 years) tall and attractive lass from

Seaford who showed she really knows how to handle a car. We hope to see more of her!

Anne? What about me?

Frankly I wasn't doing badly. More often than not I'd finish on the podium, at least in my unmodified sports-car class. And being acutely aware of the limitations of the car I was driving, I'd take some satisfaction from finishing third behind Murray Carter's Corvette and Wes Nalder's Jaguar.

Motor sport was a big deal in Melbourne in the 1960s, far more than it seems to be today with so many other distractions. Getting your driver's licence on your qualifying birthday was a rite of passage, and meeting and helping your mates with their cars most weekends was an obligation.

Although I was something of a loner, there was a circle of like-minded people destined to become important parts of motor sport and of my life. People like Jon Leighton, a bit older than me, but a guy who was good to know given that his dad, a millionaire developer, was the builder and, at the time, owner of Sandown. And Tim Schenken, a young hot shot originally from Sydney, four years younger than me, who'd go on to win the World Sportscar Championship for Ferrari alongside Ronnie Peterson just a decade later. You could rely on those guys for help when you needed it, just like they'd rely on you.

The true heroes of the time, like Harry Firth, were way out of our orbit, unless we had the money to spend in their shops. Bob Jane and Norm Beechey, the pioneers of touring-car racing as we know it, were already showmen, working the media, the public and the customers in their dealerships for all they could get. And they were stars. Sometimes my opinions get in my way. I didn't like either of them then and half a century on nothing's changed.

You knew you were doing okay when the trade started to notice you. I turned up at a race meeting at Winton in central Victoria and my re-treaded tyres were rejected by the scrutineers. I wasn't allowed to race. That's when the man from Dunlop called me over and gave me four new tyres. That was the first sponsorship I ever received and it meant so much.

At VW, Gordon Bingham and I were keen to 'help' the factory by racing their cars. Never mind George Reynolds. We ended up being given a pre-production Beetle shell and some spare parts, and with that we built a race car. I know I raced it at Sandown because there's a picture of me in the dirt off the track there, but my only clear recollection of the car is of it on its side after tipping over on Warrigal Road.

All that racing . . . all that money going out and none of it coming in. It couldn't go on. The crunch came when Monash sent me my results, or rather the lack of them. Their letter suggested I might like to consider other options and that there were a hundred young Australians breaking their necks to take my place. I rationalised that no degree meant no continuation of the cadetship, so it was time to activate the emergency airline ticket. The final indignity was offering the TR3 for a quick sale to a local motor-sport identity who was also a used-car dealer. I'd paid $1200 for that car. I got just $200 from Bob Jane.

3

CHANGING UP

CANADA IN WINTER CAN BE A COLD AND UNFORGIVING PLACE, ESPECIALLY when your sole means of income is selling pots and pans door to door. I'd arrived home for Christmas 1963 and I was seriously conflicted.

In Dad's eyes, I'd not exactly covered myself in glory in Australia. In my view, I'd found my calling. Motor racing is what I wanted to do. Australia, largely, was the place I wanted to do it.

Firstly I had to make some money, and there wasn't much coming my way from the family.

The father of a school friend, Jack Christie, owned Canadian Cookware—a range of pots and pans. For all I cared they could have been brushes or encyclopaedias. The same principle applied. It didn't matter what you were selling as long as you sold something, because your only income was from commission.

Jack was an aspiring rock musician. I was going to be a racing driver. We both knew this short period of door-to-door retail was going to look sensational when people wrote our life stories.

Our technique was innovative, purpose built for success. Rather than knock on the doors ourselves, we'd get others to do it for us. We'd stop the first young woman we saw on the street and offer a free spatula or cake server in return for the names of two or three of her friends who were either married or thinking of getting married. Seriously.

It was a different world in the 1960s. In those days, in polite society you needed an introduction if you wanted to meet a girl, so to accost one in the street was outrageous. But it worked. Soon enough Jack and I were making several sales a week, and for good money. You had to be brazen, and quick on your feet. There was one night I was on the lounge-room floor with an intending bride, pots and pans laid out all around us, when her parents came home. Her dad did not recognise me as his daughter's fiancé or as anyone else he knew and his response was pretty decisive. Next day though, I met up with the young lady and she bought my collection.

Jack was the driving force who unrelentingly pushed me to go motor racing. Throughout that winter he encouraged me hard to follow my dream. I wish I'd reciprocated because he never made it into music.

And that's how I came to be at Watkins Glen, invited into the Team Lotus pit in the late afternoon after they'd had a rubbish day. Sir John Whitmore, the second baronet of Orsett, Essex, had uncharacteristically failed to finish, and Mike Spence, the son of a Berkshire garage owner, had been able only to salvage a class second.

Both were just a couple of years older than me but Sir John was already the British saloon-car champion in a Mini Minor, and had come second in class at Le Mans in a Lotus Elite sharing with Jim Clark. Mike had raced a Lotus F1 car in the 1963 Italian Grand Prix, and he had just received the call up to be Number Two to Jim Clark for both the British Grand Prix in two weeks and for the remainder of the season. Neither was there when I walked in.

The Team Lotus garage was nirvana. It wasn't a garage actually, but a tent. Inside were the two white Lotus Cortinas with their Sherwood green stripes down each side. The US Road Racing Championships had been inaugurated by the Sports Car Club of America the previous year, largely for big-bore sports cars, and it was soon to morph into the incredibly successful CanAm series. Texan Jim Hall had won that day at Watkins Glen in the very first Chaparral 2 sports car, and Ken Miles had won the over-2-litre GT class for the fledgling Carroll Shelby team. They were already superstars in supercars but alongside them were the production cars—a massive battle between Porsche, Alfa Romeo and, for the first time, the Lotus Cortinas. They were competing for the pocket-books of real-life car-buying customers.

Ford was on a roll in motor sport. Henry Ford II had determined that motor racing was the way to bring life to his brand. Ford might have been the biggest car-maker in the world at the time—one in every five cars on the planet was a Ford—but most of them were boring and Henry wanted that to change. In 1963 he'd gone so far as to make a takeover bid for Ferrari, only to be rejected by Enzo Ferrari when negotiations had progressed so far they'd even started designing the logo for the new company. The stumbling block was that Henry wanted the sports cars but didn't give much of a fig about Enzo's beloved F1 division. You don't turn down Henry Ford.

Ferrari's rejection, from a company that Henry no doubt regarded as a minnow, led Ford to look aggressively elsewhere. So FoMoCo began a relationship with a company even smaller than Ferrari, the Lola Car Company of Great Britain, with the view to building their own Ferrari-beater. The car would be the GT40, which later would win Le Mans.

In London Henry had hired the editor of Fleet Street's *Sunday Dispatch* newspaper as his new PR man, not just to be a flack but to take custody of the company's European brand image. The editor was Walter Hayes, and although he knew little about motor racing at the time, he was to become one of the greatest influences on the development of the sport.

One of Hayes's first moves was to approach Colin Chapman, the owner, designer and team manager of Lotus cars, another minnow, and give him the contract of a lifetime. Hayes asked Colin if he could design and build a high-performance version of Ford's nice but plebeian Cortina, and could he please turn out 1000 of them quite promptly to meet the homologation rules of Europe's Group 2 championship. Colin did not say no.

The Cortina had already been racing with some success as a single overhead cam GT but, to take it to the next level, it needed what was for the time a somewhat revolutionary twin cam, along with a close-ratio gearbox that could be taken from Lotus's recently released Elan. The engine was built by two former Lotus employees, Mike Costin and Keith Duckworth. They had left Lotus to start a small engineering company named for abbreviations of their surnames: Cosworth. Partially because of the success of their Cortina program, Cosworth would go on to be chosen to develop the world's most successful F1 engine, the Ford Cosworth DFV (double four valve). It won 155 F1 races from 262 starts between 1967 and 1985.

Lotus was in charge of the rest of the Cortina. Reducing weight was vital. Lightweight panels were used for door, boot and bonnet, and lightweight casings surrounded the gearbox and differential. Suspension and brake changes were radical. The leaf springs fitted to the rear of the GT, which were the bane of my existence in the TR3A, were gone, replaced by vertical coil springs and dampers. They were so successful they became known as the Chapman struts, after their inventor. Along with the stiffer chassis and the MacPherson strut front end, the suspension package gave the Lotus Cortina that wonderful wheel-in-the-air stance that characterised a small car being hustled hard.

All that meant a lot to me. I hadn't chosen the Lotus Cortina team by accident. They were my target for exactly the reasons of their determination, their aggression and their professionalism. And yet, right then and there, it also meant nothing. I was standing on the cusp of success . . . or disaster. If only I'd had a cake server in my pocket to offer one of the mechanics so he could help me take the next move.

And then Ray Parsons stepped forward. He was an Australian and one of the country's many motor-racing success stories. Not only was he in charge of the mechanics, he was also an accomplished driver and, in those early days of Team Lotus, pretty close to being one of Colin Chapman's inner circle. Ray had been at Indianapolis three weeks before. Two months before that on the flat, featureless Sebring airstrip track in Florida, he had been co-driver to Jim Clark when they'd finessed the Lotus Cortina to 21st outright and second in class in the 12 Hour Endurance race.

People in Australia say I have a strong Canadian accent. Over there they think I'm an Aussie. It was enough to strike a rapport and to extract, not exactly a commitment, more like a vague offer. If I was to turn up at the next round of the championship in three weeks at Greenwood Roadway, somewhere south of Des Moines, Iowa, they might be able to find something for me to do. 'Look us up when you get there.' I'd never heard of the place. Few people had. Greenwood opened in 1963 and closed in 1966, surely the shortest life span of any permanent circuit, a victim of its own inaccessibility. 'Sure,' I said. 'I'll be there. And thanks.'

I'd hitched a ride to Watkins Glen, but the USA's Midwest was a lot further away: just on 1400 kilometres each way. Drastic measures were necessary. Dad wasn't going to comply but Mum might. And that's how I got to drive, and sleep, in a pretty flash Karmann Ghia, a VW-based two-door sports car with an Italian-designed and German coach-built body. Mum got to take the bus.

It was a huge leap of faith. There were no firm prospects and long-distance travel was becoming expensive but when I turned up in the Greenwood pits, I was welcomed with open arms and a bucket.

With me on the chamois, the cars had never been cleaner. Whitmore won that weekend. The versatile Henry Taylor, who did everything from Formula One to rally and was a member of the British Olympic bobsleigh team on the side, was second. The following year he would become competitions manager of Ford UK, a useful contact to have.

The resources of Team Lotus were monstrously stressed. Only four years before Colin Chapman himself had been in charge of towing his two Lotus 18 F1 cars to Continental events behind his hotted-up Ford Zephyr. These days we think of Lotus as a conglomerate. Back then, there were stories about Chapman running out of brakes in the Zephyr on the way to Reims and despatching two mechanics to drive the F1 cars on the road to get to the circuit on time. Both, so the story goes, got speeding tickets but were allowed to continue to the track.

By 1964, Lotus Cars was building 1700 vehicles a year, 500 of them Lotus Cortinas, and the company was turning over £1.5 million with a profit just under 10 per cent of that.

Team Lotus Ltd, the motor-racing arm, had split into four divisions and hired outside help to manage series it couldn't handle itself. Jimmy Clark had won the world championship for Team Lotus in 1963, so one division was dedicated to his F1 defence. Team Lotus Racing had paired with Ford of Great Britain to run the Lotus Cortinas in Britain and Europe. Another division worked with Ford of America to run IndyCar cars and the fast-emerging Lotus 30 sports-car program. And then there was a separate unit working with the English Ford Line, a distinct part of FoMoCo in Dearborn, to run Cortinas in selected American events using a wide variety of drivers. For Ford the USRRC—US Road Racing Championship—was a PR opportunity. Series points were nice, but not essential. It was showcasing Ford to a mass motor-sport audience that counted.

In the USRRC, the Lotus Cortina, a two-door sedan if ever you've seen one, was classified as a sports car. Its main rivals were the specialist Alfa Romeo TZ and the potent but lethal Porsche 904, the car even its own drivers had labelled a death trap. That the Cortina was even knocking on the door of GT-class podiums was a huge testament to the car, drivers and the team.

One week after Greenwood, in August 1964, was the race that was essential to win—the Marlboro 12 Hour on a twisting 2.7-kilometre track, short on straightaways and described locally as an extended go-kart circuit. Established for four years, the Marlboro was America's premier race for touring cars—not exactly Bathurst, but the quality of those early entries was pretty similar. There were Saabs and Peugeots, Renaults and VWs, along with a Chevvy Corvair and the Lotus Cortinas. Twenty-eight cars would start on the tight circuit—that's a track density of one car every 96 metres, which compared pretty favourably with the first Mount Panorama long-distance races where 60 cars started over 6.3 kilometres, around 105 metres per car. But at the undulating, green Maryland track, it looked like a very congested car park.

This event was so important that even Colin Chapman showed up. I did too.

Apparently my car-washing skills had been so successful that I warranted not only an invitation to continue but a bed to sleep in. No money, though. All I had to do was drop Mum's car home to Toronto, get myself back to Detroit and help drive the spare-parts truck down to Maryland. Twenty-six hundred kilometres; three days to do it. No problem.

When I look back it's all a blur. I may only have been a 'gofer' (go for this, go for that) but it's amazing to think that, in the space of two months, I'd progressed from being a coathanger on the Watkins Glen fence to being on the 'inside' of Team Lotus, wearing the British racing green uniform and driving the truck.

Mr Chapman had brought a young Scot (at the time, not *the* young Scot), Jackie Stewart, with him and, when the flag dropped at 10 a.m. he bolted, never to be seen again. At 10 p.m. Wee Jackie and co-driver Mike Beckwith were ten laps ahead of their teammates' car and 27 laps clear of the field. Sir John Whitmore, driving with Beckwith's usual British teammate, Tony Hegbourne, had the honour of having Colin Chapman change his front brake rotors when they failed at the three-hour mark, and then mounted a huge charge to give Team Lotus a rout.

My real usefulness to Team Lotus was an understanding of the geography and the local customs. They didn't know California from China Town and it helped them to have someone around who simply knew how to get from A to Z and to call it Zee. And that's how I got to travel with them for the rest of the USRRC season, my confidence, but never my bravado, growing.

Disaster was only one mistake away—you could be out, just like that.

By Mid-Ohio, I'd become a corner man, in charge of one corner of the race car. 'In charge' is probably overstating the mark. Unlike current motor-racing technique, even the mighty Team Lotus was pretty casual about who did what. And where they did it. I was working on the car in a pit area, open to all sorts of pedestrian traffic. There were people walking by, talking, leaning over me. That's how I came to put the brake pads in back to front. Thankfully quality control was in place and the car hadn't left the pits before my mistake was found. Ray Parsons was unimpressed and I was back on the wash bucket.

It was at that race meeting too that Pete Lovely, one of Lotus' merry-go-round of drivers, came in complaining that there was something loose in the boot. Turned out it was an oil drum that had been put there during scrutineering to help bring the lightweight Lotus up to minimum allowable weight. Someone, thankfully not me, had forgotten to take it out.

I learned a lot from that half-year. It was like starting at kindergarten and fast-tracking to university. Everything I saw taught me something that I knew I could apply when I had my own race team. And one of the biggest learnings was discipline. In my team, I vowed, I'd have one man assigned to one task, or series of tasks. There would be pit protocol. You just wouldn't get in unless there was a purpose for you being there. And there'd be no allowance for idle chatter.

You get one chance and you don't ever want to blow it.

The last event of the season was the Road America 500 at Elkhart Lake, Wisconsin. Team Lotus was well out of series contention by then. The Porsche 904 had won four rounds in the hands of geniuses like Scooter Patrick. Chuck Stoddard had won two with his Alfa Romeo TZ, and was to win Road America as well. In that scenario Ford and Team Lotus were both considering their options for 1965 and suddenly it was possible to see opportunity presenting itself.

It was time for the mouse to roar. 'If you're considering selling the team cars, can I buy one?'

At the time there was nothing more disposable than an old racing car. When you consider how valuable they've become today, the smartest thing a man could have done in 1964 was fill a warehouse with redundant racers and eke them out on the market, one by one, like Brett Whiteley paintings.

But Ford was interested in a lot more than making a fast buck out of me. All season long, they'd been building an image and they weren't going to have it torn asunder by the car-wash boy. It was time to lay out my grand plan. 'Sell me the car and I'll take it to Australia and win the inaugural Sandown Six Hour—or at least not disgrace you in it.' I was convinced Australia was the best course of action. In America, there was a lot of competition and a lot of money in play. I'd just seen it first-hand. Australia was much more condensed. It didn't mean the competition was any less intense. In fact, just the opposite. The Australian Touring Car Championship had entered its fourth year and this was the first time it hadn't been won by a Jaguar. The old British cats were coming off the boil. Instead, in a one-off championship race around the tight, twisting and somewhat fearsome Lakeside track in Queensland, Ian 'Pete' Geoghegan had driven a Ford Cortina GT—not a Lotus—to victory, just ahead of Norm Beechey's homegrown EH Holden S4 and Bob Jane's Jag. The only Lotus in the field, driven by Jim McKeown, had been battling at the top of the pack when he clipped a crashed car and was out. Jim would be at the Sandown long-distance race, 'But I'd be in a "works" car,' I said. 'I might even go on to do the 1965 ATCC race.'

It must have been a compelling argument, because Peter Quenet, formerly the national service manager for Ford's Lincoln-Mercury division and now competitions manager of the English Ford Line, said yes.

Then he set the price: $US4500. It was a sensational offer. When you consider how much work had gone into those cars, what condition they were in, and how many parts came with them, it was the sale of the century. I just didn't have the money. I had $1500. The rest was a stratosphere away. I gave Peter my deposit anyway, every cent I had. The car would be mine, waiting for me at Dearborn as soon as I turned up with the rest.

I went to see Dad. His reaction was encouraging. 'All you're doing with yourself is chasing around after hot tarts and fast cars.' I figured there was some wriggle room in that negotiation. Look, if a girl wanted to come and sit on my lap I wasn't going to push her away, but my priority was very definitely fast cars.

'If I can't get the money from the family,' I told Dad, 'I'll go elsewhere.' That was probably the clincher: better to keep the shame contained. We mightn't have seen eye to eye on many things, and our relationship wasn't what you'd call close, but I'm convinced to this day that, as a corporate entrepreneur himself, he just might have admired his son's determination. He wasn't about to let on though.

On the day I went to pick up the cheque from his Massey Ferguson office in King Street, Toronto, he didn't come to see me himself. I cooled my heels in the waiting room until this haughty secretary appeared, glared at me and thrust out the envelope.

But here's the thing. Dad and I never spoke of repayment. I think if he'd made Mum more aware, things would have been different, because she would have insisted on some sort of propriety between us, if only to prevent misunderstanding and friction. But I think Dad always intended the cheque as start-up seed money for the career to which I was obviously committed.

Ford, graciously, delivered the race car to Toronto, the week of the Canadian Grand Prix, just up the road at Mosport Park in Bowmanville. It was effectively my home circuit even though I'd never seen it.

Everything was happening in such a rush. In the second week of September, I'd been at Elkhart Lake laying out my grand proposal. Less than a fortnight later, I owned a works Lotus Cortina and was going to give it a shakedown at no less than the Canadian Grand Prix. Two days after that I had to be in New York to put the car on a ship to Australia in time for the Sandown Six Hour in the last weekend of November.

How to do it? Well, this was where the negotiation with Dad did become difficult. Mum's Karmann Ghia wasn't going to tow the Lotus, but Dad's company car, a Buick, would. Quick as a flash, my mate Jack Christie and I had a tow-bar on it and we were away. It's impossible to say why Dad agreed to that. Looking back through the ages, I can only think this was his way: able to help with everything he could, except giving of himself.

The great, soon to be late, Mexican driver Pedro Rodríguez won the non-championship 1964 Canadian Grand Prix in a

Ferrari 330P run by the North American Racing Team (NART). I came second in class in the supporting sports-car race and I've no idea who won. It was just the best experience, to that point, of my life.

By then I was in love with the Lotus. I knew every contour, every beautiful characteristic, how it felt to sit at the wheel, how the pedals felt under my feet. It was just as I'd expected. On fresh tyres, on the undulating track over 60 kilometres, it was everything I'd dreamed. At the beginning of the year the original Cortinas had been beset with understeer, just ploughing on in the corners and scrubbing off speed. But all year long Team Lotus had been developing the handling, fitting stiffer and stiffer anti-roll bars until they achieved a car that could be thrown into a corner. Its only response when you chucked it in was to dig deeper and try harder. You sat low in the car in a bucket seat that was bolted to the floor. There was a big, thin three-spoke steering wheel in front of you, a tachometer behind it and not much else. It was just perfect. Simple and perfect.

A day after the Grand Prix, Canadian authorities didn't want it to leave the country. Jack and I were at the border at Buffalo, heading for the New York docks, and we were learning about Customs and carnets for the first time. The car was all right but we had it loaded to the roof with spare parts and that looked decidedly dodgy. Jack was always a better salesman than me and he got us through. Then at the port, the teamsters declined to load it until we'd separated the parts. Again Jack found a box for them and held me at bay as the precious cargo swung precariously above the hold. 'Be nice to them,' he cautioned, 'or you'll have nothing but bits.'

The Sandown International Six Hour Touring Car Race was a big deal. It marked the coming of age of international sedan-car racing in Australia and, while it had to compete with the Bathurst 500, it had settled on far more liberal rules, which resulted in 23 different makes of car being represented in a field of just 38.

And what a field. British Motor Corporation in England had entered a works Mini Cooper S for Paddy Hopkirk and John Fitzpatrick, both of them aces. BMC also brought out rally stars Timo Mäkinen and Rauno Aaltonen, and they'd sent another car for Australia's Mini-kings Peter Manton and Brian Foley. Indy 500 winner Rodger Ward had originally been entered in a Ford Galaxie but he'd been swapped into a local supercharged Studebaker Lark when the promoter's money had run out. There was a Galaxie though, to be driven by wealthy British peer Sir Gawaine Baillie, alongside local motor-racing aristocrat Lex Davison. Alfa Romeo had sent out a works Guilia for their Targa Florio winner Roberto Bussinello. There were two Lotus Cortinas entered, one for Bob Jane with George Reynolds, the other for New Zealander Jim Palmer, who'd invited the winner of the Marlboro 12 Hour, Jackie Stewart, to join him.

Then, at what you might call the eleventh hour, I sent a telegram: 'Desire enter Lotus Cortina Six Hour race. Stop. Letter following. Stop. Allan Moffat.'

Could it be I'd miscalculated the strength of the opposition?

My car at least won the immediate pre-race publicity. The ship was late, trapped in the Panama Canal, and it would not make Melbourne in time. Instead, it docked in Brisbane and the Lotus was offloaded, along with the spares, and transferred to a freight aircraft. I was at Eagle Farm late on Friday afternoon to fly back with it to Essendon but when I entered the fuselage it was surrounded by packages and was nearly invisible. We took off after dark and arrived in Melbourne after midnight.

We rushed to a workshop and began preparation. Frankly the word 'rush' is misleading. I would prefer to miss practice and qualifying and turn up with a car that I know is race ready rather than be at the track half-prepared. And that's what we did. We got to Sandown after the circuit had closed on Saturday afternoon.

Race secretary Max Newbold was incredibly accommodating. I'd secured Jon Leighton, son of the circuit developer, as my co-driver, and Max arranged with officials to let Jon and me get a few sighting laps in. I was to go first. The track marshal gave me the all clear and I was away. Up the back straight, Dandenong Road at the top of the hill, down through the esses, under the Lukey bridge . . .

Squinting into the sun, I saw at the very last moment that someone had pulled the metal boom gate across the track and locked it.

So many things go through your mind, so quickly. My hand went to my mouth. I was determined that if I was to crash into the thing I was going to protect my teeth. But in the same instant I realised the only way out was to spin the car immediately.

Around we went and the left rear hit the Causeway, a low bridge, with a fearful thump. Thankfully the damage was superficial. The suspension didn't need a rebuild, and Jon and I were able to each get three laps in to qualify to start at the rear of the grid.

As for the official who waved me onto the track, I used to see him at race meetings in future years. I never spoke to him again.

Next day the race was to start at 11 a.m. With no practice time, we were at the back of the field, down around the corner on the main straight. We were late getting there. At the last moment, scrutineers had decided we couldn't race with our Plexiglas® windscreen even though we were entered in the outright class, which gave us greater freedoms.

So a Lotus Cortina in the pits was scavenged and a 'safety' windscreen fitted.

Race drivers should think fast. It's the mechanics who think slow. At that particular moment, I don't know what I was thinking. I was so far back I couldn't see the starter's flag. I was still trying to get the complicated seatbelt untangled and properly organised when I heard this huge roar—well, two, actually. The first was from the 7-litre Galaxie as it boomed up the back straight with Lex Davison at the wheel. The second was from the massive Sandown grandstand crowd cheering the start. I simply leapt in, forgot about the belts, and drove the first stint to the pit stop without them done up.

It was an amazing start. At least it amazed me. The big Galaxie, which had been five seconds faster than the field in qualifying, just powered away. But six minutes after the flag, I'd moved from 28th to thirteenth and, before the first half-hour, I was up into second.

Forty minutes later the Galaxie lost its brakes and hit the fence at Peters Corner, returning to the pits for panel work and new pads. And then I crashed too. I'd just moved to the lead, the first time in my life I'd ever been in that position.

I had no idea what to do.

Whether it's motor racing or running a company like my dad, you have to be able to visualise what's ahead, anticipate a situation and have a clear idea of how to handle it.

My solution was to hit the fence.

The car wouldn't re-start. I got out, found a low-tension lead had come off and replaced it, determined that the suspension was okay, got back in and headed for the pits. Officials held me there. They wanted to make sure the car was safe, and not rely on my optimistic judgement.

By the time we got underway, we'd dropped way back in the field and by half distance I was only then back up to ninth.

At just after 2 p.m., with Lex Davison at the wheel doing around 140 km/h, the Galaxie lost its brakes again and went straight on at Peters, exploding the heavy 30-centimetre timber railway sleepers that made up the safety fence—all, that is, but one, which captured the two-tonne car and held it swaying over a 10-metre drop into the reservoir. 'The big bitch almost killed me,' Davison told a shocked Baillie in a quote that's become part of local motor-racing folklore. Officials waved yellow flags for a few laps, compressed the field, and set up hay bales around the car, which could not be moved. Then we got back into it.

Long-distance races can be cruel. Jackie's Lotus engine blew up on the back straight. Bob Jane's car lost its front brakes. Jane asked officials for permission to disconnect them and just drive on the rears, but they refused.

With one hour to go, I was sitting a bit unhappily in fourth position when a slower car moved in front of me. I jinked to the in-field at Shell Corner and rode out a 300-metre slide all the way past the pits until I rejoined in the braking area for Peters next to the Galaxie.

Bussinello won the 1964 Six Hour faultlessly, seven laps clear of the field. Peter Manton and Brian Foley were second in the works Mini, ahead of the official Ford Australia Cortina GT of Geoff Russell and John Raeburn. I was fourth, and thankfully, first in the Open Class. It was a result I could happily telegram back to Peter Quenet.

4

ALLAN MOFFAT RACING

AN OLD BRICK-AND-TIMBER WORKSHOP, A FORMER SERVICE STATION, AT 711 Malvern Road, Toorak, Melbourne became the headquarters of Allan Moffat Racing, from my first Lotus Cortina right through to when it was ploughed under by developers in 2015.

In the early days, the owner and his wife worked in the front half and pumped gas at the street side. I had the rear on an earthen floor made rock hard by the years of garage grime that had been dumped on it. Even after I could afford to buy the place, it was years before I converted it to concrete.

It was never the pristine premises that you see race teams in now or that defined the top US teams back then. Hermetically sealed clean rooms for engine and parts assembly weren't on the radar and conditions were so rudimentary that even a simple thing like a wheel alignment was sometimes a lot less than precise.

But it was at least the equal of the Australian motor-racing working environments of the time, most of them attached to the service divisions or other premises of the racing stars, who in one way or another were supported by their business interests. Jane and Beechey were car salesmen on a grand scale. The Geoghegans in Sydney had taxis and a used-car lot specialising in top-end high-margin sports cars. Frank Matich, arguably Australia's first homegrown professional, was running a service station out the front of his workshop. There was no way you'd call them hobbyists. They were serious about their racing. But they at least had other income sources and some, like Jane, built substantial businesses on the back of their motor-racing success.

My situation was somewhat different. There was no support mechanism. A bit like Frank Gardner, Paul Hawkins and Tim Schenken, I'd struck out on my own; unlike them, I was looking to the States rather than Britain for my start.

I was back living with my Yugoslav landlady and I was existing from hamburger to hamburger. And 711 Malvern Road was, for me, a giant leap forward in realising my ambition.

I was just six months into my plan to become a professional racing driver. At Indianapolis, I had vowed to myself that I would invest two years. If it didn't work out, well, too bad, but I was going to seriously try. Already I had a car, premises and a class win under my belt in a long-distance race; not the outright win I'd planned, and that hurt a lot even though I knew I was on a learning curve.

Most importantly I had an invitation to return to the USA with the possibility of doing some racing. When Peter Quenet sold me the Lotus Cortina he mothballed the remaining two team cars. 'It might be okay,' he'd hinted, for me to make use of them in the States. Meantime there were races to run and titles to chase—all good for the résumé.

My target was to be back in Indianapolis at the end of May 1965 for the Indy 500, where Team Lotus had invited me to join them in a minor capacity, then on to Detroit to meet up with Peter. For six months I threw myself at domestic racing, and at making myself truly useful to Ford Australia. That's important. It doesn't matter how good you are, or think you might be, unless you attach yourself to a factory you're going nowhere. Four weeks after Sandown I won the Victorian Short Circuit Championship at Hume Weir. You'd have thought that I would have been over the moon but, for me, there was no great delight in winning—maybe a degree of personal satisfaction because I'd justified the work I'd put in, but no more. You can't bank emotion.

That subdued reaction, so early in my career, was perhaps a bit surprising to some, but it's always been part of my make-up. I tend not to get too excited about winning. If only I could apply the same philosophy to losing. I hate it.

The big race I wanted to claim was the Australian Touring Car Championship, a winner-take-all one-event title, at Sandown in April. It came less than two months after Lex Davison, a doyen of Australian motor racing, had been killed at the circuit when his Brabham Climax crashed on the back-straight kink. Lex, the coroner found, had suffered a heart attack at 43. It was a bizarre fortnight. Just one week later, Lex's protégé, Rocky Tresise, a 21-year-old from Toorak, whom I vaguely knew, was racing at Longford in Tasmania with the team's blessing. 'Lex would have wanted it,' they said. Rocky went off on the main straight and was killed, taking a photographer, Robin D'Abrera, with him.

Lex's passing was big news in Melbourne. The fatal coincidence within the same team cast something of a pall over motor-racing's inner circle, but it was a different era. Today there'd probably be a public outcry and a call for greater safety standards; at least questions would have been asked. At the time, shocked as we were, we just got on with preparations for the touring-car championship.

When I had bought the car from Ford, I'd earmarked this event. Touring-car rules were changing and they favoured my Lotus Cortina. Jim McKeown in the Shell-owned Team Neptune Cortina was the person I saw as my greatest rival, expecting the old school in their bored-out hot-rod cars running under antiquated rules to drop away.

How wrong I was.

Bob Jane and Norm Beechey had both secured new V8 Ford Mustangs over the summer break, complying with the latest regulations. They were obviously a giant step forward. Even the Mini Cooper S and the six-cylinder Holden S4 had found new legs.

Jim McKeown broke his engine in the race and Beechey went on to win the first of his two Australian touring-car titles. Jane blew up, Pete Geoghegan punched his Lotus Cortina into second, and right on the line I was passed by Brian Muir's Holden for third position, hardly the result I'd been targeting, but my tussle with 'Yogi' Muir, a noted hard man, did my reputation some good.

A fortnight later Ford mounted one of the biggest PR campaigns ever undertaken in Australia. To prove the durability of their locally manufactured Falcon, they staged a 70,000-mile (112,650-kilometre) marathon on their newly opened test track in the You Yangs outside Melbourne. Their plan was to run six Falcons non-stop for nine days around their 3.5-kilometre handling track at an average speed of 112 km/h, all under the scrutiny of CAMS timekeepers to set a multitude of national and international records. It was about as big a deal as it gets, then or now. It had been devised by Ford's local PR man Les Powell and, while initially they had recruited 23 drivers to rotate through the cars, the sheer scale of the task overwhelmed them and they parachuted in another ten to help out.

As much as was possible in such a short time, I'd become part of Ford Australia's catchment of Ford-friendly drivers, so here I was, one of the team screaming around a coarse-chip surface on radial tyres that were pretty well unsuited to the task. Some cars crashed, one rolled, and the mechanics did a sensational job undertaking track-side repairs in a paddock without running water or town power. We slept in caravans and, while the other guys were a bit put out by the camp meals, I was eating consistently better than I had in a long time. And we hit the target, each of us covering just on 1000 laps.

On the last day Henry Ford II turned up from the USA. He had flown in his private jet, unusual for the time, and caused a major media riot. It didn't occur to me to hitch a ride back to the States—in fact, Henry would not have known any of us by name. But the local Ford guys did and the fact that I managed to complete my stints without incident was duly noted and, I'm sure, contributed to my career.

I flew back to the States in coach, the Lotus Cortina tucked up at 711 Malvern Road. On 31 May 1965, dressed in British racing green overalls, I held out a Dixie cup on the end of a modified broomstick so Jim Clark could have a drink in his pit stops en route to becoming the first Briton ever to win the Indy 500 and the first person to set a race average speed above 150 miles per hour (241 km/h). His Lotus 38 Ford was the first rear-engine car ever to win the race. Jimmy would go on to win the World F1 Championship and become the only person ever to achieve the Formula One–Indy double in the same year.

I was there because my mates at Team Lotus had asked me. Sure I was cleaning cars and components in a pit garage so pathetically narrow that mechanics had to take parts out into Gasoline Alley to work on them. But I especially requested to be Jim's water-bearer and the singular honour was granted to me. That night I was in Colin Chapman's room having drinks as part of the winning team. Jim was just so pleasant. That day at Indy lives with me as one of the greatest experiences of my motor-racing life.

There's a photograph of the team on the grid: Jim in the car, Colin Chapman alongside and me at the rear quarter. It just couldn't get any better—but it did.

Soon I was in Detroit, knocking on Peter Quenet's door. In my life I've been blessed with several guardian angels, people who for no apparent reason have decided to help me, sometimes above all others. I was dead broke, no car, no obvious prospects. Peter gave me the use of a couch at his own home, and use of a works Lotus Cortina at his office, along with a part-time mechanic.

The only proviso, if you could call it that, was that I race locally in the Detroit area so I could help keep the Ford brass motivated. There was a big motor-racing culture in the Motor City. It was the common ground between workers and managers, and there was huge competitive needle between Ford and General Motors.

First time out at the Detroit track, Waterford Hills, my Lotus Cortina blew away the local Chevrolet Corvair heroes Don Eichstaedt and Jerry Thompson. The win was made even better because both were engineers in the General Motors technical centre. The Ford guys at the track were ecstatic.

While Waterford would remain my home track, I was gradually allowed a little more leash. We took the Lotus Cortina to Mosport to race in open competition. This time it was my turn to be trounced. Sir John Whitmore, driving for Team Lotus, lapped me before he broke; I managed to salvage third. Sure Team Lotus was using the latest works BRM engine and I wasn't, but clearly there was still some learning to do.

At the Marlboro 12 Hour, I had the celebrated Bob Tullius as co-driver. We were in the top six when a wheel broke out on the track and Bob came back on foot. I pulled on my helmet, ran out to the car and drove it back on three wheels. We'd lost so much time that we were the last of the classified finishers but at least we finished. It's not a good look to fail to finish and I told Bob that in reasonably forceful terms.

The rest of the short season flew by and Waterford Hills was my stamping ground. Then it was time to return to Australia and have another crack at the Sandown Six Hour.

No used engines for me. I had a brand-new Team Lotus BRM engine. With all their racing commitments, Lotus had run out of capacity and they had subcontracted the manufacture of the twin cam to another F1 team, BRM, winners of the World F1 Championship with Graham Hill in 1962. Those engines were flyers.

I had raided New Zealand for this next, glorious, attempt at the Six Hour. Jim Palmer, the country's foremost resident open-wheeler driver, had agreed to co-drive. And Allan McCall, a top Kiwi mechanic with Team Lotus, and later with McLaren, had accepted an airfare home to help run the car.

'Boom. And away we go,' Bill Tuckey wrote in his *Wheels* magazine report of the race. 'Moffat got away incredibly from the seventh row to third place in the 300 yards to Shell corner. Moffat came out of Peters first and went for the doctor up the back.'

It was a good start but not destined to last. Instead of bringing victory it was to be one of the low points of my life.

Halfway through we blew a tyre and then lost the electrics and had to take several unscheduled stops to fit new batteries to keep going.

We'd worked our way up to second outright when Jim pulled to the pits with just four minutes to go. 'The diff is about to pack up,' he said.

'Well, get out there and finish,' I replied.

First Tullius, now Palmer. It was becoming a constant theme. Jim accelerated out of the pits and I started to walk towards the victory dais for the ceremony. 'Too bad,' someone said to me.

'Sure,' I replied, 'but we're still on the podium.'

He pointed to the kink in the back straight just after the pits and there was my car. Stationary. When Jim floored it out of the pits he'd torn the last remnants of the diff alignment to pieces. He'd also torn out my heart.

Everything—and I mean everything—I had was in that car. In fact, I was in the red. There were serious bills to pay. Next morning Allan McCall knocked on my office door at 711 and resigned on the spot. It was the honourable thing to do. I was convinced the diff had been misaligned. Drivers just don't do that damage no matter how brutal they are, and both Jim and I were easy on the machinery. Allan went on to become chief mechanic for Denny Hulme's winning McLaren in the CanAm series and then built his own open-wheelers, the Tui, named for a New Zealand honeyeater.

Later that week I was driving again. Jack Brooks, once the CEO of Sandown, owned a car park in Lonsdale Street in the Melbourne CBD and he gave me a job as 'car jockey'.

It could have been worse.

The year before, in 1964, Australia had introduced mandatory conscription into the armed forces to source human cannon fodder for its entry into the Vietnam War. Many fine young men—nashos—were being called up for national service. A ballot was conducted among twenty-year-olds. If your birthdate came up, then it was goodbye to the next two years of your life—or worse. It was the lottery no one wanted to win. It didn't affect me, because I was both too old and Canadian, and therefore ineligible on two counts. Canadians had, in fact, a different take on Vietnam. Canada had become something of a safe haven for similarly affected young Americans. Draft-dodgers were pouring over the border. Meantime, just up the road in Wagga, two twenty-year-olds were serving their time: Peter Brock and Dick Johnson were both in the same boot camp—only a hut apart—and they never met. Neither of them was racing yet but both were mad keen motor-racing fans.

On Boxing Day, I'd be mighty close to them at Hume Weir, Albury, in what turned out to be the successful defence of my one and only title, the Victorian Short Track Championship. Perhaps they were in the crowd. If they had been, they would have seen me win at the slowest possible speed, conserving everything I could of my meagre resources. Even tyres and fuel counted.

I was to later learn that my conservative drive at Hume Weir did a lot to save my career. Unbeknown to me, I was under scrutiny. The sport's governing body, CAMS, had already called a clandestine meeting of touring-car competitors to discuss my 'forceful' driving. The obvious intention was to ban me, or at least impose severe penalties. To my later surprise, it was the drivers I'd treated with the least respect who stood up for me. Their attitude was 'Give him a go. We'll sort him out on track.'

There's a lot to be said for counter-seasonal motor racing. The Tasman open-wheeler series in Australasia pioneered the concept, bringing the best open-wheeler drivers to the southern hemisphere during the European winter, keeping their driving skills current until the F1 season restarted in the spring. I was a fan of the idea, hampered only by a lack of funds to do either successfully.

But a New Year's gift had arrived. Peter Quenet wrote to say that he'd make cars and engines available if I'd like to contest the 1966 Central Division (CENDIV) Touring Car series in the American Midwest, starting in May. In that year the Sports Car Club of America transformed the US Road Racing Championship into the Trans Am series, destined to become the birthplace of muscle cars. The CENDIV was a lesser category. My heart was set on doing the Trans Am, but there were no offers on the table there.

For the next five months I set out to be truly counter-seasonal, racing where and whenever I could in order to be race ready for the US . . . meantime continuing to park cars in Lonsdale Street to pay the bills.

The path to success is not just about the racing. It is about being in the right place and being seen. At the Tasman series round at Sydney's Warwick Farm, I met up again with Ray Parsons, who was running Jim Clark in the Lotus 39 Coventry Climax. It was a poor Tasman for Jim, by his standards anyway. Although he'd win at The Farm, he'd suffer three retirements in eight races to come third in the series, just ahead of my Sandown co-driver Jim Palmer.

The Tasman had become a race-car supermarket. The northern hemisphere teams would bring down last year's stock and dispose of it to eager Aussies. Jim Palmer had bought the

Lotus 39 from Team Lotus and Ray asked me to handle the delivery to New Zealand. I was to be paid in kind: F1 tyres from the Lotus that would bolt straight onto my Cortina.

Jim McKeown had become both my nemesis and my benchmark. Whenever I saw his Team Neptune Lotus Cortina, in my mind it had a huge target painted on it. I'd now raced Cortinas against some of the best drivers in the world, and I knew Jim's engine was the best of the best. It allowed him to do things other drivers couldn't. Whatever it had, I wanted some. I chased Jim up and down the east coast and across to Adelaide and I never beat him. While the Mustangs and Beechey's new Chevy Nova would sprint off into the distance, Jim and I staged huge battles behind them.

Our best was held for last, the 1966 South Australian Touring Car Championship. For the first time I unleashed the Team Lotus tyres. It was a huge battle and neither of us won. We swapped the lead, went off the track, spun, traded paint and broke the outright touring-car lap record. Jim was disqualified for receiving outside assistance to recover from his spin while I failed to finish due to a tyre blow-out on the last lap. Our parting words weren't kind. Every panel—bar the roof—on Jim's car was dented. Mine, not much better, went straight into the hands of its new owner. I needed the money to pay my remaining Aussie debts and for the airfare back to the States.

God, it was good to be in the States that season.

I was running hot, the car was sensational and my two Aussie mechanics—Vince Woodfield and Barry Nelson—were geniuses. They could strip an engine in a dusty car park and make it go even faster than before. They built an engine, using nothing more than ingenuity, which was every bit as good as the works engines. We won our class in the first two CENDIV rounds.

They were tough times, and good times.

None of us was drawing a salary. We were on a mission, each of us committed to our shared success.

Dan Gurney once told me: 'Don't waste your time waiting for the phone to ring. If you want to be serious about your racing, start your own team and promote like hell.' I could see my chance looming.

The official Ford team in the Trans Am series was British-owned Alan Mann Racing. Despite having superb drivers like Jacky Ickx, Frank Gardner and Sir John Whitmore, and the best of engineering talent, the red-and-gold-painted Cortinas were having a hard time of it against the new lightweight Alfa Romeo GTA, a rocket ship of a car.

Alfa, with Jochen Rindt on board, had trounced Ford at the Sebring Four Hour. Later to become Formula One's only posthumous world champion, Rindt had already become famous by winning the 1965 Le Mans 24 Hour race in a Ferrari 250LM he'd set out to deliberately break. Legend has it Jochen had a hot date waiting back in Paris and, because the LM was hopelessly outclassed, he'd determined to destroy it early and hot foot it to the Sixth Arrondissement that night. Instead it proved indestructible; he just kept getting quicker and won the race.

Using a combination of logic gleaned from Gurney and Rindt, I figured the next round of the Trans Am was a place I wanted to be. It was like playing hookey. I put the CENDIV on hold and went AWOL to chance my arm in the big game.

There was no Ford backing for this one. Vince, Barry and I piled into our Ford Econoline van and towed the Lotus Cortina 1000 kilometres to Mid-America Raceway for the 500-kilometre race. There wasn't a lot of money left, so I let my co-driver cough up for the gas. I have a policy of never selling a drive but co-driver Dan could well afford it. His surname is the giveaway: Gerber. He was the baby-food heir.

We got there two days early and I started to do laps in the Econoline. Now long since shut, Mid-America was almost 4.5 kilometres around, with trees taller than Mount Everest on each side and lots of 90-degree corners. It was a difficult track and it took a long time to learn it.

I must have done 50 laps in the van and it was only because of that training that, in qualifying, I was able to take class pole position, faster than the Alfas, faster than the works Fords.

And that's when my luck changed for the better, forever.

A guy in a plain white shirt walked up to me in the pits: 'Not a bad effort on a used set of Dunlops,' he said. I looked closer. He was wearing a very discreet name badge that said Goodyear. 'With your permission I'd like to set you up with a good set of tyres.'

The guy's name was Mike Babich and he was Number Two in Goodyear Racing.

He walked over to the Alan Mann truck to talk to their team manager, a lilting Englishman by the name of Howard Marsden, later to figure strongly in my Australian racing. It was the first time I'd met him too. Marsden's response was pretty forthright—'We can't afford to help others'—and he denied Goodyear America access to Goodyear Europe's tyres. Mike's reaction was equally blunt. Realising, as he put it, that he was dealing with an asshole, he got into his car and roared off into nearby St Louis and secured my tyres himself.

In the race, the distributor blew up—same problem as we'd had at Sandown. Goodyear, though, was hooked. By being his typical obstructive self, Howard had done me the biggest favour of his life.

'At the next round, New Hampshire, we'll have a bigger truck than those bastards from England,' Mike said. 'If they ask you for as much as a valve cap, tell them "no", as forcefully as you like.'

Next day, back in Dearborn, Goodyear sent around two technicians to talk to me about specifying tyres especially for my car. They'd build those Goodyears at their plant in Akron, Mid-Ohio, not source them from overseas. It was the start of a career-long association that has never wavered. I'm a Goodyear man, and they support me. It was not a case of 'do I need tyres?'; it was 'how many?'

It is impossible to understate a circumstance like that. It was a turning point in my career and a once-in-a-lifetime opportunity for any driver.

The 1966 winner at Mid-America was an Austrian racing under an Australian flag. His name was Horst Kwech and he too would play a role in my career. Like me, he was running as a privateer but for Alfa Romeo, diving in and out of both the CENDIV and Trans Am races.

At the next CENDIV round, at Grattan Raceway, Michigan, we raced the wheels off each other.

It was a very special race for me, the only one my parents ever attended. Mum had lured Dad, allegedly reluctantly, to the hilly campground course and things weren't looking good. Kwech took pole and Dad looked worried. Then it rained and I nailed the Alfa under brakes for the win. My folks went home happy.

Bryar Motorsports Park in Loudon, New Hampshire, was the next round of the Trans Am. It had been a go-kart track until its owner, Keith Bryar, a Baptist minister, extended it to 2.5 kilometres. Goodyear's truck was one of the biggest in the small pit area.

The bottom line is, I won the race. Not the class, the race. Against Mustangs and Plymouth Barracudas and Dodge Darts.

I had won a round of the 1966 Trans Am series outright.

Okay, I don't get excited. It's not about the emotion. But when I received the trophy they also handed me a cheque for $US1200. Now *that* got me excited. To me it was $12 million. I'd never seen winnings like it.

That night at the official dinner I walked past Kwech's table. 'Bad day at the office,' I quipped.

'Not really,' he said.

'What did you think when I lapped you?' I asked.

'I thought you'd blow up like you always do,' he responded.

'And what did you think when I lapped you the second time?'

'I thought I'd better get my finger out.'

The next day my happy world exploded. The enemy, as it turned out, was from within.

•

I'd expected a reaction from the Alfas and maybe even from the usual outright contenders, but it was Ford's own team, Alan Mann, who raised a protest. They couldn't believe that one of their drivers—Australian Frank Gardner, the British touring-car champion—could be beaten by me, a nobody.

They demanded that my engine be surrendered to BRM Competitions UK for checking.

I asked Peter Quenet if they could do that. He said, 'Only if you agree, but it would be a good idea if you go too.'

I gave them the engine and, by appointment, hopped on a plane a little while later and went to England, first class, at Mann's expense. By the time I got there, they had already pulled the engine to pieces. First, it was perfectly legal. Second, it was developing serious power, in excess of 170 bhp (brake horsepower), not bad for a team of struggling Aussies. It's more than likely the Ford guys noted a few of our mods for their own development.

To my mind, Alan Mann had shot himself in the foot. He had reacted badly and was looking like a man with a team under pressure.

My own stocks were rising. As long as I didn't get ahead of myself, get boastful or make promises that I couldn't keep, what would be the chances of doing as Dan Gurney had suggested: running my own team? The English Ford line in Dearborn had so far had two suppliers to run their works team: Lotus and Alan Mann. Was it feasible that the next year they could have me?

In Britain, I had visited Ray Parsons at Lotus. In Ray's mind, he was first and foremost a driver. Team management and mechanical work were just what he did between drives.

My suggestion was straightforward: 'Join me, form a two-car team and let's take on the Trans Am.' He agreed. Just like that, he agreed.

Things were moving fast. Money matters in motor racing but, if you don't have it, you find another way. I bought an insurance write-off Cortina body for $75 and with Ray's special components, including quite a few engine components from BRM, built our second car. The cars looked good too. We painted them gold with green stripes and a green roof, clearly distinguishing them from any other Cortina. Any connection with Australia's national colours was coincidental.

We tested the new car at Waterford Hills and it felt as good as the Number One. We debuted it in the 1966 Marlboro 12 Hour but inexplicably there was water in our fuel. How does that happen by accident?

By the time we got going, we were thirteenth outright and eighth in class. There was no option but to move on.

To all intents and purposes, I was now a team, and Peter Quenet was keen for me to supplement the Alan Mann cars in the final rounds of the Trans Am, a Six Hour in Texas and a Four Hour in California. Four cars were better than two when it came to taking on the Alfas.

Tentatively, I made a radical suggestion. Instead of hiring two local co-drivers, why not bring in people we knew and trusted? I suggested my 1964 Sandown co-driver, Jon Leighton, and a genuine Ford hero, Harry Firth. Harry had won the Armstrong 500 and the inaugural Bathurst 500 for Ford—the last time in a Cortina—and he'd won the Ampol Around Australia Trial in a Cortina GT. He'd even nursed home a Cortina 220 to win the baby-car class in Bathurst. His workshop in Melbourne had become the *ex officio* Ford Australia team.

Peter immediately agreed and paid for them to come. That was a surprise. Already I was sensing a difference between being a down-and-out privateer and an emerging works team.

Green Valley Raceway, outside Fort Worth, Texas, was a combination drag strip and 2.6-kilometre road course. It lacked drainage, relied on hay bales for safety, and the rubber laid down by drag cars made grip questionable. And it rained. I aqua-planed off and hit one of the hay bales.

Honestly, at that moment on the track, I'd lost concentration.

For me it was a big lesson. I'd shouldered so much responsibility for this two-car effort, I'd been working nonstop and worrying unceasingly. Ray had joined me as equal team manager and, while he had much more experience in that role than I did, I was still the boss.

The 'off' would influence my view of team ownership and structure for the rest of my career. You can be a team manager or you can be a lead driver. But you cannot be both.

Harry Firth was fantastic. The race was half-day–half-night and, when darkness fell, he drove like the rally star he was. He pulled back four of the six laps I'd lost and brought us up to second in class behind Kwech's Alfa. Then a throttle cable fell off and he dropped another six laps and had to start again. This time he got into 'man possessed' mode. On a track with questionable grip, in the pitch dark, he set a new under-2-litre lap record. We finished fourth in class and ninth outright. Ray Parsons with Jon Leighton was third in class and seventh outright.

One week later, on 18 September 1966, we were racing at RIR, Riverside International Raceway, the race track stuck in the middle of a Californian sand dune.

To get there we drove 2200 kilometres across the bottom of America in two days and then Harry surprised us again. He removed the cylinder heads from both our cars and took them to a local machine shop where he performed some magic.

It's not that I didn't want the details, but Harry wasn't called 'The Fox' for nothing. All I needed to know was that his work was legal and quicker. He assured me it was.

Harry came down with the flu that weekend so I drove solo. My job, if I could, was to spoil Horst Kwech. For four hours we raced like crazy for second in class, while Frank Gardner sprinted ahead to score the Alan Mann team's only victory of the series.

I couldn't stop Horst.

The points he gained for second were enough to give him not only class but also outright victory in the championship.

It had been a promising performance. In something well short of the full season, the Fords had pulled back lost ground on the Alfa Romeos. And I'd also won the CENDIV championship, almost an afterthought.

5

HAND TO MOUTH

IN ITS FIRST YEAR, THE TRANS AM SERIES HAD BEEN A HUGE SUCCESS.

American fans had fallen in love with the big 5-litre V8 muscle cars, and all eyes were increasingly on the race for outright.

Our class struggles were becoming something of a sideshow.

Ford had almost blown it in 1966 by not supporting an outright team. It was only Jerry Titus's win in the final race at Riverside for Carroll Shelby's Mustang team that had secured the Manufacturers' Championship for FoMoCo. For 1967 Ford contracted Shelby to run a two-car works team, effectively parking the Alan Mann 2-litre outfit. The big question was: did they really need an under-2-litre-class effort at all?

Peter Quenet was not exactly strapped for budget but he had to mount a really good case as to why his English Ford Line should continue to invest in a Trans Am class that was under threat not only from the Alfas but also from the new Porsche 911s.

Naturally, I had the solution. I knew where the world's most powerful Lotus Cortina engine lived. It had to be putting out in excess of 180 hp, maybe more. If we could secure that engine for the Daytona Three Hour—the first race of the 1967 Trans

Am season—and win, then Peter would have a strong case to put forward. He agreed.

Next stop Jim McKeown.

It had to be a well-reasoned approach. I could hardly say to an arch-rival, especially one I'd left on questionable terms several months before, 'Can I borrow your engine?'

We went about it like a military exercise. The mechanics shipped back to Australia a full works BRM Lotus Cortina engine and drive train. I contacted Les Powell at Ford and he gave me a Cortina body shell, and over Christmas, in the 711 Malvern Road workshop, we built a Lotus Cortina, the equal of anything we had run in the States. We entered it in the January 1967 Calder meeting.

The aim wasn't to win. It was to evaluate our car against McKeown's, but only we knew that. He had no idea he was in some sort of test.

The long straights at Calder provided ample opportunity to determine which of our engines had more grunt. The answer was plain to see. Jim was a second a lap faster than me, all of it in straight-line acceleration.

Norm Beechey won, Jim was second and I was third, desperately clinging onto the Neptune car, and obviously down on power.

More than ever, I wanted that engine.

There's an apocryphal story that Jim and I met clandestinely in the dark of night on a park bench away from the politics and intrigue that surrounded the deal. It didn't happen that way, but there was still a lot of talking to do.

There were people who told Jim not to trust me. There were conflicting sponsor interests, especially from oil companies. But ultimately Jim liked the idea of racing at Daytona. 'Take my engine, take me' was the deal and I was happy to accept.

Daytona International Speedway was built by the France family, founders of NASCAR, as an alternative to using the original Daytona Beach road course. It's a fearsome 4-kilometre tri-oval with a 6.1-kilometre 'sports-car' course built into its in-field, utilising all three 32-degree-banked corners of the oval.

We were so on top of our game. Using Jim's engine, I took class pole position from Peter Gregg's new Porsche 911 and Horst Kwech's Alfa. In the race the Cortina took off, opening quite a gap on Gregg. Then on lap 25, with my future as the owner of a Ford works team looking increasingly certain, there was a noise that I'd heard only once before in my life: a buzz saw. It was a screeching banshee of a noise so loud it completely filled my senses. I pulled my feet up just as the floor started to buckle and switched off the engine—a difficult manoeuvre when you're at 200 km/h on a steeply pitched banking. The flywheel—the big buzz-saw–like wheel that connects the engine to the gearbox—had torn loose when the bolts holding it on had sheared. I coasted to the pits, out of the race and out of a career.

It turned out that when Jim's guys in Melbourne had prepared the engine for shipping they had fixed the flywheel with non-standard bolts—from a Holden just to add to the misery—and they had not been replaced.

I will never forget the look on Peter Quenet's face when he gazed into the sorry mess of the engine bay: 'I cannot in all conscience recommend to management that we proceed with a factory team this year,' he said. The implication was obvious. I might have found the best Cortina engine in the world but I couldn't guarantee its reliability.

In the pressure cooker of Daytona, I'd failed in a very public arena. That was exactly what the Ford PR machine didn't want.

Jim took his engine home to Australia.

A Lotus Cortina would not win a round of the Trans Am that year. It was the start of Porsche's class dominance.

I'd never seen Peter get mad before. He was a lovely, understated Englishman who privately enjoyed motor racing. In fact he owned a stove-hot Ford Anglia that he ran in club races at Waterford Hills. We'd occasionally tune it for him. But that was personal and this was business. No one messes with Ford, let alone one of its own executives. His career was on the line, probably more so than mine.

Several days later, when the heat came out of a mutually distressing and embarrassing situation, Peter was left with the remnants of his Alan Mann Lotus Cortina team, now redundant, and bequeathed them all to me.

The Cortinas were never going to be serious contenders. For the first, and only, time in my life I raced for starting money. As a low-cost alternative to fielding a works team, Ford was offering $300 'assistance' for every car that entered a Trans Am race. I had three working cars and Americans keen to drive two of them while I raced the third. Vince Woodfield moved on, collateral damage from my failure to live up to the promise of 1967; at twenty years of age, Barry Nelson became chief mechanic, and another Australian, Peter Thorn, a friend of Barry's, joined our privateer effort.

We were living sparsely, if not rough. No one was paid a salary. I doled out meagre expenses for food and fuel. We had been borrowing workshop space, but paradoxically we were now too big for it. I found a place across town that I could use for free. It was so big that I was able to buy a three-person campervan and park it next to the race cars: that became our home.

The pay-to-play Americans were hard on our race cars and most of the starting and meagre prize money we earned was spent on repairs. The best result I managed was fourth in round three at Green Valley where I was increasingly using my mirrors, not something that has ever made me happy.

Moving around the country was expensive and we agreed to what in hindsight were some pretty dodgy schemes.

If NASCAR had its roots in bootlegging then we figured running high-octane race fuel across America in 44-gallon containers for other teams was comparatively low risk. That is, until the truck we were driving seized its gearbox on a railway crossing with 30 containers on board. We pushed it to one side and happily my relationship with Goodyear came into play. While not revealing our cargo, we did ask if they could assist with alternative transport to get us to the race meeting. Within one hour, seriously, a brand-new Hertz prime mover arrived at the roadside, hitched us up and we were away, complete with cargo.

At round five, Mid-Ohio, luck found me again. Texan Ford Mustang owner George Kirksey, a former sports writer and part owner of a major league baseball team, sacked his regular driver—'just one of those things'—and approached me.

Would I take on the car, just for this race?

I could have said: 'I don't know.' The Mustang was three times the cubic capacity of my Cortina, weighed 50 per cent more, was bigger all round and ran on drum brakes. And besides I had my 'trusty' Cortina—which was leaking money—there.

There was no way I was going to say no.

I was itching for the chance to drive one of these things, and here it was—on offer. Five hundred kilometres later we'd finished third outright, disqualified later for refuelling with the engine running. Not my fault.

Kirksey promptly invited me to a non-championship round at Watkins Glen, the Manufacturers' Challenge. The main opposition was the Roger Penske Chevrolet Camaro driven by the great Mark Donohue. He was universally known as 'Captain Nice', a soft-talking engineer with a world-beating driving talent who would give you all the time in the world in the pits and then drive away from you on the track. He was to die a decade later as the result of a race crash in Austria.

I'd met millionaire race-owner Penske only the once. I was sitting in the office of Larry Truesdale, head of Goodyear's Racing division, in Akron, Mid-Ohio. I had a good relationship with Larry. He used to invite me to stay at his home whenever I was in town and that morning we'd driven over early to his office from his home, arriving just on 8 a.m. Suddenly this guy, Penske as it turns out, arrives, shoves me on the arm to move me to one side and starts to talk to Larry as if I didn't exist. It was incredibly rude, a show of power and an example of the sort of arrogance that just doesn't wash. I know these days Penske has a god-like reputation and the patina of a sweet guy about him. But first impressions count.

Anyway, at Watkins Glen, the Kirksey car streeted the field. We finished second and were then elevated to first when the 'winning' car was found to be running a 5.7-litre engine in a field limited to 5 litres. Mistakes happen.

After that the phone started ringing and offers started coming in. It was great but it wasn't what I'd wanted. Being a gun for hire isn't nearly as secure as team ownership, my goal, but at the time it was a lifeline.

The phone call that really counted was from Ford's Mercury division. I suspect Peter Quenet was behind it. The Trans Am series that year was the embodiment of Ford versus General Motor rivalry and it was good for showroom business for both auto-makers.

General Motors was fielding its Camaro through Penske. Ford was shooting itself in the foot by having two of its divisions—Ford Mustang and Lincoln-Mercury Cougar—competing as separate brands.

The Mustang and the Cougar were virtually identical under the skin. Each time they took points from each other they were giving Chevrolet a free kick.

Fran Hernandez, from Mercury, had decided to increase the official Mercury team's strength to four cars, run by Bud Moore, in an attempt to claw back points and I was asked to drive for the last four rounds.

In my view it wasn't my finest hour, but others differed. Three DNFs (did not finish), two of them not my fault, and an out-of-the-points finish in the final race were the sum of my contribution. On paper it didn't look good, but in that last race I'd actually achieved the team's objective. I'd been sent out to block, to deliberately spoil the field. And it seemed I'd been successful.

'Are you planning to be in this business for a while?' Captain Nice, the rising star of Trans Am, said to me at dinner that night.

'I'll try my best,' I replied.

'If you carry on like you did today, you won't get far,' was his response.

Bud Moore overheard the exchange. 'If you hadn't done what you did, I would have fired you,' he said.

For four races, I'd been in a works team, running against the best big-bore touring-car drivers in the States, if not the world, and when the car was going I'd learned a little more about what it takes to be at the front of the field. Ford Mustang won the title by two points from Mercury. Chevrolet was outclassed.

I'd driven well but at the end of the season I was out of a job again.

Barry and Peter helped me conduct a fire sale of the Cortinas as well as a Brabham BT15 open wheeler in which I'd had one run and one win at Waterford Hills using a Cortina engine, and then they returned to Australia.

There was no reason for me to follow them. There was nothing in Australia for me and there was a girl in Detroit, although that relationship had an end-of-season feel about it too.

•

I don't know—do you make your own luck or does luck find you?

I was sitting in a Ford cafeteria in Dearborn with Peter Quenet when a Ford legend came up to chat. Roy Lunn was head of Ford Advanced Vehicles and one of the founders of the renowned 'skunk works' Kar Kraft, a Ford-owned but virtually off-line high-performance development cell. He'd been integral in the design of the Ford GT40, Henry II's revenge on Ferrari, which had won the Le Mans 24 Hour race in 1966 and 1967, and would do so again for the next two years. Roy was not quite Enzo Ferrari, but he was close.

'What are you doing now?' he asked.

'Starving, except when my friends take me out,' I replied.

He offered me a job at Kar Kraft: $1000 a month and all the food the canteen could provide.

Let's get that in perspective. At Ferrari, in Maranello, the factory is connected across the road to its in-house test track, the famed Fiorano course where any day you can hear the wail of an F1 car intermingled with the equally evocative sounds of road cars being worked out.

At Ford, there's the giant River Rouge plant and one-and-a-half kilometres away there's the Dearborn Proving Ground.

In 1924, Henry I had built his own airfield. Because he owned his own lighter-than-air airship, it also featured the world's tallest mooring mast, so Henry had somewhere to park his dirigible. Over the years, as the lighter-than-air fad faded, the airfield morphed into the Dearborn test facility with a ribbon of roads used for component evaluation of Ford's day-to-day products. For high-speed testing, there were other proving grounds in faraway places like Arizona. Then, at Henry II's direction, Ford Advanced Vehicles was born, followed in 1966 by Kar Kraft, housed in a building that opened directly onto the test track—just like Maranello. With the global technical headquarters just across Oakwood Boulevard, DPG—the Dearborn Proving Ground—came alive.

For some people, being a test driver would be the ultimate prize. For me, maybe not. It's a repetitive process. Sometimes you're doing nothing more than mileage accumulation, hour after hour.

And the engineers are in charge, not the drivers. One of the engineers with whom I worked closely was Lee Dykstra, later to become a big part of my racing efforts. We worked well as a team. With my race experience, I was able to provide meaningful feedback. And we were working on some of the product that was most evocative to me: the Mustang Boss 302 and the Boss 429. We were also using as a test mule the very first mid-engined Ford Mustang sports car, developed by Roy Lunn five years before.

The Ford course was a mishmash—a long straight, a flyover, off-camber corners, switchbacks—a typical test track, not Fiorano at all. At one stage I held the test-driver lap record, pretty close to a sackable offence, and I'd also beached a car in a snow drift because testing was year round, even in the depths of a Detroit winter.

The value for me, apart from the mileage I was clocking up and the money I was saving, was that I was in the Ford fold, totally visible. That's how I got the call-up for the first and second rounds of the 1968 Trans Am title. They were to be extremely long-distance races—the Daytona 24 Hour and the Sebring 12 Hour—and I was to be part of the official works Shelby team. Driving for Carroll Shelby was a huge honour as well as an opportunity. He was one of the sharpest operators in the business. Jacque Passino, Ford's head of motor sport, a man who lived in the stratosphere of Ford's executive echelon, once said of Shelby: 'The old chicken farmer is so dumb that I have to have three lawyers around me or I'll lose my wallet and my pants.'

Jerry Titus and open-wheeler driver on secondment Ronnie Bucknum, two guns, were to drive the lead car. I was to share the Number Two Mustang with none other than Horst Kwech. Although we weren't young by today's standards we were, then, young guns and we were both eyeing something more permanent with Shelby. Bucknum had made it known he wouldn't be seeking the second drive for the year.

Twenty-four hours around Daytona in the second-best Mustang in the world was something to savour. You can't win the race on the opening lap and I was careful to hand the car over to Horst in good condition at the first stop. If only he'd done the same for me. On the next stop he jumped out and didn't say a word. Trundling down pit lane, I found the steering so tight that I could hardly manoeuvre around the cone markers out onto the track. For two laps it was beyond dangerous, especially on the banking.

The way to drive Daytona's banking is to let the bank steer you. You get in a groove and stay there, modulating your position by throttle control. With this car I was having to apply really heavy steering adjustment, narrowly avoiding other cars.

Even with an obvious problem you don't want to make an unscheduled stop, not ever, but there was no choice. I tore into pit lane and, when they opened the hood, they found the whole spring tower had pulled away, leaving the front suspension totally unsupported. In the race for the Shelby Ford works seat, score one for H. Kwech. You never want to be at the wheel of the car when it breaks and he'd neatly handballed that honour to me.

Titus and Bucknum won the 1968 24 Hour.

A month later at Sebring I broke my golden rule. When the flag dropped I was away, leading for the first hour until I was overhauled by Mark Donohue, who was to win the series for Penske Chevrolet. When I handed the Mustang to Horst it was perfect but, with one lap remaining of his long stint, the engine blew. At least he hadn't been able to get me back behind the wheel before it broke.

After Sebring, with the rest of the events regarded as sprints, the need for two drivers per car ceased. Titus was nominated lead. Kwech got the Number Two.

There's no comeback. You have to accept whatever happens. I went back to Kar Kraft, mightily disgruntled.

The projects there were good. We were working on something called the Mustang Mach2, a mid-engined Shelby 302 with a ZF five-speed transaxle at the rear. It would never see the light of day as a Ford but it was to become the DeTomaso Pantera, built in Italy and later sold back in the States through Ford's Lincoln-Mercury division.

The 302 Boss Mustang program was also in full swing.

At least I was revenue positive. For four months I worked hard, paid off my debts, got bored. It was mid-summer in Detroit, stinking hot and I was pacing the cage.

From Australia, John Sawyer telephoned me, then came to visit. John, a quietly spoken, determined sort of guy who was renowned for his organisational ability, was running Bob Jane's motor-racing division. Sawyer had previously worked with Australian Porsche distributor Norman Hamilton on his early Spyder hill-climb car and then with Stan Jones, father of world-champion Alan, on his locally made Maybach and then his Maserati 250F when he won the 1959 Australian Grand Prix. John moved to Bob Jane in 1961 and engineered the Jaguar with which Jane won the Australian Touring Car Championship (ATCC) in 1962 and '63. He came with a decent pedigree.

John was seeking the very latest Mustang for Jane's 1969 ATCC assault. It would be the first year the championship had moved to a series rather than a one-race screamer, and that put a whole different perspective on car preparation and longevity.

John asked me to introduce him to the right people and to help in local representation. I didn't like Bob Jane but I did like, and trust, John Sawyer. The suggestion, never put in writing, was that when Jane got his new Mustang, I'd get his old one. A drive in the ATCC in a Number Two car as a gun for hire was not exactly where I thought my career would end up, but it's an indication of my desperation that I accepted. As it turned out John Harvey, Jane's lead driver and a man with whom I'd later share great motor-racing moments, had been injured in a race crash at Bathurst and I was gifted a couple of his drives late in 1968.

The wheels fell off, literally, in a one-off appearance in the Lombard Trophy Race, a round of the CAMS Australian Gold Star Drivers championship at Sandown when I was in the Jane Repco Brabham. Apart from another drive in the company's locally made Elfin 400 sports car at Phillip Island, which I won, I was desk-bound and it was frustrating.

I was sitting at that desk in January 1969 when Bob Jane, himself, walked into the office, threw $500 on the table and said: 'We haven't been getting along very well.' And that was the end of my employment and the Mustang drive.

My 30th birthday was looming and I'd sold the remnants of the Australian Lotus Cortina to a young trier called Bill Fanning. With Jane's severance pay, my total bank balance was $5000. I figured I'd done more with less before and headed back to the USA.

6

THE GREATEST
TRANS AM OF ALL

IN 1969 I FELL IN LOVE TWICE.

The first time was with the Trans Am Boss 302 Ford Mustang that would become the definitive race car in my life and one of the most successful in touring-car racing in the world. It would win 101 of its 156 starts.

The second time was with twenty-year-old Pauline Dean, executive assistant to the marketing director of Coca-Cola, the first major commercial sponsor I'd ever secured; Coca-Cola became the name on the side of the Mustang. Both relationships were powerful, intense, rewarding and successful to a point, but, sadly, neither was to go the distance.

'Dedicated' is how a lot of people have described me. It is probably true although it's difficult to find the words to define the spirit within yourself that drives you towards your own goals, even in the face of extraordinary odds. I guess it's not about introspection. It's the qualities other people see in you that make the difference.

Why, otherwise, would a senior executive of Ford Motor Company in Dearborn open his door to me at a time when it would have been so much easier to refuse contact?

Sacked by Bob Jane, I wrote directly to Jacque Passino, the head of all motor sport for Ford. Like most of the Ford top brass at the time, Passino was a dyed-in-the-wool car guy, but not necessarily a motor-racing enthusiast. He was first and foremost a fast-tracked rising star for the world's most successful auto-maker at a time when its supremo Henry II had decreed motor sport was a key ingredient in brand enhancement. Jacque was easy to spot at a race meeting. He was the one in sombre suit and tie, sharply if inappropriately dressed, and keenly interested in all that was going on around him. He was absolutely no fool. 'I'm really not a performance nut,' he told *Hot Rod* magazine in a rare interview. 'I am a merchant engaged in the selling of cars.'

In his twelve years at Ford, straight from university, he had worked in sales, product planning, advertising and, most importantly, as his stocks rose in the company as a close underling of the mercurial Lee Iacocca, who was to become Ford president and who was widely regarded, somewhat erroneously, as the father of the Ford Mustang. The motor-racing brief was another step on Passino's career ladder and he intended to carry it out well. 'A performance image can help promote car sales,' he said. 'I feel that anytime a wheel turns we have to be represented and I plan to see that we are there.' The thing is, he had the authority to keep his promise.

I just thought I had to have a go. My letter to him got through to his secretary, a feat in itself, and I was granted an appointment. I guess I had some credibility: being the outright winner of the third-ever Trans Am race in one of his products must have stood for something, and backing up as a driver in his works team as well as a Kar Kraft test pilot maybe put me on his radar. But I seriously doubted it.

My grandfather always taught me to never sit down in anyone's office unless they invited you. I was high up in the executive towers and I was ushered into an office bigger than my workshop. Passino was a fearsome guy, beautifully dressed, with prematurely greying hair and strong steel glasses. He didn't ask me to sit.

I explained my case. I was a Ford man through and through. I had unfinished business in Australia—to win the national title—and a Cortina was no longer going to do it for me. I held back on saying that I wanted to cane Jane's hide, but I guess that was pretty self-evident. I concluded by asking: 'Are you able to help with a car?'

He said: 'I don't know where the cars are. Give me a couple of days and I'll see what I can dig up for you.'

He asked me where I was staying—a motel down the road which he passed every day on his way to the office. He said he'd call me there.

It was only when I left his office that I reviewed what he'd said: 'I'll see what I can dig up for you.' Not just 'I'll see what's available', but 'for you'—those were the two key words.

I hightailed it back to the motel and briefed the front-desk guy. 'Sometime, I don't know when, I am expecting a visitor or a phone call. I won't be leaving my room until then.'

I arranged for room service for all meals—not exactly a standard feature of the house. And I waited.

On the fourth day, the longest four of my life, the phone rang. It was Passino himself: 'Have you got enough money to get to Spartanburg [Bud Moore's workshop]?'

I said, 'Only just.'

He said, 'There's a car waiting for you.'

There was no mention of payment, but I figured that was to come. For the 1969 Trans Am series Ford was having a big go. Through Kar Kraft they had built seven incredibly special Ford Mustangs, the Boss 302s. Three each were to go to Ford's two works teams—Carroll Shelby and Bud Moore. The seventh would go to Smokey Yunick's NASCAR team. Their value was incalculable. I knew because I'd been a small part of the development program. Like the Le Mans GT40 assault of three years ago, this wasn't a campaign being run by normal accounting practices.

I had no expectation of even touching those cars. My goal had been to see if I could buy, at the cheapest possible price, one of the now-redundant 1968 cars. After all, nothing's cheaper than an old racing car and I figured I could still build a race winner from it in Australia.

I was at Bud Moore's workshop a day later and he wouldn't look me in the eye. I thought, *Who are you to be upset? I've come to buy used stock.* He walked me into the workshop and there, sitting abreast, were the three new Trans Am Boss 302s, each still in their grey undercoats. 'The one in the middle is yours,' he said.

Jacque Passino had done what nobody else in Ford could do, with the possible exception of Henry II. With one word, he'd made one of the magnificent seven mine. And at no cost. No cost at all.

I didn't know why then and I don't know why now. There are theories. Ford Australia was a favoured outpost of Dearborn. It was managed by upwardly mobile Americans who were using it as a stepping stone for their careers. Maybe a favour was being offered way beyond me. In the sometimes murky world of corporate ownership, Ford Australia was attached to Ford America through another subsidiary Ford of Canada, and I was Canadian—that theory is pretty far-fetched, I know. Maybe, simply, it's because I asked and someone just liked me.

When I returned to Australia that year I was immediately drafted into Ford's series production touring-car team and soon became Number One. So perhaps there was a grand plan in which the Mustang was the best incentive ever. I don't think I will ever know.

For two weeks Bud Moore wouldn't let me near the workshop floor as his guys finished the cars—mine first, because it had a pressing engagement in round three of the ATCC. I wanted so desperately to help assemble it, but I also knew I was on thin ice in this environment. I figured that if you had a gold bar in your hand, it wasn't the time to worry about its weight. I waited in the coffee shop and carried parts when asked.

A lot was happening in Australian motor racing.

For the first time the Australian champion would be decided in a series of five events. Over the previous nine years—since its inception—the title had been awarded on the basis of a one-off race. There was nothing wrong with that; in fact it was incredibly entertaining to choose a champion of champions in a sudden-death play-off. But there was also a lot to be said for the strategy that comes with a multi-state title chase and the promotional build-up that accompanies it, not to mention the opportunity to correct errors you may have made along the way.

Two rounds of the championship would have already been held by the time of my return, one won by Pete Geoghegan and the other by Bob Jane, both in Mustangs. Even if I won the last three races, if Pete came second, he would still take the title on accumulated points. But the cars of the day were fragile, and finishing at all was never assured. I was in with a chance.

The second major change in motor racing was the emergence of sponsorship on cars. Under some sort of Queensberry rules of sporting purity, advertising on cars had been prohibited by motor sport's governing body, not just in Australia but throughout the world. Teams used all sorts of subterfuge to get around the ban. Cars were painted in sponsors' colours, leaving it to only the more astute observers to get the connection. Jack Brabham famously arrived at an early race meeting with his Cooper Bristol emblazoned as the ReDEX Special. ReDEX, an oil additive, had paid for half the car and deserved its recognition. But officials forced Jack to cover the sign—which he did with thinly attached brown paper that blew off on the first straight.

The Mustang may have been free but I needed money, lots of it, to run it and this was an opportunity to provide a big-name sponsor with exposure in a brand-new medium. Even as I was in the USA a colleague, former radio announcer and sometime motor-sport entrepreneur Don Gibb, was sending a prospectus to potential backers. It seems so fundamental but so many people seeking sponsorship come at it from the perspective of what's in it for them. They see sponsorship as a one-way flow of necessary, even deserved, assistance. For me it's always been about what I can provide my valued business partner in return. Look after them and they'll look after me.

Coca-Cola was interested.

They were big in surfing and rock-and-roll at the time. Both provided lifestyle exposure, which was all about the Coke image. Surprisingly, while Coke was a national brand, it was actually owned by a grouping of independent bottlers, one in each state. It wasn't until 1977 that they would consolidate. My proposal had gone to Victoria and landed on the desk of its visionary marketing manager, David Maxwell. My offer was not the giant breakthrough David was constantly seeking, but it was the opportunity to have a small experiment on the side. My Coke backing—promoted hard by me, well covered by the media and accepted by the fans as a massive boost to motor racing—was, in the context of the company's other involvements, a pretty cheap sponsorship. 'It's affordable, so let's do it' was David's response and I had two reasons to be grateful to him.

The second was Pauline Dean, his gatekeeper, who, wisely for one so young and pretty, had already developed a deep suspicion of the motives of surfers, rock musicians and now racing drivers. It would take some time to break down that barrier.

Back in Spartanburg, I was still getting the cold shoulder from Bud Moore but the mechanics, with whom I'd struck up a good working relationship, had given me a heads up on when the car would be out of there, so I entered the 1969 Southern 60 at Sandown and booked passage for myself and the Mustang on a part-passenger, part-cargo aircraft out of New York. My car was well ahead of the US's own program and it would be the first Trans Am ever to race and win anywhere in the world. If only I'd dared to ask why, and how, I'd been fast tracked, maybe year one would have turned out differently.

The drama started in the air. I'd hopped a plane to make it to JFK International in time to supervise the loading of the car but we got stuck in a massive mid-air holding pattern. We'd advanced to fourth slot for landing when the pilot came on and said we were low on fuel and had no option but to divert to Washington.

I arrived in New York late that night to be told the Mustang had already been loaded and would I please take my own seat. I finally persuaded a steward to peep in the hold. He did and reported there was a big grey car back there that looked like it was going faster than the plane. Only then could I sleep.

In Melbourne we were possibly not as well prepared as we would have liked. The Trans Am was delivered to a holding yard and my only way of moving it to the earthen-floor workshop at 711 Malvern Road in a timely fashion was by towing it. Not on a trailer: I hitched a rope to the front of the world's most valuable race car and flat towed it behind my Econoline van. Peter Thorn, back from our Cortina adventure in the USA, was at the wheel of the Trans Am, judging his steering and braking moves off my brake lights and signals.

At '711' we examined this beautiful gift for the first time on our own terms. It was an incredible piece of engineering—not a Mustang at all. For a start it had been made lightweight by a process of elimination that has stood the test of time throughout race-car development. Every component was examined and lightened where possible. Every non-essential item was removed; every steel panel made lighter by drilling cheese-holes in it—even the window winders were shortened to remove weight.

By getting the car beneath the minimum weight for the category, it was possible to strategically place ballast to alter the front-to-rear handling to make it the best-mannered, most-controllable Mustang of the time in the world. Fuel tanks were dropped lower and the engine was discretely sunk in its bay to provide a better centre of gravity and even better handling.

Seam-welded panels, braced suspension towers and one of the world's first integral tubular steel roll cages improved structural rigidity to the point of a very lightweight Sherman tank. Aerodynamics were enhanced by minute means. Trim 50 millimetres from the height of the radiator support panel and you get a shovel nose that cuts through the air.

The Trans Am had disc brakes all round—a 'so what' by today's standards but for the time it was a breakthrough so great that two years later officials forced us to go back to drums on the rear to comply with their 'new' regulations. How that could be a step forward I never understood. Suspension, however, was by leaf spring at the rear, just like sulkies and horse carts, again required by category regulations, but Kar Kraft's engineers and test drivers, me included, had made them the best they could be.

The heart of the car was supposed to be the 302 Boss engine, a massive improvement on the tunnel-port Windsor engine that had been spectacularly unsuccessful in the 1968 season. The Boss, transferring its power through a heavy-duty Toploader NASCAR-style transmission, was going to give me everything I needed—power, grunt out of corners, exceptional braking and nimble handling the like of which no other Mustang could deliver.

Kar Kraft had truly crafted the Mustang. I respected that. In all the time I owned it, I never changed a spring or a roll-bar setting. You shouldn't try to improve on perfection.

We didn't start the car in the workshop. We'd save that for Sandown.

Peter Thorn painted the Mustang red. Most people assumed it was Coca-Cola's corporate colours but we weren't that sophisticated and neither were they. It was nowhere near Coke's colour. We thought the car looked so good that we wanted to paint it Ferrari red. Peter, a panel beater and spray-painter by trade, mixed three Dulux colours—Deep Red, Fast Red and Bright Orange—and applied three coats. He did all that on the earth floor and left it to air dry. I promised Peter the first thing I'd do when we won some prize money would be to concrete the floor.

That was necessary for another reason too.

Ford Australia had given me a surface plate, a machined platform of steel that allows you to accurately build and measure the weight balance of a car on each of its corners. It is an amazing piece of engineering, almost magic, and it was to be the centre piece of both 711 and my race-car construction for the rest of my career.

We arrived at Sandown, scene of my Cortina frustrations, for its first hit out and the car wouldn't go. It started with a magnificent cackle and I drove out of the pits, heading for the back straight, when it stuttered and stalled. Back in the pits we went over everything. When things go wrong, there's no other way. You just work hard until you find the problem. Mechanic Barry Nelson, also back from the USA and, like Peter Thorn and myself, just privileged to be working on the car without any thought of salary or recompense, started blowing down the fuel line. The electric pump was not getting fuel through to the engine.

That's when I chased the line all the way from front to rear and found under my driver's seat a surplus of rubber fuel tube tied tightly in a knot. We undid it and shortened it. Fuel flowed and we were away. It was so good to drive—no power steering, but the steering got lighter the faster you went. No power brakes, but you knew exactly where you stood with the pedal pressure and I never lost a brake in all the years I drove it.

To say the car created immense interest was an understatement. A guy from Ford arrived and placed a huge blue Ford decal on the car. I politely removed it and replaced it with a discrete white one that I'd brought from the States. A person from Ampol put a sticker on and I left it there because I assumed money or kind would follow. It didn't.

Then the opposition turned up.

Norm Beechey was the first. He walked straight into the Coke tent and leant heavily on the right front fender, testing the suspension. Then he turned around and sat on the bonnet.

I said, 'You don't need to sit on my car any more.' I don't think I said please. Bob Jane was next and he simply looked. He was almost polite. Then Bryan Thompson, a talented privateer from Shepparton who'd bought Beechey's Mustang, simply dived under the front of the car to have a look at its mechanicals. He was wearing a white race-suit at the time and he cut his ear on the arrowhead low spoiler lip, emerging with blood pouring down his cheek and over his clothes. I wasn't sympathetic.

Pete Geoghegan saved his welcome for the track. He drove into my door on the first corner.

Okay, so that's how it's going to be, I thought, and got out of there fast.

At its first race meeting, the Mustang won three races out of three. It was something to write home about.

The car had just scored the first-ever win for the Trans Am Mustang anywhere in the world. I thanked Jacque Passino profusely and sent him pictures but I also told him I was surprised the car was not as powerful in a straight line as I'd expected and that it was very highly geared, meaning it was not jumping out of corners or getting off the start line like a jackrabbit.

Jacque did some investigation and that's when it was discovered that in their haste to get me on my way the Bud Moore team had fitted the car not with the new Boss 302 engine but with the troublesome tunnel-port engine from the 1968 season. Because parts weren't readily available they'd also given me a Toploader gearbox built for NASCAR, the American oval series popularised as Days of Thunder. It did 190 km/h in first gear, great for a rolling start on a speed bowl, but not so good on a road circuit.

Was it possible that Bud didn't share the same respect for my efforts as Jacque?

A new drive train, Jacque promised, would be despatched for the third round of the ATCC on the converted World War II airstrip at Mallala in South Australia.

In the meantime there was money to be made, necessary if we were to keep the show on the road. Motor racing had always been the playground of the seriously wealthy, but it was also emerging as a lucrative spectator sport. Promoters who had the foresight to build an amphitheatre-like layout to give fans ringside seats were in a position to make a fairly major sum, especially if they weren't paying their performers, and very few people were getting paid. Unlike some of my better-heeled rivals I was in no position to give it away. I established a fee for service.

It was such a closely guarded negotiation that even now I'm loathe to reveal it. But if the agreement was in cash and not kind, like an engine or new tyres, it was a four-figure sum that usually started with just the number '1'. One promoter was already enlightened. Peter Brock, who'd started to become a crowd favourite in Victoria in a Holden-engined Austin A30, was shocked when Oran Park promoter Allan Horsley offered him a slightly smaller sum, undemanded, to cross the border into New South Wales. It was only much later that a few of us, owners of our own teams without other visible means of support, started an entrants group that formalised our money-making agreements with the circuit owners.

At one point I ran seventeen paid weekends straight. The pace was punishing and it cost me three burnt-out mechanics, but at least I was earning money from my craft.

At Oran Park the Mustang was again a hit in the regional Toby Lee Series where it came second to local hero Pete Geoghegan, and it was not yet on the scoreboard of the touring-car title.

When I go motor racing, nothing else matters. Total concentration is an absolute requirement, but that Oran Park weekend I relaxed my principles. Pauline's parents owned a hotel just down the road at Goulburn so I invited her, in her official Coke capacity, to come to the race. Cautiously she agreed, as long as her brother John could attend personally as a chaperone. That night we found ourselves at an after-party at the nearby home of the Hon. John Dawson-Damer, a British aristocrat and major motor-sport enthusiast who was to amass a wonderful collection of Lotus racing cars; he was killed in one of them at the finish line of the 2000 Goodwood Festival of Speed. John's home was an original two-storey colonial with a tree-lined driveway on over a hundred hectares. The house also had a grand piano, which I was playing, poorly. Pauline had been taken aback by my on-track persona but she said later it was this new view—which surprised even me—that softened her resolve. Small steps were being taken.

Mallala, my first round of the ATCC, was a disaster and it was a forebear of the season. The new engine flown in from the States put me on the front row of the grid alongside Jane and Geoghegan. But two laps later, it blew while I was challenging Jane for second. Motor-racing engines are very specialised units. They are built with components—crankshafts, conrods, pistons—to rev hard and high and sustain immense stress for long periods. When we pulled this one down we found it to be bog standard. I'd been sent not a racing engine but a completely stock unit. It was as if I was being sabotaged.

One of our special guests at Mallala, a track on a wind-blown plain some 70 kilometres from Adelaide and not easily accessible, was the South Australian bottler for Coca-Cola. Our Coke money was coming from one source—Victoria—and from the other franchise holders only if they saw some merit. New South Wales was already on board, not totally willingly, but at least complying. The guy in Queensland was happy for us to run there, and to promote his product, but paying was another matter. David Maxwell had implored his South Australian counterpart to go and see for himself. He did so somewhat reluctantly, and by the time I'd walked back to the pits from the stranded Mustang he, his wife and daughter were already gone on the long drive back to civilisation. It was the last contact I ever had with him.

There's one word to describe the Mustang's first season and that's 'harrowing'.

Seasons two, three and four were better but the Mustang never did win the ATCC, and that's a cause of immense disappointment to me.

In 1969 it never even got on the board, never even scored a point, despite becoming one of the most recognised and followed cars in the series. It even suffered humiliating DNFs and DNS (did not start) in some of the non-championship races, as we worked to sort it out. From 1970 to 1972 it cemented its position as one of most successful and admired cars in the country.

In the 23 ATCC races it contested until its enforced retirement at the end of 1972, it won ten, finished on the podium another four times, claimed 14 pole positions, and set four lap records. It figured in some of the most controversial incidents in the championship, starred in front of the biggest crowd ever at Oran Park and played a lead role in the touring-car battle regarded as the greatest of all times. Yet in the annual title fight, the best it could manage was a second and a third.

In search of more power for the 1970 season I'd tried to fit a 351-cubic inch (5.75-litre) engine. It was so heavy, the winch lowering it into the car bent. It changed the whole handling dynamics. The Mustang was built for cornering speed and, with its tall gearing and good torque out of corners, it was surprisingly quick on the straights. Put the big engine in it, however, and all that mid-corner speed went away. So I stuck with the 302 Boss and settled for handling and corner speed over horsepower.

Norm Beechey went the other way. He built a Holden Monaro with 6.0 litres. It was a rocket ship in a straight line and a boat anchor in the corners. It was to carry him to the title, but not without a fight.

Beechey had already made his feeling for me known at Calder the previous year. In mid-1969, in a non-championship race, he brake-tested me on the warm-up lap. We weren't even racing when he slammed on his brakes in front and left me nowhere to go but into him. I saw him size me up in his rear-vision mirror before he did it. It was a deliberate tactic to at least unsettle me and at most damage me enough to put me out of the race before we'd started. It didn't work for him. It fired me up and, with my brand-new bonnet bent out of shape, I blasted past into the first corner and won, putting him off in the process.

In the first round of the 1970 championship, I'd taken pole on the wet Calder track but there was nothing I could do to stop Beechey pushing past. Then his ill-handling car hit a back marker and he had to stop to pull the Monaro's guard off the wheel. My win that day, my first in the ATCC, was also the first time since the title began that someone other than an Australian had won a round. Beating Beechey felt good.

It was, however, to be my last win of the season. In seven races I claimed three pole positions and a podium at Sandown. But I was T-boned by Pete Geoghegan off the start at Warwick Farm and I was black-flagged for passing under the yellow flag at Lakeside, past the crash that destroyed Chris Brauer's ex-Bob Jane Mustang.

The year did have an upside. Midway through the season, I'd made a flying overseas dash. The day she turned 21, Pauline was off on her own kangaroo tour to Europe without a defined return date. She was working for a celebrity doctor in London, delivering actress Mia Farrow's twins, and travelling when she could.

I'd been pretty relentless in my pursuit so it was sensational when I received a telegram (you sent them in those days) saying: 'In Amsterdam. Have found my engagement ring. Send money.' I responded: 'It's the price of a crankshaft, but go ahead.'

Looking back, I can see how steely on-track resolve can be interrupted by matters of emotion. I flew to Britain, picked

Pauline up and made a quick trip to Toronto to introduce my folks to their intended daughter-in-law . . . all the time ignoring my race program. But at least we waited until the end of the race season to be married in the Goulburn Catholic Cathedral. Ford turned on a black Falcon GTHO as our wedding car. With that settled, I was looking forward to 1971.

Then organisers changed the touring-car rules.

Six litres were apparently no longer enough. Now they allowed seven. Bob Jane, an arch lobbyist for the increase, took maximum advantage, importing a 427-cubic inch (7-litre) Camaro. Jane had always been good at yapping—convincing officials either by persuasion or force of personality that his ideas were worthy of their support. At the time I was more interested in immediate matters, like car preparation and living from day to day. That corporate blindness on my part cost me dearly in those first few years.

But the Mustang still handled better than Jane's Camaro and I won the first round at Symmons Plains and was leading the second at Calder when the engine overheated and stopped.

Sandown was a ridiculous farce. The track suited Jane's Camaro but, when it stuck in gear, I took the lead and was heading for victory until an official spotted something, unspecified, hanging beneath the Mustang. There was no visible oil leak and no sign of danger but they black-flagged me anyway and called me to the pits.

A black flag is a pretty ironclad instruction, but I chose to stay out. For five laps, I drove the wheels off the Mustang, building up a gap between me and Jane. It was only on the last lap that I dived into the pits. They looked underneath, said it was okay, and sent me on my way as I knew they would. I took the chequered flag in first, 40 seconds clear of the field. Then the stewards of the meeting convened and disqualified me for disobeying the flag. You have to pit immediately, not when it suits you. My appeal was dismissed and I was disqualified. Zero points and my loss was everyone else's gain as they shuffled up the points table.

At the Queensland circuits, Surfers Paradise and Lakeside, the Mustang came into its own. It took pole position, fastest lap and the race win at each circuit—the perfect trifecta, twice. My points would have been looking even better if Beechey hadn't put me off the road at Mallala.

One round remaining at Oran Park and Jane led the series on 34 points from Geoghegan on 32 and me on 31. Effectively it was winner take all.

That Grand Final day was when the growing pulling power of top-end motor racing was confirmed. Oran Park attracted its biggest crowd on record. Police bulletins were issued to tell people to turn back because the track was packed beyond capacity, but turning back was difficult too, because the roads were gridlocked. The next day the *Sydney Morning Herald* carried an aerial photograph showing traffic queues for kilometres and a dark mass of humanity at the race track.

I took pole position and rather than tell the story myself, here's the race report from *Racing Car News*:

Moffat ran away with the race, winning the start while Jane missed a gear and for three laps was third behind Geoghegan as Moffat drew out a useful temporary margin. Jane then started to inch closer but on lap sixteen he was leading as Moffat found the Mustang stuck in second gear and rolled to a temporary halt and Geoghegan, too, howled past.

Moffat then started a great comeback drive pulling in Jane's 15 second lead at around a second a lap. At just after half distance he caught Geoghegan, dancing the red Mustang from one side to the other looking for a way through and finally in desperation holding to the outside of the long first corner loop to gain the inside running on the drop into the esses, cannoning off Geoghegan's door and away after Jane again.

Then the unbelievable happened—a spectator drove a Valiant Pacer road car onto the track. It entered the circuit at the esses and was almost bundled off it by Moffat. So hard was Moffat concentrating on the task of overtaking Jane that afterwards he had no recollection of the road car. (The spectator pulled up at the pit entrance and was taken into custody.)

Over the final six laps Moffat was relentless in his pursuit, driving superbly and was right astern of Jane in the final corner. Which of course was just one lap too late. Moffat had turned in some of the most spectacular and intense driving ever seen.

I lost the championship by six points, a black flag and a momentarily jammed gearbox, a fault of the Toploader that can only be cured by coming to a complete stop. By today's standards, the Toploader was pretty rudimentary but in its time it was the best—what I'd call magnificently useless. There was some comment that it was pride that kept me going, that I was driven by some sort of egomania, wanting to prove my ability. I knew my ability. I just wanted to win the race and the championship. And, as tough a competitor as Jane was, the more pressure you put on him, the more likely he was to make a mistake.

Organisers changed the rules again in 1972. The maximum engine limit was reduced to 6 litres—a bit late, I thought. Drum brakes were required for the rear—why in goodness' name they'd do that beggars belief. And, to provide an even playing field, 2-litre cars were allowed to score class points equal to outright and pick up bonus points for outright positions. In other words, they could win the title. It was also to be the last year of these regulations. The following year, under completely new regulations, the Mustang would be ineligible, so it was now or never.

I won the first race and retired in the second after cutting a tyre in a clash with Jane. Bathurst was the third round and it would become renowned as the best touring-car race of all time.

There were 13 laps of the 6.2-kilometre circuit and I had pole in a car that was everything it was supposed to be across the top of the mountain. Jane led from the start but by the time we got to Conrod Straight the Mustang was in the lead with Pete Geoghegan in the Super Falcon GTHO passing Jane for second. For the next six laps, Pete and I swapped the lead at various points of the circuit. It was amazing racing and then a mist started to cover my windscreen. The big GTHO was pumping out oil all over the front of me. It was impossible to see. I made the mistake of turning on the windscreen wipers and it just made vision worse.

I dropped almost 200 metres behind. We were still averaging 150 km/h and pulling 270 km/h down Conrod—long before the Chase was built—and the only thing to catch you when you flew over the second hump was a barbed-wire fence. That's when I made the decision that the only way to catch Pete was to put my head out the window and the only way to do that was to take off my seat belts and perch on the side of my bucket seat. It was the most dangerous, worst-considered thing I've ever done in my racing career. I broke the lap record like that and by the end of Conrod on the last lap I was alongside him, but on the wrong line. He won. I was second. Here's the race report again:

> Just what Moffat pulled out of his soul over those last three laps can only be guessed at, but one observer with top credentials detailed the following:
> a) that Moffat had his rear wheels off the deck over the last hump on Con Rod
> b) that the Mustang's spoiler and brake scoops were scarred from where they hit the ground before Moffat could start to brake
> c) that Moffat had undone his belts so he could put his head out the window
> d) that the Mustang finished the race with an almost opaque screen and oil dripping off the front panels.
> It was the stuff legends can be made from.

I protested against Pete for his oil spill but by then his crew had had plenty of time to clean up the GTHO, and when stewards met to consider their verdict that night they determined that, because I'd set a new lap record on the second-last lap, if any oil had been leaking, it couldn't have been so bad.

Politically that race was most important. I'd resisted using the Super Falcon GHTO Ford had built for me. They could not get it to handle and I knew my Mustang was vastly superior. For obvious commercial reasons Ford wanted me in the Falcon. They sold Falcons in Australia, not Mustangs. So when Pete beat me in the Falcon, to a degree the Ford guys had scored a victory. They could say, at least privately, their car was better than mine. It wasn't so. Pete had taken his Falcon off-line and his own engineers had done some marvellous work to make it work—minus, of course, its oil leak. But it would lead to more pressure on me to abandon the Mustang—something I would never do.

Two weeks later at Sandown, I set pole position, won the race and claimed fastest lap. At Adelaide International Raceway, for the first time in the Mustang, I was on pole alongside the unrelenting Jane. For the first fourteen laps it was incredibly physical, so much so that we were both shown the bad sportsmanship flag. Jane hesitated at the flag and I took the lead, but with just seven laps to go the Mustang filled with smoke. I headed for the pits and came back out in fourth.

Warwick Farm was the next round and it was to be my undoing in the championship—a victim of a litigious competitor who'll win at all costs. I had pole with Jane alongside me and he passed me down the long Hume Straight on lap seven. Four laps later he left an opening coming onto the double-apex Causeway and I went for the gap. We touched and he spun off. At the end of the race he was at my window, raining punches at me. 'Stop it,' I yelled. 'You'll lose your licence.' Instead he protested against me, claiming I'd been dangerous in my passing manoeuvre and spun him close to marshals. I was called to the stewards and, at the end of the day, it was announced I'd been reprimanded. That wasn't enough for Jane. He appealed to the motor-racing tribunal, a power above the race stewards.

I went to Surfers Paradise with that pending decision hanging over my head. In fact, I'd had to hire a lawyer to counter his lawyer—but Jane's lawyers were always the best.

At Surfers I took pole and fastest lap, but my throttle cable broke and I idled into tenth position, out of the points. The tribunal was not favourable. They deemed I'd shown insufficient caution and had been the cause of Jane's spin. With that, I was no longer in championship contention and I'd ultimately finish third. For some people that would still be a good result. For me it may as well have been last.

The Mustang won the final race of the series at Oran Park, and that was also the last race of the championship in that form. It was fitting, I think, that the accolade of that final win should fall to the red car.

It was not so fitting that long before compulsory drug testing I was asked to give a blood sample. I hate needles, but I complied because I had nothing to hide and to make a fuss would have played into the hands of the competitor who suggested to officials they should test me. I said nothing.

I think it was probably the first drug test in our sport.

Officials also said nothing, especially when the results were all clear.

After Oran Park I just could not part with the Mustang. For the next two years I raced it as a sports sedan, a lesser category, both in Australia and in New Zealand, while I won the 1973 ATCC in a Falcon.

Coke pulled out. I found a new sponsor in male toiletry company Brut 33, sharing their patronage with such noted sports luminaries as Muhammad Ali and Barry Sheene. It wasn't a happy relationship. I had to chase them for money and they showed little appreciation. The Mustang was, of course, successful but I refused to cut and shut it like a lot of sports sedans. It deserved better than that. It deserved to be kept as original as possible. To my eye it looked horrible in its green-and-silver livery and I couldn't wait for it to be red again. It changed colours once more in the summer of 1975 when we raced in New Zealand in Union Shipping Colours. Its last race was against local hero Jim Richards in January and it performed up to par, although Jim won on much wider tyres that could fit beneath his modified body work.

On one of our New Zealand trips, we had it parked at the local Ford dealer's showroom. At 3 a.m. a group of guys from the winning team snuck in and took it silently out the back to a hoist to try to discover for themselves what made it so fast. They only had to ask me.

I kept the Mustang for another twenty years, moving it from garage to garage, never wanting to be separated from it. It sat on the magic surface plate for a long time—a monument to its success.

•

The old cliché is that the only way to make a small fortune out of motor racing is to start with a large one. In my post-driving team-ownership days I was to experience the full brunt of that statement.

In fact, I was forced to sell up just about everything, including the Mustang, a valuable asset. For two years I had it on consignment to specialist race-car builders Holman and Moody in the USA. There were a lot of Asian buyers around in those days with briefcases full of money. I thought it would fetch maybe $400,000 or $500,000, but there were no takers. Then Australia's foremost enthusiast collector David Bowden made me an offer that the bank did not allow me to refuse. He snapped up the car by clearing a debt of just $140,000.

David has made her red again—not exactly Peter Thorn red—and when I was given the honour of driving her at the Australian F1 Grand Prix in Melbourne, I found that, after all those years I'd spent keeping her as the factory intended, she'd been interfered with.

The steering was heavy, she was sluggish in response and, although David has told me I'll be the only one apart from his family to ever drive her, I'd simply rather not.

7

A family holiday in Manitoba Province, Canada. My father Arthur, mother Evelyn, Gordon and myself.

In South Africa—my first powered vehicle, the scooter I rode to school. I remember it as a Goggomobile.

My very first car—the mighty 1935 flathead Ford Fordor. I'm on the right fender.

The Triumph TR3 became progressively faster—or at least I did. It was possible to set it up in a drift.

At the wheel of the 'works' VW Beetle—all four wheels off the track but with the power still fully applied.

My first year as a Team Lotus mechanic, 1964. Gofer, actually. Cleaning the windscreen was an important job and I took it seriously.

Two of my greatest early motor-sport influencers, 1964—Ray Parsons (left), who gave me my start and later became my Lotus Cortina teammate, and the amazing Colin Chapman, the genius behind Team Lotus.

After my first race in the Lotus Cortina, in the sports-car race at the Canadian Grand Prix, Mosport Park, 1964, with my great mate Jack Christie and the second-place trophy on the bonnet. Jack got to wear the official Team Lotus mechanic's overalls.

Past and present. My guardian angel Peter Quenet (middle) on the bonnet of the Lotus Cortina with me (left).

I became part of the Lotus Cortina. The 'steering wheel' I'm holding is actually the brake-light garnish.

This was the natural body language of the Lotus Cortina—two wheels, perfectly balanced and on the absolute limit. That's how you drove them for maximum effect.

With my father,
Arthur Moffat, 1965.

My favourite photograph of all. On the main straight at Indianapolis after Jim Clark won the Indy 500 for Lotus in 1965. He's in the car. Team owner Colin Chapman is kneeling in front of the cockpit and I am second from the right, proudly wearing my Team Lotus overalls.

At Daytona, 1967—my car and Jim McKeown's engine. Left to right: me, mechanic Vince Woodford and Jim McKeown. It was the day one career door shut.

A very historic picture. The Mustang in its original grey, sitting on jacks in Bud Moore's workshop along with two sister cars, prior to being built up. I wasn't allowed near it so this is a spy shot I took in 1969.

The mighty Mustang Trans Am—still in its grey undercoat—arrives in Australia after its flight from New York, 1969.

On the earthen floor of 711 Malvern Road, with the Mustang still to be painted, 1969. Left to right: Barry Nelson, me, Peter Thorn and Brian Fellows. We shared the workshop with trucks from the local bakery.

In 1969, on the warm-up lap of a non-championship race at Calder, Norm Beechey 'brake-tested' me, putting a dent in the nose of my Mustang. Payback came shortly afterwards when I was able to press him into error. Despite the nose damage that implies I hit him, I never touched him.

Calder Park. One of the few times when the Mustang stepped out of shape.

I was always hands on. Here I'm using a micrometre to check the bearings of the Trans Am's engine, an intricate task, 1969.

A close encounter with Pete Geoghegan put me into the fence in the Warwick Farm esses. It all looks okay from the A-pillar backwards but check out the front left-wheel position and angle.

The very early days of the Brock/Moffat rivalry—Peter in the six-cylinder XU-1 Torana and me in the Falcon GTHO at Warwick Farm.

My first Bathurst 500 win, 1970. Emotion overcame me.

Al Turner was a hot-shot marketer and race-team developer at a time when Ford was relying heavily on high performance to sell cars. I looked up to him. Still do.

Ford's Super Falcon, pushed onto the hard stand at Lot Six, 1970. You can see from the surrounding wire fences and weeds that Ford's race headquarters were devoid of pretention.

In 1971 Bob Jane (right) promoted a Formula Ford 'Race of Champions' at Calder. Three times world champion Jack Brabham (centre) won it, but not before I'd booted him from behind, putting myself out of the race.

At Calder, for the 'Race of Champions' in 1971, after I ran up the back of Jack Brabham's Formula Ford and retired hurt . . .

It's wet in the Philippines and a racing driver doesn't need slippery shoes, so Fred Gibson found the perfect solution for getting me to my car, c. 1971.

Keith Horner did more for my Ford career in Australia—and for my life in general—than any other. The look on my face says it all—RESPECT.

When a beer carton jammed on the radiator, Ford wanted me to stop and remove it. I refused, causing great angst, but I won that 1971 Bathurst race by not pulling in.

Getting physical—my Mustang versus Bob Jane's Camaro at Calder, 1972. You tried to be smooth and precise but in this form of competition being forceful was the key arbiter of success.

Shadowing Pete Geoghegan in the Super Falcon in the Greatest Touring Car Race of all time at Bathurst in 1972. The Mustang's windscreen is so smeared with Pete's oil that I cannot see.

Just the most perfect race car of all time. My Trans Am Mustang, in the studio. All the right stickers on. Sensational.

HO HO HO

THE FORD FALCON GTHO WILL FOREVER BE ENSHRINED AS THE GREATEST muscle car ever built in Australia. The Holden Monaro didn't come close. That it was so quickly supplanted by the nimble Torana and its siblings puts it in the shade. The HO on the other hand was purely and simply the first, and last, of the supercars.

It was born to win Bathurst and when its reign came to an end, so did Ford's factory support of motor racing. There's no more powerful epitaph than that.

The GTHO, and Holden's response to it, created the golden era of production touring-car racing in Australia. The tribalism that had characterised Ford versus Holden rivalry, handed down from father to son, had been simmering before then, but a comparatively brief half-decade of ferocious on-track rivalry cemented it. From that moment on you were either a Ford man or a Holden man. Whole families embraced either the Blue team or the Red team.

Harry Firth was the cork in the bottle. In 1968, as the unofficial head of Ford Australia's racing program, he looked to have Ford's motor-racing future all locked up. He'd won Bathurst and its predecessor at Phillip Island for Ford on four occasions in a Falcon and a Cortina as well as the first Australian Rally Championship in a Cortina. Some said his blood ran blue, but it wasn't true. Harry, as I'd discovered in the USA, was a mercenary. He would go where the winning was sweetest.

In 1967 he'd masterminded Ford's Falcon GT program at Bathurst. Driving with Fred Gibson, who saw and drove the 4.7-litre Falcon for the first time only on the Friday of the race, he won the 800-kilometre event, but only three hours after the chequered flag, when he'd persuaded lap scorers that they were wrong in giving first place to the identical car of brothers Leo and Pete Geoghegan. It was going to be a Ford victory anyway, but it was a measure of Harry's competitive spirit that he fought for it to be him, even against his teammates.

In comparison, Holden was in the wilderness. They had not had an outright competitor to field that year and they were suddenly, acutely, aware of the power of motor sport on their buying public, so they hastily prepared a 327-cubic inch (5.4-litre) coupe version of the Kingswood—the Monaro—to respond in 1968.

Australia's first touring-car champion, David McKay, was doing his best to become Holden's equivalent of Harry. McKay's Scuderia Veloce, 'Team of Speed', was one of the most powerful in the country, providing an umbrella for all sorts of racers to compete under, quite reasonably in return for a fat fee. David had come to an arrangement with Holden and, although not a works team in name, he had entered three of the Monaros paid for by General Motors.

This was an incredibly big deal. It's impossible to overstate how important motor racing was to the two giants of the Australian car-manufacturing industry—Ford and Holden. It became their public battleground, not just for the hearts, minds and pocketbooks of customers, but also for the enthusiasm and support of their dealer networks. The two biggest-talking, hardest-nosed sales and marketing chiefs in the business—Keith Horner for Ford and John Bagshaw for Holden—were slugging it out in a way no one had seen before and that most likely will never be seen again.

The marketing guys were big on bravado. Holden was the market leader. Ford was coming for them and, if you had enough swagger, you could make millions by jumping on the express train with either of them.

Harry's Ford victory in 1967 had hurt Holden badly. But they couldn't enter motor sport officially because head office had a blanket ban on direct participation, so they approached a third party to make it happen.

David McKay was in Surfers Paradise for a race meeting. Here's his story, verbatim, on the day the Holden Dealer Team was born:

'Staying at the same hotel [as me] was Max Wilson, boss of GM-H, his sales director John Bagshaw, Holden dealer Bill Patterson and his local manager Jan Woelders, both known as advocates for changing the GM worldwide no-motor-sport policy.

'We were sunning ourselves around the pool when suddenly Bill Patterson said to me, "How much would it cost for you to run three Monaros in the 500?" We kicked this around for a while. I explained that, as the Bathurst regulations required standard cars, there was no great cost involved apart from careful assembly of all components that should be done at the factory. My team would only be involved on receipt of the cars and we would take them to Bathurst, run them and perhaps win.

'I pulled a figure out of the air, perhaps $10,000, which seemed a lot to me but obviously delighted the others and the next thing I knew we were in business.

'Could I register a business name Holden Dealer Racing Team and enter the cars under it? Yes, I could, pinpointing the birth of the team that was to turn into a multi-million dollar company.'

As it turned out, neither David nor Harry won.

That honour went to Bruce McPhee, a privateer who drove all but the minimum one lap that, by the rules, he had to hand over to his co-driver, Barry Mulholland. The pair, if you can call them that, was in a Monaro on road-going Michelin tyres that were so bald at the end that sparks came off their steel belts as they made contact with the road. The first Ford was seventh.

McKay brought his cars home second and third, but it was his inaction immediately after the race that contributed to him not going on with the Dealer Team.

'A competitor came to me, saying I should protest against the McPhee car, which he knew to be outside the rules.

'He alleged McPhee had modified the braking system in a way which would increase the supply of hydraulic fluid to the front discs and that was why McPhee had a relatively trouble-free race whereas all the other Monaros had been plagued by stops for new brake pads.

'I considered my position in the few minutes remaining before the expiry of the half-hour allowed after the end of the race for protests to be lodged.

'I liked McPhee and I thought the General would see the publicity value in a privateer beating the unofficial works cars. After all, they were all GM-H cars and surely it would be counter-productive for the "heavies" to stamp on the little guy. So I thanked the informant and declined to protest.

'But I was quite wrong about the General's reaction.

'He was in it to win it with his own cars.

'I wasn't really surprised when I wasn't asked to run his entries again.'

David pointed out that the General Motors executive team watched the race from a hotel in Sydney's Kings Cross, 'about as close as they could get without fear of guilt by association and getting a rocket from New York'. He had been on his own in that pre-mobile-phone era and he'd made an error of corporate judgement from which there was no return.

There were two big events in 1968. The second was the world's greatest long-distance road event, the London–Sydney Marathon. It was run right after Bathurst, leaving Crystal Palace in the heart of London in late November and arriving at Sydney's Opera House a month later, having ploughed across countries that are today war torn and closed. Contested by teams from throughout the world, Firth and McKay would face off again—Harry with three works Falcon GTs and David with three works Monaros.

Again, neither was to win. A tiny Hillman Hunter driven by Scottish ace Andrew Cowan snuck across the line. But, in the tussle between Blue and Red, Harry's Blues came out decidedly on top, with a podium, sixth and eighth. David's Reds came twelfth and fourteenth, and David failed to finish after his co-driver, my old VW 'colleague' George Reynolds, rolled the Monaro on the second-last day of a very long competition.

And that's when the cork popped out of the bottle.

The marathon had been extremely tough and Harry's efforts were exemplary. Maybe someone at Ford would recognise that— just a pat on the head. But, according to him, he got nothing. Something was definitely wrong with his relationship with Ford. Meantime, across town at their Fishermans Bend headquarters, General Motors was none too pleased with its results. Who knows, perhaps David had made a promise he couldn't keep, but on top of Bathurst it was too much.

The upshot was ruthless. Within days, a week at most, David was out of Holden and Harry had received a lifesaving blood transfusion.

Lifesaving? It happened this way. In 1968 Ford knew it was in trouble in Australia. Its short-lived global chief Bunkie Knudsen, hired from General Motors by Henry II in 1968 and fired by him just a year later, had commissioned deep research into Ford's all-important performance image in Australia and the findings were that it was five, maybe six years behind the USA. The fix was to send in someone who could write and implement a strategy to put Ford in front in the arms race. The Ford executive they chose was the guy who ran the highly successful Lincoln-Mercury drag-racing program in the States, an unashamed 37-year-old hot-rodder named Al Turner. When Al came to Australia on a look-see, he met with Harry and, in his own words, 'determined there wasn't room in the Ford operation for two strong personalities, especially when our way of doing things was so different', so Al fired Harry. 'When I first came he was still employed by Ford,' Al said. 'I called him in and told him we no longer needed his services.'

The exact timing of the dismissal and Harry's retention by Holden is a bit murky, but the inescapable fact is that Harry got very lucky. Notwithstanding the Holden lifeline, he was out of a job at Ford. Not many people knew that. Certainly Harry used to claim the move as entirely his decision. 'It's a better deal, cock' was his take on it.

The ramifications were wide reaching and pivotal in Australian motor racing.

In the time-honoured tradition of hostile takeovers, Harry did his best to rob Ford of its armoury of experience. Several of his Ford mechanical team were high on his hit list and Ian Tate, one of the best wrenches in the business, made the move. Harry regarded Fred Gibson, his 1967-winning Bathurst co-driver, as a protégé and was sorely disappointed when Fred, always his own man, made the decision to stay put. Fred's Road and Track garage in Sydney was doing a lot of business for Ford, including running its New South Wales press fleet, so his call was financially grounded.

Without Fred, Harry started his own version of a star search. His criteria were simple: he wanted someone who was young, quick, had mechanical ability, with no current ties and no baggage. He got Peter Brock, then racing his own Holden-engined Austin A30. It's worth contemplating: what would have happened if Fred had taken the leap and gone with Harry? Where would Peter have ended up? It's untenable to think that a talent like Brock's would not have been recognised. But who knows?

Meantime at Ford, gung-ho managing director Bill Bourke—a big-talking American, sometime confidant of Henry II who'd go on to become executive vice president of Ford USA and who made his name in Australia by declaring 'no Japanese-made car will ever find a place in an RSL car park'—had had enough of using hired help. Bunkie Knudsden had given him Al Turner and that was just fine. Ford would use motor racing in Australia to forge a path up to and past Holden in the sales race.

Al was already aware of the Bathurst-winning Falcon GT, a car Bill Bourke had fought hard to get approved by the US Ford product planners, who'd initially objected on the basis that nowhere in the world would the Falcon ever be positioned as a performance car. Well, it was going to be in Australia, because that's what they made on the local assembly line. Bill got the Falcon GT and he got Al Turner.

Across the road from the Ford Broadmeadows plant at Thomastown in Melbourne's north was a group of nondescript factory buildings in Mahoneys Road, known only by their lot numbers—Lot One, Two, Three, and so on.

Al secured Lot Six, a red-brick building surrounded by cyclone-wire fencing with a lock on the gate. The lock was necessary because the area, then, was not a safe environment.

In later years it had a starring role in the *Underbelly* television series on criminal activity.

Lot Six was the original skunk works. Al recruited and moved in there an elite group of specialised engineers. There were twelve of them, headed by Al and supported by John Gowland, the Ford guy who'd been Harry's wing man all through his London–Sydney campaign. The recruitment program had been highly successful. Simultaneously, performance-components builder Repco was shutting down its Repco-Brabham engineering works in Melbourne and three of the key people who'd been on Jack Brabham's F1 world-championship-winning support team were on the loose. With Jack's personal recommendation, Al hired them for Lot Six.

When you think of Ford, you probably think of a huge bureaucracy, one of those corporate monoliths, awesome juggernauts, that plough down everything in their path. That's probably pretty close to the truth, especially in the retail sector, but within that huge, grey mass there's a nucleus of guys who know and respect each other and make things happen.

That was the situation I walked into when I arrived back in Australia in 1969.

I went to Ford to seek help for my Mustang only to find they were already waiting for me to assist them with their domestic motor-racing program. My reputation both as a test driver and as a long-distance racer had preceded me.

The timing could not have been better.

'No,' they said, they did not want to sponsor the Mustang. They didn't want to know about it. Ford didn't sell Mustangs in Australia, so their appetite to even see it run was limited to peripheral badge promotion. (That refusal would be a continuing source of contention between us, and it would lead to huge arguments and amazing offers.) What they wanted was my testing expertise. Race craft was secondary. If I'd spent the best part of a year tooling around the Dearborn Proving Ground under some of the best engineers in their business, then they wanted me for this project.

Al Turner put it this way: 'My boss, Bill Bourke, gave me a whole heap of grief. What was I doing hiring a Canadian? Why couldn't I get an Australian race driver to head the program? Well, I didn't know any Australian racing drivers, but I did know Moffat through Kar Kraft. I knew he came highly recommended as a guy who could test all day and give consistently good feedback. I needed that because I didn't know where I was with the car.'

Holden was expecting Ford to arrive at Bathurst with a new Falcon GT. They, after all, were going to field the new 350-cubic inch (5.7-litre) Monaro, the first one built by Harry Firth.

What they didn't know was that Ford was building, under the strictest of security, a Falcon purpose built for racing. It would have Handling Options—HO for short. 'Actually,' Al Turner said, 'that wasn't its first name. It was always HO but it initially stood for High Output. As a marketing strategist, as well as a race team manager, I thought that was not too politically astute. So when we rolled it out and the media asked me what it stood for I told them Handling Options.'

Handling, or lack of it, was a big issue for cars built in Australia at the time. David McKay got himself fired from his job as motoring writer for the Sydney *Sunday Telegraph* for a forthright story on how poorly the Holden Kingswood SS wandered at speed. Holden wasn't happy with the exposure. Advertising dollars counted, pressure was applied, and McKay was out. 'I heard later from the then young touring-car driver Peter Brock that he'd been asked to give his opinion of the SS and that subsequently GM-H had indeed improved the stability by better damping—more suitable shock absorbers,' McKay wrote after the act.

Later Holden made a big deal of the handling of its cars. The Commodore's chief engineer (soon to be Holden's managing director) Peter Hanenberger was dubbed 'Handling-berger' by motoring journalists for his work in building a performance car that was also safe.

But Ford was there first. The HO was the benchmark.

There were two divisions of touring-car racing in Australia at the time—confusing now as it was then. My Mustang would compete in the ATCC in 'Improved Production', which meant—along with the cars of Bob Jane, Norm Beechey and Pete Geoghegan—it could be extensively modified. But the Bathurst 1000 and other endurance races would be run for production cars with strictly limited modifications. Not only that but they had to be 'series' production, which required 5000 of them to be built internationally or, if they were an Australian-designed and -made car, 500 would have to be proven to be built here for registration. That regulation was to prove a real sticking point and, as the power war escalated between Ford and Holden, CAMS—the controlling body of the sport—was persuaded to reduce the locally made 'series' numbers to 200 for 1970.

The touring-car title may have carried a lot of prestige but the cars that raced in it, with the exception of Beechey's 1970 championship-winning Monaro, were all imports with little to no relevance on the showroom. You don't 'win on Sunday, sell on Monday' if there's nothing to sell. Keith Horner and John Bagshaw turned to Bathurst.

I must have done more kilometres around Ford's You Yangs test track in the GTHO than I did in the 70,000-mile Falcon Endurance run. Whatever Ford did in development, it wanted it kept under wraps. There was no point in going to a race track where spying eyes could catch you out. The You Yangs track had a high wire fence around it, armed guards and dogs. Seriously. It used to be sport for journalists to sneak up on the compound and capture scoop photos of new models. In those days a shot like that would be front-page news, such was the electrically charged atmosphere of the car sales environment.

Repetitive testing is part of my DNA. Al Turner determined that the other drivers in the loosely formed Ford team—Fred Gibson, John French, Bo Seton and Pete Geoghegan—didn't have the same qualifications to turn the miles. Call it dogged determination or lack of imagination, it's just something that I do and that throughout my career I have insisted on doing. You can only improve if you've got the miles under your wheels.

The guys at Lot Six were good engineers, but not necessarily race trained. There's a big difference between meeting corporate expectations and jury-rigging a solution to meet an immediate race-track need. It was my guy, Peter Thorn, who, while not part of the Lot Six inner circle, built an aluminium aerodynamic spoiler for the GTHO to keep the front end grounded and to mask cooling air from the brakes. In race trim, the HOs needed to have their brake pads at a constantly high temperature. The spoiler was the first production-car aerodynamic device in Australia, and it became the trademark of the GTHO series and a beacon for performance-car enthusiasts. The lack of it, also, would be my downfall in a later Bathurst race.

Al Turner was a big fan of the front spoiler. Back in his drag-car days, he'd defied Lincoln-Mercury aerodynamicists who swore putting a mask on the front of the car would simply increase frontal area with no direct benefit. Al argued that they were being theoretical, that a race car was an imperfect object and not subject to direct logic. In fact his very first spoiler on a Funny Car shaped an entire industry, increasing downforce and top-speed stability with no reduction in speed. Because the car was more manageable, it could be pushed harder.

That 1969 HO was a good car but handicapped by narrow wheel rims, so getting the power down was challenging, and by brakes that for repetitive activity didn't match the car's speed potential. But the 351 Windsor V8, with a bigger four-barrel carburettor and engine modifications to match, didn't have to be revved beyond 5500 rpm and you let the torque do most of the work.

Ford sprung the GTHO surprise on the dealer force and the public in August 1969, and we raced less than a month later in the Sandown Three Hour. I was teamed with Queensland veteran John French, a guy who's figured in several of Australian motor-racing's greatest moments, especially with Dick Johnson, and to this day he makes the claim, tongue in cheek, that I was his co-driver in the Sandown race.

I'm happy to go along with the gag but the ground rules had been clearly set by Al Turner. From my first race with the Ford team, I was the Number One. Why? It's what I'd been working for and frankly what I deserved. I had a natural touch with the production car, light on the brakes—squeeze, squeeze, squeeze, not stamp, stamp, stamp—and the same with the throttle. I could maximise speed out of the car without shredding tyres or burning brakes. 'Allan was always the Number One,' Fred Gibson said. 'With the Mustang he was the star so he was the one Ford wanted to promote, but he was also the best. His real forte was his unbelievable throttle control.' Kind words from the guy who'd already won Bathurst, and who had the most to lose from my promotion.

Al Turner went one step further: 'Allan was used to driving a car with a Detroit Auto Locker differential, and the others weren't. He knew instinctively to hold off flooring it until he was out of the corner and he actually heard the locker click into place. That way, when he got on the gas, he wasn't tearing the tyres to pieces by only putting power down through one driven wheel. He was unbelievably smooth and easy on a car.'

John French and I won Sandown and led home a Ford 1–2–3. It was a sensational debut for the car.

Then we went to Bathurst and were deflated. It was a truly embarrassing, frustrating and unnecessary situation and, to a degree, it drove a wedge between members of Ford's race team management and myself.

Series production cars raced on series production tyres—not by regulation, but as a result of availability. To win Bathurst on road radials was an achievement but Turner could see huge advantage in putting the works HOs on racing rubber and streeting the field. We discussed it, the two of us, and we both had good contacts at Goodyear. Although I'd spent hours, days, testing on high-performance road tyres and the cars were set up for them, Turner and I both knew the advantage of changing to race tyres even without testing.

Ford imported container-loads of Goodyears, and needed them all. Al distributed them among the chosen few of the fourteen Ford entries, but there's always an information gap between the factory and the privateers. Pretty soon we realised that, if you drove the tyres too hard, they would make contact with the top ball joint of the suspension wishbone and the outcome could only be catastrophic. Not too many people knew that. There was a way to 'massage' the ball joint but not too many people knew that either, because it was pushing the limit of the rules, and it wasn't a guaranteed fix. Even if there was no clearance problem, there was a preservation mode you had to adopt to get any reasonable mileage out of the tyres. I was on top of it.

The race started badly. Sydney driver Bill Brown rolled his Falcon over Skyline and caused a multiple-car pile-up that decimated a quarter of the field. Luckily I missed it. I'd found a false neutral in the gearbox and pulled to the side of the track in the Cutting to get it sorted out, dropping almost a lap, which completely changed my race strategy. When I arrived at Bill's accident, the big red Falcon was upside down in the middle of the road with smaller crashed cars around it like sucker fish on a whale. I manoeuvred around the debris and got on with the job. An hour later the other HOs started to blow tyres. Pete Geoghegan, leading the race, exploded his at the top of the mountain and descended Conrod Straight at high speed with rubber flaying to get to the pits. In the afternoon, while just 200 metres behind leader Colin Bond, and closing, Bo Seton had a blow-out and rolled the other GTHO works car.

Al Turner had made the decision to be the executive director of our race effort and he had installed John Gowland as crew chief. They both put me on safety watch while they debated what to do with me. 'Allan drove the car differently to everyone else, and I was confident that his tyre management was within the data parameters we'd established in testing,' Al said.

'But there was panic in the pits. How could we leave him out there and take a risk with his life? So I went along with bringing him in for the unscheduled stop, which cost him his shot at a race win. Of course his tyres were exactly as I expected them to be, but I went along with the panic decision.'

They'd pulled me unnecessarily to the pits for fresh rubber, only to discover heaps of meat on the tyres they removed. They just didn't trust that I could manage the situation.

'Bill Bourke called me to his office the next day to explain,' Al said.

'Before he could say a word I said, "I screwed up." It took the wind out of Bourke's sails: "How am I expected to chew you out when you don't even offer an excuse?" We did make one change. Bourke insisted that from then on I had to take direct responsibility for team management. I'd chosen Gowland as my successor in the Ford works team. Now he was out.'

Harry's Holden won—with young Colin Bond at the wheel of the Monaro along with Holden engineer and racer Tony Roberts. Bruce McPhee, now in a Falcon but on road XAS Michelins was second; third was Peter Brock alongside Des West in another Monaro; and I was fourth, with Alan Hamilton, one lap down. Fourth place was galling. It was my first-ever Bathurst and I should have won it. It's frustrating when I look at the results. It was Peter Brock's first Bathurst too, the start of our rivalry, and he came third.

There was a tradition at Bathurst back then that the major manufacturers would reserve full-page advertisements in the next day's papers. Only one of those spaces would contain a quickly made advertisement claiming victory, while the others would swiftly replace their winning claims with generic substitutes— families picnicking with their cars and the like—as if there'd never been a motor race. Ford, however, built a special ad. 'We were deflated', it screamed, and cast the blame on Goodyear. It was poor form and caused me a lot of embarrassment.

I resolved that, as I was Number One, I'd be treated like one. It wasn't as if we didn't have a system. Al had resolved a protocol for pit-board signals, the only communication between car and driver in those pre-radio days. If one of the mechanics held out the pit board, it was for information only. If Al was holding the board, it was to be absolutely obeyed. But it was a one-way communication and that just wasn't good enough. You had to put faith in the man in the car. We discussed that frankly, and agreed it would be different in future.

Everyone went up a huge notch in 1970. Series production had become the big buzz for spectator involvement and, although change would turn out to be three years away, the writing was on the wall for improved tourers in the national touring-car championship.

I used the GTHO to win the three-round Tasman Touring Car series, and Fred Gibson won the hugely popular Toby Lee Series at Oran Park. Meantime, at Lot Six and in the You Yangs, we were working on the next GTHO with more power and more call on brakes and suspension. Across town, Firth's Dealer Team was going the other way. They had taken the lightweight, nimble Torana coupe and begun turning it into a six-cylinder race car—the XU1. Even Chrysler was getting into the act with its six-cylinder Pacer, later to evolve into the Charger.

In that one year Ford had become the last V8 standing.

The next GTHO, to be known logically as the Phase 2, used the new 351-cubic inch (5.75-litre) Cleveland engine (Cleveland and the previous Windsor engines are named for the Ford plant in America in which they're built), giving more power and supposedly greater reliability. Everything about the car had been beefed up and the lessons we'd learned at Bathurst the previous year had been adopted. Race rubber was now the norm and the car was set up for it.

Sandown, the long-distance race before Bathurst, is as much a set-up for Mount Panorama as an event in its own right. Paradoxically, it is harder on components, especially brakes, than Bathurst so you go there to try to break the car.

Mine didn't. Driving solo, I won Sandown for the second time in succession, but I was the only Falcon not to have problems. Fred Gibson with Bo Seton was the next Falcon home, six laps behind in sixth place.

At Bathurst I set pole position in the first session, then blew the motor, requiring a quick engine change and the use of the third and last session to run it in. The HOs were quick. To put it in perspective I was five seconds a lap faster than the first Torana, driven by Colin Bond, and while that didn't indicate race pace, over 130 laps it still adds up to better than ten minutes or a three-lap advantage.

The Australian Racing Drivers' Club, promoters of Bathurst, allowed us to drive solo. It was an amazing concession and one that I was quick to take up. There's nothing better than getting in the groove and staying there. These days the pace of a long-distance race is such that it is pretty much impossible to do the event in anything other than 'sprint stints' but, in 1970, being as one with your car and nursing it through its changes in performance made for a perfect solution, minus one small, very personal, consideration.

I was in the lead, pulling in for a pit stop that would take perhaps two minutes—incredibly long by today's standards but then it was pretty impressive. Although I couldn't exit the car I figured I could time a pretty necessary comfort break to coincide with the pit stop and I was doing that, belts loosened, zip undone and feet up on the pedals so they wouldn't get wet, when a television pit reporter arrived at my window. Happily my chief mechanic Peter Jeffrey managed to shield the camera, but I conducted the interview on national television while urinating. I stormed out of the pits not completely recovered and it took the length of Mountain Straight to get everything back in place and to restore my composure.

My first Bathurst win wasn't easy. Teammate Fred Gibson, sharing with Bo Seton, had retired early. Al Turner had given a third Ford factory drive to Bruce McPhee—the man more used than anyone else to doing the race solo—and he was always in striking distance. When smoke started to pour from my engine bay in the last hour, he started to close, reducing the gap from more than 30 seconds to less than ten. That's when Al Turner took over the pit board and told him to hold station. For the first, but not the last, time in my Bathurst career, team orders were to play a part in my victory. I could have perhaps held him out—who's to know—but I was nursing the car and there was no guarantee it would last if it came under pressure. Peter Brock had his own problems. He was thirty-seventh, the lowest result you'll ever see for him on a scoreboard.

The Falcon GTHO Phase 2 was anything but easy to drive. Fred Gibson and I used to say to Al Turner: 'You're so lucky to have us driving for you, because these cars are a heap of rubbish.' The Cleveland engine had nowhere near the torque of the superseded Windsor and you had to rev it harder to get something out of it. That led to vibration and lubrication problems, both of which I'd experienced, especially towards the end of the race. For some of the private teams the engine problem was critical and I was aware that some people were having to speed to dealerships as far away as Sydney to source new engines after practice. Driving higher up in the rev range required a totally different throttle technique. You really had to work at the job. Once you got the car out of shape, it was very difficult to get it back.

Fixing all that was our goal with the GTHO Phase 3. By now there was an expectation that there'd be a new model in time for the next year's Bathurst.

Both Al Turner and Bill Bourke were on their way out and up. As a Ford lieutenant, Bourke had done his job. He'd worked with Keith Horner to reinvigorate a network and make Ford a genuine alternative to Holden. He'd defended the Falcon against extinction when Dearborn decided it should be replaced by the US-designed Torino and he'd persuaded head office to let him build a design centre in Australia. As much as anyone and more than most, he had contributed to the future of the Australian automotive industry. He appointed plant manager Brian Inglis, later to become Sir Brian, as his replacement. Australia was hardly autonomous from headquarters but at least now it had its own voice, in its own accent. Bourke went on to run Ford Asia Pacific (FasPac) out of a separate office in Melbourne, so in that respect he was still overseeing Australia. Al Turner left more suddenly and mysteriously. One moment he was there . . . the next his new assistant was running the show. Al was sequestered by Bourke. FasPac had been having huge difficulty building a multi-purpose jeep-like vehicle for the Philippines and other South-East Asian markets, so Al got the job not only of designing it, but building it. When Bourke moved on to become head of Ford Europe, Turner went with him, ultimately falling back into Ford motor sport in the 1980s until a clash of ideas and policies with his then boss, Mike Kranefuss, forced his departure from Ford to Chrysler, where he worked hand in glove with Lee Iacocca on the rejuvenation of the brand, building concept show-cars like the Prowler and the Viper.

Al's Lot Six successor was Howard Marsden, who'd annoyed my Goodyear connections so mightily in the States when they'd asked for some of his Alan Mann Cortina tyres for my car and he'd refused. I was inclined not to like Howard either, although, when they asked for my opinion before hiring him, I'd been as neutral as possible in my assessment.

The management styles of the two special vehicles managers were chalk and cheese.

You might have had your disagreements with Al Turner, but you knew he was on your side. He'd work a 9–5 day over at Ford's Broadmeadows headquarters, pushing paper and doing all the things responsible line managers do. Then he'd make his way to Lot Six, take off his tie and work with the guys until 10. He'd buy their dinner, take a genuine interest and he'd spend whatever it took to get the job done.

That was probably, ultimately, a contributing factor to his downfall. Lot Six was absolutely secret-squirrel. Big cheeses from the factory were curious and occasionally, if invited, they'd be given limited access. Al didn't need their 'help'. One night there was a rattle at the gate, which was always kept locked. Al looked out to see the head of finance. 'Quick,' he said. 'Turn out the lights, there's no one here.' The guy went away. He was Jac Nasser, later to be promoted to head of Ford Australia and ultimately to become the world president of Ford.

Howard Marsden, on the other hand, was a Yes Man. He would do whatever it took to keep the peace, which meant, in my terms, that I was never fully confident that he was pushing the case for motor sport. Later in the GTHO program, I became aware of a paper he'd written for senior management, outlining the scenario for Ford's withdrawal from motor racing. It may have been one of those either/or documents but the fact remains that Ford did withdraw under Howard's watch, and to this day I'm convinced more could and should have been done to prevent it. There was a team joke about Howard and money. He ran the team so you'd expect when they went to lunch or dinner he'd pick up the tab. Not Howard—it was invariably 'I've left my wallet in the truck' or 'I have no cash'. It got so that when team members were around without him they'd say, 'Let's do a Howard', pat their pockets and ask someone else, usually me, to pay.

'Howard wasn't the sharpest tack in the tool box,' Al Turner said. 'I can understand why he and Allan didn't get along. Allan has always been the most driven of people, super competitive. If you didn't support him or weren't capable of supporting him, he had no further use for you.'

Howard did, however, build a sensational Phase 3.

It was so good that Mel Nichols, destined to become one of the most internationally acclaimed high-performance motoring journalists, used *Sports Car World* to call it 'simply one of the best cars in the world, a true GT that can take on Ferraris and Astons on their own terms . . . a classic car worth buying to keep a lifetime'. Ford built 300 GHTO Phase 3s and they cost just $5250 each.

The Cleveland engines had been made more reliable and the suspension was stiffer with heavier front and rear anti-roll bars. The rear brakes, still drums, were larger, but the front discs had a completely different set up with smaller calliper gaps, creating a lot more heat. The big improvement was in power delivery. The HO was already fast enough down Bathurst's Conrod Straight but I wanted more speed up the hill. New gearing gave better acceleration in short bursts between the corners, but there was a need to keep the tyres in one piece and the brakes intact because they'd be working so much harder at every corner. It was all necessary if we were to hold off the Toranas, which had been made more powerful and even more nimble.

We failed dismally at Sandown. Heat build-up in the front brakes pretty much seized them. Peter Brock won for Torana. The first Falcon home, driven by Murray Carter, was five laps down. But Sandown is built to prepare for Bathurst. Hardie-Ferodo, Bathurst's naming rights sponsor and a brake specialist, could not afford a brake version of our 'Deflated' story and they sprang into action. In just three weeks they devised and built an entirely new pad shape and compound. So successful was it that, for the first time, the top three finishers completed the entire event without a pad change.

In October 1971 I won Bathurst for the second year in succession despite the best efforts of Ford management to stop me.

I'd taken pole position, 13 seconds faster than my lap record of just two years before in the original GTHO—that's how far development had come. The team was around me. John French was second on the grid, Fred Gibson third. It was a Falcon lockout—the first 'other' was Leo Geoghegan in the new Chrysler Charger in seventh slot.

I led the race from start to finish. Not even Bill Brown's second horrendous crash in three years slowed me down. Brown rolled his GTHO along the fence at McPhillamy Park, slicing the car virtually in two. From my seat it looked unsurvivable, but he walked away with a black eye. Stirling Moss once said that when he sees an accident he goes faster, because he knows everyone else would be slowing down. I've never really thought about it or tried to psychoanalyse myself. My concentration is pretty intense and so anything extraneous really doesn't affect me at the time.

But journalist Bill Tuckey had obviously been inside my head:

Typically [Brown's crash] did not seem to bother Moffat. Moffat was capable of being the coldest, most unemotional person amongst his drivers' peer group. It was a product of his need to raise his concentration to supreme levels to overcome his lack of natural flair—the kind of flair that came naturally to Peter Brock and Colin Bond. Moffat always had to work harder at being as quick as Brock (which in his heyday he was) and incidents like passing the Bill Brown wreckage on that most awful of Bathurst corners would certainly have upset him less than it did Brock.

It's not a debate I ever had with Bill. But I don't believe him to be right. I think I had the right stuff in the right order.

My big concern later in the race was to stop Ford stopping me.

Somehow, in high winds, I'd picked up an empty Coopers beer carton across my radiator and there was a strong chance it would send engine temperatures soaring. The team hung out a lap board to tell me, and pointed to the pits to bring me in to clear it. Al Turner wasn't there, but it was my 1969 Goodyear story all over again. Marsden was telling me to pit, and lap after lap he was getting more demonstrative. Sir Brian Inglis, the new managing director of Ford, was telling Howard to make me do it. And Ford hierarchy was backing the boss. What kind of fool was I to stay out and risk blowing up the car and robbing Ford of its works victory? Well, I was the kind of fool who was in charge of his own work-space. I had one eye constantly on the temperature gauge and it wasn't moving. The car's vital signs were good. There was no loss in power, no change in throttle response; even the brakes were holding up. I stayed out. At one stage I did make a signal to the pit that was effectively one finger raised. I later explained I intended to win by one lap, which I did.

There was so much anticipation about the following year. If the Phase 3 was this good, what would the Phase 4 bring? Holden was already working on a V8 for the Torana, and Chrysler was developing eight cylinders for the Charger. After two years of namby-pamby six-cylinder nonsense, the message had finally sunk in. V8s rule!

We were at Oran Park on 25 June 1972 when the bombshell struck. The Sydney *Sun-Herald* had a front-page story: '160 MPH "Super Cars" being built for Bathurst'. Because of CAMS rules, 200 of each model had to be built, which meant that most were destined for our roads. The story was written by Evan Green, one of the best and fairest motoring journalists (who ultimately went on to become a director of General Motors-Holden, although that was long after this story was written). The outrage was immense, firstly at the circuit, where Harry Firth sought out Evan and gave him a character reference like no other. But then the wildfire spread. The man behind it all was another journalist, Harvey Grennan, who was then working as press secretary for the New South Wales transport minister, Milton Morris. The minister was carving a reputation as Mr Road Safety, introducing the breathalyser, radar traps and the compulsory wearing of seatbelts. His major failure was that he hadn't been able to convince the minister for works to upgrade the roads, which were in a poor state and killing more people than any other cause.

Here's Grennan's confession: 'Evan Green had just taken up the job as motoring editor of the *Sun-Herald* and was looking for a big story to establish his credentials. We chatted about the pending Phase 4 mentioned in a confidential Ford dealer bulletin and touted as the fastest four-door car in the world's history, and Holden's and Chrysler's plans to produce more powerful cars for that year's Bathurst.

'I came up with the phrase "bullets on wheels". That was enough for Evan.

'On the front page of the *Sun-Herald* the minister was "appalled at bullets on wheels being sold to ordinary motorists". Other media took up the story with gusto. It filled the airwaves and devoured trees.

'The reaction from Ford, with cars on the production line, was hostile. I had to hold the phone at arm's length when the company's Sydney PR man, Max Ward called. It was a dumb response.

'Holden was a lot smarter and I suspect had an ulterior motive. It had a good relationship with Morris and sought a meeting with the minister. The company did not seem too unhappy at the prospect of CAMS rules being changed.

'If Ford had sought the minister's ear—he was a good listener—who knows how the supercar saga might have played out?

'Three days after the *Sun-Herald* story Morris upped the ante by calling for a national ban on the registration of supercars. He was quickly joined by his Queensland counterpart.

'Government sales were a huge slice of the local car-makers' business so the pressure—and implied threat—was immense. The following day CAMS announced the regulations would be changed to discontinue "series production car" races and to allow manufacturers to modify production cars for racing.

'This was the day supercars died because in the flash of a press release they were no longer relevant to Australia's Big Race.

'CAMS rules had created the phenomenon of the supercar and CAMS rules killed it off just as effectively.

'The next day, Friday, Holden announced it would abandon plans to build and race a V8-powered Torana because of "concern expressed by government leaders". I'm sure it was suppressing a huge sigh of relief.

'The axe fell on the GTHO the following day. Ford announced it would discontinue production and seek government guidelines for the production of performance cars.

'The same day Chrysler abandoned further development of the Charger R/T and pulled out of Bathurst. The whole saga had taken just six days.'

Peter Brock won his first Bathurst 500 in a barely improved Torana XU1 from John French in a Phase 3 GTHO and Doug Chivas in a Chrysler Charger. It was ironic, and somewhat fitting, that all three brands were represented on the podium.

I had a terrible time. In atrocious conditions—rain and grease and mud, the first time it had rained in the big race—Howard Marsden had made the decision to run without front spoilers, which made both handling and brake management difficult. I was leading early but had a spin at Reid Park on the way up the mountain under pressure from Brock. Then I was given two one-minute penalties for starting my car in the pits before refuelling had been completed. I had a flat tyre, then my brakes failed so badly that in the second half of the race I had the rears disconnected and ran on the fronts alone. If only the officials had known. I finished ninth, eight laps down on Brock. Arguably that was a better position than my Ford teammate Fred Gibson, who rolled at McPhillamy Park. But only arguably, because sometimes you just want something to be over.

For what it was worth, the points I picked up contributed to Ford's victory in the newly minted Manufacturers' Championship, held over five rounds, of which Bathurst was one, and I won two others.

It was the end of an era.

Four GTHO Phase 4s were built before the cease-production order. Three were race cars and one, I know, was destroyed in a road crash. The only fully built-up road car is in the hands of a Sydney collector who rarely shows it.

8

FORD FINALE

THE MOST POWERFUL MAN, BAR ONE, IN FORD AUSTRALIA WAS STANDING on the other side of my Ford Mustang, parked on the surface plate at 711 Malvern Road, and yelling at me.

Keith Horner, sales manager and my guardian angel at Ford, was furious.

But then I was equally obstinate.

It was a confrontation like no other and Pauline, usually so up-front with Keith and other supporters, was doing her best to fade into the background.

Keith wanted me to stop racing the Mustang. I was having none of it.

This was more than a Mexican stand-off. This was a potentially career-changing moment and, in my mind, racing at a hundred miles an hour, the outcome could go either way. But I had to stand my ground.

In 1970 Horner, Bill Bourke and Al Turner had decided that Ford had to be in the main game—the Australian Touring Car

Championship, with a locally sold car. Ford had dominated the title. For the past five years its Mustangs had claimed victory and, before that, under the original Appendix J rules, it had broken Jaguar's four-season stranglehold with a one-off win by Pete Geoghegan in a Ford Cortina GT. Only Ford and Jaguar had won the championship in its ten-year history. The scorecard read Jaguar, 4; Ford, 6.

But now Norm Beechey, who'd won the title for Ford in his Mustang in 1965, was preparing a locally made Holden Monaro GTS350 and was going to launch a massive lunge for the prize.

It was more than Ford could bear. They wanted the Mustang gone and a Falcon in its place.

Even in the midst of their Bathurst-winning Series Production campaign, Bourke and Horner turned to Turner and his Lot Six team, and demanded a Falcon that could beat Beechey.

'Spare no expense,' they said. But of course that was rubbish. If it had been an open-chequebook campaign, they wouldn't have stretched the Lot Six resources so thin and they would have recognised that designing a racing car from the wheels up required an entirely different mindset to modifying a series production car.

There was a lot of optimism involved, mainly Turner's.

He had come from a hot-rodding and NASCAR background; he was a larger-than-life character, and no problem was ever going to be insurmountable. His rationale was that the mighty Ford Mustang had been built on a Ford Falcon platform, so all the suspension mounting points and all the key chassis parameters would be the same. It should be a relatively easy task to transfer everything learned in the Trans Am program directly to a local Falcon.

You couldn't fault his enthusiasm, but you had to question his logic.

If the mighty Kar Kraft in the USA had failed in its first attempt to build a winning Trans Am Mustang in 1968 and had to rely so heavily on specialists Carroll Shelby and Bud Moore to bring their 1969 cars (including mine) up to speed, then what chance did a skunk works in Mahoneys Road, Thomastown, have?

Well, came the reply, look at Beechey. With a lot of help from Holden and from a genius young race-mechanic-turned-engineer Lou Mallia—whom I'd later poach for my team—he was building a Monaro that looked like it would have the goods. They were even cheeky enough to call it a Trans-Aus as a nose-thumbing exercise to my Trans Am.

Beechey had used his first attempt with a Monaro to win a couple of ATCC races in 1969, although Pete Geoghegan won the title with his Mustang. Now that CAMS had opened the regulations for 1970, it was time for him to have a proper go.

Surely the might of Lot Six, with the vast global resources of Ford's motor-racing network, could match a backyard operation from Brunswick. Well, it was hardly that. But Bourke and Horner were convinced. The Super Falcon program was officially ordained.

There were to be two cars: one for me and one for Pete Geoghegan. He'd already won the title five times, more than anyone else, and was regarded as the best in Australia to muscle big, unwieldy cars to do things beyond their theoretical capability.

Al partitioned a special sealed section of Lot Six and the boys got to work in early 1970. It was never realistic that the Super Falcon would challenge for the title that year and, as history records, Beechey did win a reliability-plagued season with three wins out of seven rounds. Pete brought his Mustang home fourth, his worst result in the Improved Production era, but at least it was better than my sixth.

I think we both thought the Super Falcon program couldn't come soon enough. It may have had its problems but you couldn't fault its intent. We both would have loved to compete for the title in a Falcon, a car far more relevant to the buying public, but it was taking some time.

On a bitterly cold day in mid-August 1970, accompanied by Ford's top brass, the Special Vehicles division trundled the first built, my car, onto the track for a demonstration lap. It looked sensational, real eye-candy. Without doubt it was the best-looking Falcon ever built. All the proportions were exactly right and the CAMS relaxation on wheel dimensions meant that the Minilite mags filled the wheel arches and made it look like it was doing 300 km/h while standing still.

But the program was running way behind. That day the car was fitted with a well-worn series production engine, so it was more show than go. With that engine fitted, down on power and torque, it felt pretty good. It was only when they fitted up the race engine with its massive 620 hp that the car's handling inadequacies became so disappointingly apparent.

A race car depends on its structural rigidity. You can put the most powerful engine in the world into it, but it will only be counterproductive if you can't transfer the power to the ground. Worse, if you have a chassis that is unresponsive, it can rob you of stability, safety, driver confidence and lap times. It can become undriveable, and in a nutshell, that was the story of the Super Falcon.

The Ford brass were getting twitchy. Even as Beechey was winning the title, they pushed Al Turner to get the Super Falcon on the track. I was already a non-event in the 1970 title with the Mustang, so I agreed that, for the last round at Symmons Plains in Tasmania, I'd leave the Mustang at home and take only the Falcon.

It's a challenging track, built at the back end of the Launceston grazing property owned by the Youl family. John and Gavin Youl had been great racers in their day, and doesn't everyone want a race track in their backyard? The back straight has a massive kink in it where vehicle stability is paramount. And at the end of the front straight is a downhill drop-away left-hand hairpin that winds a chassis up into knots. In between are ess-bends and fast-transition right-to-left corners that let you know you're alive.

I managed six laps that practice session and claimed pole position.

Straight off the trailer, the car's first two laps were tenuous. There was smoke billowing from the engine bay and, although I'd not brought the car up to speed, I was already getting signals that told me all was not well. We got right to the last ten minutes of the final practice before we were ready to go again. This time bravery overcame finesse. I brutalised the car in a straight line and, where I would have been getting far greater corner speed from the Mustang, I was pounding in under brakes, getting it turned in and then squirting it again in a straight line. It was like driving a F5000 open-wheeler car—immense power, but no great mid-corner ability. I went across the line with a time 0.3 seconds faster than Jim McKeown's Porsche 911 to secure the Super Falcon's maiden pole. And it was right on the finish line that the engine blew, massively. There'd be no racing for the Super Falcon the next day.

Ford thought it was a promising start. I thought there was a long way to go before I'd give up the security of my Mustang, even with its reliability challenges.

Keith Horner didn't agree and he came to 711 to tell me so.

Keith Horner was my biggest fan in Ford. He was much more than a client or a boss; he had become a friend to Pauline and myself. We'd eat dinner at each other's homes and he'd mentor me on matters of life and love—I had issues with both.

He was also one of the toughest operators you've ever known. As sales manager he lived and breathed the monthly registration results, could not abide failure and hated Holden with a passion. With Bill Bourke he'd recognised that the key to success was not only Ford product but Ford people. And the people he most cared about were his dealer network. They were his front-line troops, the people who actually talked to the customers and sold cars to them.

He and Bourke embarked on a program to make their dealers millionaires. The more successful they became, the more sales

Ford would make. He'd find promising young operators in the network and encourage them to go into debt up to their ears to buy a dealership. At the very least they had to mortgage their houses to the hilt, not just as a sign of good faith but to ensure their full and absolute commitment. He wanted them in their place of business before dawn, cleaning the cars if that's what it took, and he didn't want them to see the sun on their drive home. But he'd also back them 100 per cent, with funding and product. So many of Ford's star dealers were created that way, guys who are millionaires today. There's even one who can boast a billion.

In that super-charged atmosphere, motor racing was important and Keith used me as a tool in his motivation program. It wasn't only about winning; it was about schmoozing. If I was a Ford star, then I had to be the most accessible Ford star in the business. If that meant nights on the town with the Ford dealers—and, boy, did they like their nights on the town—then that's what it took. I've never been a big drinker—it's sort of counter-intuitive if you have to have your wits about you—but I played the game. One time I used a public phone box, badly, to call Pauline to come and get me. She found me on a park bench in Fitzroy Gardens, not the safest place to be in Melbourne in the 1970s, especially if you had a recognisable face and you were under the weather.

I don't mean to make Keith sound crass. He wasn't. He was genuinely sensitive to everything going on around him. My life was hardly balanced and there was a lot of pressure, financial and emotional. We struggled and we battled and nothing was ever easy. Keith recognised that and insisted that Pauline and I go away for a few days to Dunk Island, at the company's expense, to chill out and mend fences. That was the act of a friend more than one of a man protecting his investment.

At 711 that morning, we welcomed Keith with some trepidation. I knew what was coming. He'd made it abundantly clear that there was much greater value for him in having me in a Ford Falcon than in a Ford Mustang.

The conversation, not sitting but standing around the offending Mustang, started with a massive offer. 'The time has come,' he said, 'for you to join the Ford dealer program.'

Consider Allan Moffat Ford—prime location, heaps of support, and money would never again be a problem. It was a program they were soon to undertake with Jack Brabham at Bankstown in Sydney at the end of his international career, and for Jack it was certainly a success.

But for me there was a condition. No more Mustang; Falcon would have to be my future.

I just couldn't do it. I was in my early thirties, a first-time Bathurst winner and, most importantly, I was living my dream as a professional racing driver with a career that was just starting to come good. And that's how what started out as something positive quickly turned ugly. Pauline said we assumed positions on either side of the Mustang like tennis players on either side of the net. Except neither of us was lobbing winning shots. We were just sluggers.

Apart from Symmons Plains, I'd done a lot of testing in the Super Falcon that year. The car was so badly engineered it was dangerous. It was always a problem—lap times were off, handling was off, tyre wear was terrible. I told the Lot Six guys this and they didn't appreciate the honesty. I wanted to go into 1971 with my Mustang.

The compromise Keith and I reached was that, should the Super Falcon be ready, we'd take both it and the Mustang to the race tracks and let the times and set-up decide which one to run.

As it turned out, I never raced the Super Falcon in the season. In practice it was never a contender. The tension within Ford was rising.

In order to raise more funds for the program, Keith called a meeting of his department heads and asked each of them how much of their budgets they were prepared to give up to contribute to the motor-racing purse. Not one of them made an offer, a surprise in itself. So Keith walked around the table and told each of them how much he'd be taking.

Those were different days.

In the fourth round of the series at Surfers Paradise, Ford gave my Super Falcon to John French and he brought it home fourth, despite a massive spin, after a race-long battle with Pete Geoghegan in his Mustang. 'Surely,' Ford said, 'that proves our point.' No, it didn't. The car was not a race winner and Frenchy had overdriven it like a crazy man. You just couldn't spend, or risk, your life like that.

The next round was at Mallala, that totally flat windswept plain outside Adelaide, and we tested beforehand. I had to do something. The car was everything I said it was. In that state, it was undriveable at race speed.

During the test I contrived to get Al Turner into the car. He thought we were just going to have a conversation, but once he was inside, the door was slammed and we were away. I drove that car as best I could. This was not a plot to scare him and, besides, he knew what constituted good driving and what didn't. As we squirmed down the straight with the torque of the engine trying to turn the car sideways, as we turned into the corner with the chassis flexing so much that there was no control, and as we powered out of the corner with so much of the car's drive being lost in wheel spin, he knew.

We returned to the pits and he ordered the crew to put the car back on the trailer and return it to Melbourne. Effectively my commitment to the Super Falcon program and the torture it was causing me ended right there.

Pete Geoghegan went the other way. At the Lakeside round of the ATCC, Ford once more put John French in the Super Falcon, this time Pete's car, and he lifted front wheels and slid rear ones to finish one lap down in fifth place.

Pete put a proposition to Ford. Give him the car (done), give him a bag of money (done) and he'd turn the old d-d-d-dog (Pete had a terminal stutter) into a race car.

Turner had already moved on to his next project, effectively disappearing from Lot Six. There were some who said he was a victim of his absolute commitment to, and failure with, the Super Falcon campaign, but honestly, there was more to Al in Ford than that. It can't have helped, though, that the program wasn't a success. Marsden had no stomach for a fight, so the deal with Pete was done.

In a back street in Brookvale on Sydney's northern beaches was a small(ish) engineering workshop run by a brilliant engineer called John Joyce. He was an Australian motor-racing success story. He'd worked at Lotus Cars in Great Britain during Colin Chapman's formative years and risen to the role of chief development engineer. John was just one year older than me and he'd returned to Australia in 1968 to start his own company, Bowin Designs. He was to build 56 very successful open-wheeler cars between then and 1976, when motor-racing's law of diminishing returns overtook him and he diversified into low-emission industrial and domestic cooking products, which were so much ahead of their time. John died, young, of a heart attack in 2002.

It was to John that Pete took the Super Falcon and he performed the miracle that Lot Six could never achieve. It was never going to be the best-handling Ford on the track, but with Pete's considerable skill it was capable of being contained. It was that car which Pete used to beat me at the Easter Bathurst meeting in 1972—the race ordained as the best of all time.

Pete campaigned the Super Falcon throughout the 1972 season and finished fourth to my third.

You couldn't have written a better script.

In the last round of the 1972 championship at Oran Park, the last race ever to be held for this classification of car, Pete took pole position in the Super Falcon with me alongside him in the Mustang. After a race of mishaps and scrapes, I caught the Falcon with three laps remaining and passed it to win the final ATCC race under Improved Production rules. It was fitting that the Super Falcon, the car with so much promise, was second.

•

Ford won its ATCC with a Falcon in 1973, and I was at the wheel. That year was absolutely epic. It started with my win in the ATCC in the GTHO 3, then we passed the ball to a new car, the Falcon coupe dubbed the Superbird, which delivered me my third Bathurst victory, but the season then ended with me in hospital after an inexcusable call by Howard Marsden. Above all, it was the year that could be said to have started what became known as the Brock versus Moffat era.

Ford pulled out of motor racing at the end of the season. Now who would have predicted that, given that they'd won the touring-car championship and Bathurst?

The new set of rules effectively merged series and improved production. It removed the need for those cars to be suitable for road registration, although, in the fashion only CAMS can manufacture, that exemption was still surrounded by grey areas.

At Ford we took the decision to run the ATCC with the tried and proven GTHO Phase 3s, but then to switch to the new XA two-door Falcons for the Manufacturers' Championship and, of course, Bathurst.

The ATCC was first to be run over a busy eight rounds right around the country in just sixteen weeks.

The writing was on the wall at round one in Symmons Plains. On pole position was Peter Brock in the Holden Dealer Team Torana XU1. I was alongside him in the Falcon GTHO 3. It hadn't been easy; I'd hit a slower car, a Torana, in practice and done a fair bit of damage. But in the race I sped away from Brock at the start and he couldn't catch me.

Next round, Calder Park, and the old guard was rapidly changing. Bob Jane was more than miffed that he'd been relegated to a Torana under the new rules, so he read them again and figured that, with a bit of manipulation, he could enter his red-hot 1972 championship-winning Camaro—which he did, and put himself on pole alongside me. Brock was third. Rain turned the start into an organisational disaster. Some cars had sped to the pits for tyre changes and were then told they couldn't start because the field was already in the starter's hands. Brock ignored all that and started anyway, but was then black-flagged and disqualified. I got the jump on Jane but later in the race he overtook me to win—only to have CAMS reverse their decision on the Camaro's eligibility, so I scored maximum points after all.

At Sandown Brock pushed me all the way to the last lap, then literally pushed his Torana over the line when his fuel pump packed up and he ran out of gas with petrol still in the tank. The cheers from the grandstand for Brock's heroic effort were greater than those for my win.

Sandown should have been a triumph for me, my third victory in succession, but it was a tragedy. Midway through the day, I got the call every son dreads: your dad is dying.

Mum and Dad had retired the year before and moved to Victoria Island off Vancouver, where everyone from the plains goes to get some sun. Dad in his never-ceasing way had found work at, of all places, a men's-wear fashion business, and he and my mother were settling down to enjoy a deserved long time together. They were only in their early sixties. In the past decade, we'd been getting on okay, but there was still a long way to go for both of us. For Pauline and me, the racing business was an intense time, but for the past couple of years we had enjoyed the much-cherished Christmas holidays at Dad's beloved Hilton Hawaiian Village on Oahu. We'd meet there and he'd be the king of the beach—a title my family said I later assumed.

As soon as the race finished, I was on a plane. Those were the days when you used to lock your passport up in the safe at the bank, and on top of that it was Sunday afternoon. To this day I have no recollection of how I did it, but I left Australia and returned without a passport. I can only guess it was someone at Ford or Pan Am who arranged it. I flew by myself, sleepless, as I recounted the hits and misses of our life together and apart.

I got there too late.

Dad had lingered for four days, but I wasn't in time to say goodbye. I'm by no means unique. So many families have had the same experience. There's just so much emptiness, so much you wanted to say, so many fences you wanted to mend. I stayed as long as I could, made sure my mother was safe in the hands of my brother, and I was back in Western Australia for the Wanneroo—now Barbagallo Raceway—round of the championship two weeks later. It was Brock versus Moffat the whole way and, with a deflating front tyre, I had to make the Falcon as wide as possible to hold off Brock as he went to the dirt to try to slingshot around me to the flag.

At Surfers Paradise, on a wet and slippery track, I was leading Peter when I spun, lapping traffic. Third wasn't first but I was starting to look at the championship points and thinking it was best not to risk the title for a race.

We went to Adelaide and tied to the tenth of a second for pole position. I figured Adelaide was mine to lose because the long straight suited the Falcon.

That night we tucked the car up for bed in the workshop of Bib Stillwell's Ford dealership and in the morning it was gone.

Race-car theft is not something you expect. In the early 1960s Dan Gurney was racing a BRM open wheeler in Australia and he'd suffered a similar fate at the little-used Ballarat airport circuit. But his car had only been driven from the hangar, where it was garaged, to hay bales on the track, where it crashed. Mine was simply gone.

A lot of things happened quickly. At 4 a.m. the police started a dragnet. Bib Stillwell's people offered me a brand new XA Falcon off the showroom floor but there was no way that could be prepped in time. The race organisers scrambled and rescheduled the race start to give me as much time as possible. All to no avail. Then Murray Carter, one of the leading Ford private entrants, stepped forward. 'Take my car,' he said. It was an act of extreme generosity, and I did my best to repay him in coming years after Ford withdrew from the sport, making sure he was always up to date with the latest modifications to the Falcons. It's not always possible for privateers to get that help. But I know for a fact that wasn't Murray's motivation. He'd entered the sport in the very early 1950s when it was a lot less professional, and he was first and foremost a sportsman.

The rules said I had to start from the back of the field, not from alongside Brock. He battled a sticking throttle the whole way to win. I brought Murray's car through the field to finish second, a lap down. My fastest time in Murray's car was just 0.2 seconds slower than Peter's best lap but I'm pretty sure he wouldn't have been on full noise.

Six days later the police found my car abandoned and bogged in a ditch in the Adelaide Hills with only superficial damage. A pretty special induction system I'd been working on was missing from the front seat.

The thief had left a note: 'My apologies Allan. Sorry we inconvenienced you, but what a beaut car it was. I hope you go on to beat the Toranas, Allan. Sorry about the spare carby but we had to hock it for fuel. What a thirsty beast it was. The Phantom Hunter.'

A fortnight afterwards police arrested a 22-year-old labourer and charged him with car theft.

It was only to be expected that with these new rules CAMS would sooner or later start to enforce them, or at least check to see if we were all complying. It was one of the great frustrations of the sport at the time that there was a real them-and-us attitude, rather than us all co-operating to get the best result. Later CAMS would appoint Harry Firth to become their chief scrutineer—a case of setting a thief to catch one, but at least it created a more equitable playing field.

At Oran Park they caught Harry. In the race Brock slipped past me in lapped traffic to win but in post-race scrutineering they found his Torana had oversize exhaust manifolding, delivering extra power, and he was disqualified. I got his points and won the ATCC for Ford Falcon with one round to go.

It had been a huge battle with Peter, and our respective legends, if you can call them that, were established. We'd raced wheel to wheel throughout and never swapped paint. That was the thing about Peter. He was fast, clean and reliable to race against. We both knew exactly how far we could push each other. Aretha Franklin had sung it all when she released the hit single 'R-E-S-P-E-C-T' just six years before.

Brock won the final round at Warwick Farm after the Fords suffered oil surge as a result of their wide tyres creating much higher cornering forces. Both my and Fred Gibson's cars blew engines. It was the last race for the Ford Falcon GTHOs as Ford factory cars and it was a sad way for their era to end. But they were champions.

For the Manufacturers' Championship we'd been developing the new XA Falcon two-door, dubbed the Superbird by the marketing department. It was based on the XA sedan, naturally, but was lower and therefore more aerodynamic. Howard Marsden's development had been hampered by a rolling two-month strike at the Ford factory, which affected Lot Six as well. John Goss, the Tasmanian tearaway (who'd go on uniquely to win both the Australian Grand Prix and Bathurst), had become something of a pioneer by racing an XA GT in the ATCC, finishing just one race in the points as he battled the teething troubles.

There was a lot of speculation about the XA two-door. Would it simply be the banned Phase 4 in disguise? Was the marketing name Superbird a nod to the Super Falcon and, under the new rules, would much of the development work there be used in this new car? Both were pretty close to the mark because, from anyone's perspective, it would have been a crime to waste all that development investment. So we got four-wheel disc brakes, the Phase 4 Holley carburettor and the exhaust headers, and we got sump baffling, which tried, with only limited success, to head off the oil-surge problems Goss had been experiencing all year and which we tasted at Warwick Farm.

The coupes took to the track in brand new livery: white with blue stripes—effectively the American Shelby Cobra colours.

I put the new car on pole in the Chesterfield 250 at Adelaide International Raceway and was leading in horrible, wet conditions until the alternator blew up. A quick pit stop moved me back to third behind teammate Fred Gibson, who had a long overdue win. Kevin Bartlett in John Goss's car was second.

In the Sandown 250, prelude to Bathurst, I turned pole into a DNF when my engine blew just as John French's had a few laps previously. I'd been disconcerted by the sight of Pete Geoghegan's coupe stranded at the back of the circuit on three wheels. He'd been in the test mule in which I'd done many miles and it turned out the back wheel fell off when the hub cracked. Since it had been decided Pete would share the drive with me at Bathurst there were a lot of learnings to be had from the debriefing session after the race. Brock and teammate Bond clean-swept the Sandown 250 ahead of John Goss and Fred Gibson. The Toranas were the only cars on the lead lap.

The Australian Racing Drivers' Club had done something massive for Bathurst. Encouraged by the club's general manager, Ivan Stibbard, the race had changed from being the Bathurst 500 to the Bathurst 1000. 'Five hundred' referred to miles so, in the metric age, it was positively antiquated. 'But you can't have a race called the Bathurst 804,' Stibbard said, which was the exact conversion, so he increased the race to 1000 kilometres.

Along with Pete Geoghegan, I won the first 1000 in 1973. It was a close call on two fronts.

Firstly, Peter Brock was in strong contention. He'd started from the front row alongside pole-sitter John Goss, while I was on the second row. Brock's co-driver Doug Chivas was leading when he ran out of gas at the top of the mountain. It was one of the classic Bathurst moments. He coasted all the way down Conrod and then had to push the car up into the pits, unaided, according to the regulations. Doug was 51 and frail of build, and he collapsed in the pits after his pit crew had been able to take over the pushing.

My own problems, again, related to time. I was to take the majority share of the driving but Pete, no slouch, had to do his bit. Midway through his stint his hands started to cramp. There's absolutely no explanation for it. The Falcon wasn't that heavy to drive and Pete was Mr Muscle anyway. But it happened and he called in early. The rules allowed each driver only three-and-a-half hours at the wheel at a single stretch. My job was to stay in for all of those three-and-a-half hours and get to the finish line before they ran out. It was a close-run thing. I crossed the line with just two minutes to spare.

And there was no alternative.

Brock was fast closing on me with Bond close behind him, coincidentally co-driving with Pete's brother, Leo. If I'd had to stop to put Pete in the car, both Toranas would have overtaken us. But that couldn't happen. When Howard Marsden sent Pauline to the team caravan to get Pete to suit up just in case, she found him and Keith Horner over a bottle of scotch. There was no way Pete was getting back in that car.

Another tradition ended at Bathurst that day. It used to be the winners would ride around the track on the back of a truck dressed up as the victory podium accompanied by the boss of Hardie-Ferodo, George Hibbard. When I won in 1970 it took an hour to complete the victory lap as fans flooded the track and we stopped for autographs. This time we were at the top of the mountain when, at the edge of my vision, I saw a missile approaching. It was a beer bottle, heading straight for George's head. Despite the scotch, Pete's reflexes weren't that diminished. In a flash he lashed out and deflected it. It was a close call and all George could say was: 'We'll never do this again.' And no one ever did.

We blew the next round of the Manufacturers' Championship at Surfers Paradise with only Murray Carter finishing out of all the Falcons. With one round to go, the score line read Holden 50 points, Ford 49. Everything rested on the final round at Phillip Island if we were to achieve the trifecta of ATCC, Bathurst and the man-champs.

It was no secret we were having difficulty keeping tyres under the Superbird. On certain circuits, it took immense restraint to nurse them through to scheduled pit stops. This track would be one of those.

Brock was on pole but he made a strangely poor start. I charged through to lead on this most challenging of all Australian circuits. Nothing, not even Bathurst, matches that track in its requirement for absolute precision and preservation. Brock and I staged a monumental battle for 23 laps before I just had to stop for new tyres, dropping to eighth. I'd worked my way up to fourth by lap 51 when I needed two new front tyres, again.

I was second, but I knew it couldn't last. Eighty laps into the 102-lap race the wheels started to wobble, so badly it felt terminal. I screamed into the pits and looked up at Marsden on the pit box and asked him to check for flat spots, those points on the tyre that make it out of round and difficult to drive. Worse, they can cause a tyre to blow out. He looked at them in a cursory fashion and waved me away. 'Go!' he called, not wanting to lose any more time.

It seems he didn't check well enough. The vibration was worse and I was contemplating murder when the tyre blew. At just under 200 km/h I was off into long grass at the side of the track, then I hit a ditch and rolled. The impact was so great that my belts stretched and my sternum cracked. I staggered from the wreck and then collapsed. I was struggling for breath and the pain was immense. It was, at the time, the worst crash in my motor-racing career and all I wanted to do was get the guy who had not properly checked the tyres.

Holden won the Manufacturers' Championship. Because of our poor performance in the last two rounds, Ford didn't even come second. We slipped to fourth behind class-contenders Alfa Romeo and Mazda.

Ford said it had achieved what it set out to do. It had won Bathurst three times with its Falcon, and it had finally won the ATCC in a locally manufactured car of its own design. If you were ever going to quit, you'd want to go out while you're ahead.

On 25 January 1974, the day before Australia Day, Keith Horner issued a statement announcing Ford's withdrawal from motor racing. He cited greater cost pressures brought on by development needs in emission control and vehicle safety. He referenced the world energy crisis, which had struck in October 1973, just as I was winning Bathurst in a 6-litre V8. He didn't talk about industrial unrest at the factory and in Australian society generally as part of the Whitlam era of federal government. But it was there—an ever-present threat to Ford's manufacturing viability.

Sometimes you need to look at the bigger picture. These were not the times to defend what was, when you come right down to it, a publicity campaign.

Keith said: 'Motor sport has achieved a great deal for Ford both in terms of assisting us in the development of better cars as well as encouraging sales through favourable and competitive exposure.' He was right on both counts. In those days you could genuinely say that motor-racing development led to immense benefits in road-car performance, not just in speed but in primary safety aspects like handling, steering and braking. It was a lot to give up.

Keith talked to me before that announcement. It was, he said, a global directive, not just local, and there was no ignoring it. But he did mention the Holden model of dealer-funding of motor sport—a way around the factory directive—and he did encourage me to stay close to my dealer mates. His message was very clear.

9

FRIENDS AND FOES

OWNING AN INDEPENDENT MOTOR-RACING TEAM IS LIKE BEING CAPTAIN OF an aircraft carrier. You're isolated and, to survive, you need to be completely self-contained. If you've achieved that, then your only challenge is to work out what weapons you launch off the deck.

That's how I felt when Ford pulled out of local racing.

I had spent the last four years—and in reality more than that—building my aircraft carrier, and now it was time to use it in earnest.

The Trans Am Mustang was the constant. It was no longer capable of being played in the main game, the touring-car championship, but it was still a capable weapon under the more liberal rules of sports sedans. And it was still highly marketable. People wanted to see it and that meant promoters, most likely, would be willing to pay for it to appear.

One, initially, didn't.

At Surfers Paradise International Raceway, around 1974 when the Mustang had become a sports sedan, I turned up on trust, expecting to be paid on the spot. Those were different days. Appearance money wasn't exactly passed over in a brown paper bag full of cash—although that occasionally did happen, promoters being promoters.

I know of one promoter, an employee of the organising club, who lost his job because he took home the entire gate money and was found the next morning in bed with his girlfriend in a messy sea of bank notes.

At Surfers, there was an understanding I'd receive a cheque on arrival. An ensuing conversation with the promoter indicated he'd had a change of heart: 'You're here now, so you can race for prize money.' I wheeled the Mustang back on the trailer and headed for the gate. I was about to turn right onto Nerang Road when the promoter arrived, breathless at the truck door.

'Where are you going?' he gasped.

'Home, mate,' was my reply.

The money arrived instantly; I raced, and won the prize purse as well. Which is just as well, because without both funding sources the weekend would have been a loss. The prize money alone wouldn't have turned a profit. Truth be known, I'd made it very obvious I was leaving and I might have delayed a bit at the turn onto the highway in the hope he'd come running.

The word quickly spread and Allan Moffat Enterprises, a step up from Allan Moffat Racing, was confirmed as an operation with which you don't mess.

When Ford made its withdrawal announcement, I spent a couple of days in contemplation.

It's a huge step to move from being works supported, with an umbilical cord straight to the mother ship. Sure, I'd been independent before, but that was before anyone depended on me. Now here I was with commitments: marriage, mortgage, employees and a Mustang that had to be fettled. It was time to work out exactly what that meant.

I'd never really set out to be a businessman. My goal was to race cars and win. The four years with Ford had helped me achieve just that. It's arguable today whether the Ford GTHO program subsidised my Mustang campaign or whether it was the other way around. But either way, without too much deep thinking, life had become a bit easier than it had been.

For a start, Pauline and I had become investors. When the owners of 711 Malvern Road, Toorak, had decided it was time to move on, they had come to us. Their asking price for a prime piece of real estate in the middle of one of Melbourne's most exclusive areas was $60,000. I couldn't say yes fast enough. It was of little consequence that I didn't have the money. This was a big opportunity, made more so by the fact that I was the tenant and had already become emotionally committed. Ring up mortgage number one.

It never occurred to me that a race workshop with the necessary attendant noise of unmuffled high-performance engines and the occasional late-night test run up a back lane might cause some offence to the residents. That was to herald several appearances in council and the offering of promises of noise attenuation that I found difficult to keep. One meeting was to answer a petition signed by 70 residents. In all honesty, I couldn't attend that one because it would have meant lying. I sent Pauline, who was quaking in her boots but able to charm the petitioners. Much later the issue also led to the purchase of the home next door—yet another mortgage.

Until the 2000s, upmarket Toorak, the heart of the city of Prahran, had never been a big development area. Some of the most beautiful and stately old homes in Australia have nestled quietly for a century under the plane trees lining its avenues. But, just after we bought 711, a fast-talking developer slipped one by council and the area's first multistorey—in fact, high-rise—apartment block was approved. It was in Sydney Street, Prahran, 700 metres from the workshop, and we bought a sixth-floor unit off the plan. It cost a massive $25,000. Chalk up mortgage number two.

The workshop was in easy walking distance but we didn't often do that. Our deal with Ford gave us the use of his-and-hers cars. Life was good. Sydney Street had tennis courts opposite, which was good for competitive Pauline.

I've never really enjoyed sport or exercise. I've been fortunate to remain in race-shape with my only exercise being between the ears. I enjoyed watching tennis though, mainly because it was close to home. After years of rotation around the country, the Australian Open Tennis had moved permanently to the Kooyong Courts, an easy 3-kilometre stroll from Sydney Street. It was the time of the great Aussies. We watched John Newcombe take out Jimmy Connors in four sets with a nail-biting 9–7 tie-breaker. And we cheered Evonne Goolagong when she took three straight Opens after being runner-up for two successive years. To me it doesn't matter what sport it is. To see the best of the best compete at their pinnacle is inspirational, and I guess that's been my motivation. To be able to take the time to go and watch was, in my own estimation, a sign of my increasing maturity. Perhaps I was finding balance in my life.

We were to live at Sydney Street for more than a decade before the arrival of son Andrew prompted a move to a stand-alone home, a California bungalow on a huge block of land in Monaro Road, off Toorak Road; the name caused some amusement. It had its own pool and was an excellent entertainer.

There was a pattern in our lives. With 711 as our nucleus, our life existed in a tight radius of no more than a couple of kilometres. Even my parents' company house, in which I spent my late teenage years and early twenties, was within the circle, just 800 metres from 711 where, in those days, I used to buy petrol for the TR3. Strong memories there. The summers were so hot that in those pre-airconditioning days you had to lie on the linoleum floor to keep cool. In the afternoons I'd move Dad's car out into the cul de sac so I could work on the TR in the garage.

This was my comfort zone and I guess, subconsciously, I had built a force field around it.

These were things I didn't want to change. Although I'd spent my growing-up years constantly travelling in pursuit of my father's ambition and the first decade of my adulthood in the same transient state, I'd found something I didn't consciously realise I'd been seeking. Stability and security had become important to me.

That didn't mean we were living high. I'm not the greatest socialiser. Most of my time was spent at the workshop, worrying the cars and the team into race-winning form. At home, a dinner party once every few months was more than enough for me. As for eating out, Pauline was a great cook; when in town, we saw not a lot of reason to leave the comforts of home. There was enough living on the road as it was.

I'd built the race team into its own ecosystem. I hadn't been trained in management so a lot of my technique, if you can call it that, came from observation of people like my dad—a hard man—or simply from my own life experience. Looking back, I couldn't have been all that easy to work with, but I guess those who stuck with me did so because they shared the intense commitment to purpose that has always driven me.

We were innovators in so many ways. I can honestly say the concept of making one person responsible for one part of the car in a pit stop came from me. The use of large lever-like wheel braces, which enabled mechanics to apply just the right amount of torque to each wheel nut, was another. I could sit in the car with my foot on the brake and feel the nuts being tightened in sequence on each wheel. It was reassuring.

The penalty for getting things wrong, though, was severe.

We were at Bathurst and the team had gone to lunch. I don't eat a lot when I'm working and I took the quiet time to slip behind the wheel and stare forward into the middle distance, imagining my way around the track. I put my hands gently on the steering wheel, and it came straight off its spindle when the retaining nut fell in my lap.

It was one of the few times I've truly gone off my head. The thought of what might have happened if I'd gone out on track with the wheel loosely tightened and it had come off at 250 km/h down Conrod Straight was too much to bear. I stormed into the food tent and ordered everyone outside and tore strips off them. 'Get it right or go home' was the general gist of my rant. There would be management consultants who'd take me to task for that reaction, but I was unapologetic. The captain of the aircraft carrier isn't going to condone an unsafe release.

The food tent was another innovation. It is difficult to imagine now, in these days of corporate hospitality, how rudimentary our pit areas were back then. Once Pauline's dad had gotten over his initial distrust of a mature-age son-in-law with no fixed income, he had become a bit of a fan and, when he could, he would turn up in our pits with a portable barbecue. It was a gesture I truly appreciated, but it was hardly a professional solution.

'An army marches on its stomach' is an idiom I slightly changed to being 'a team races on its stomach'. Whenever we worked back at 711, which was more often than not, we'd send out for takeaway. A new Chinese restaurant, run by a widowed Chinese lady, had opened in Toorak Village. Her four sons and a daughter would do their homework in the kitchen and take turns at delivering orders. And they were already fans, revealing they'd come to Victorian race meetings, hanging over the fence and cheering me on.

I turned that to mutual advantage. Nana Margaret became our full-time pit caterer, travelling with us to Bathurst each year. Our canteen became a beacon not just for our own team, including sponsors and supporters, but also media. Whether it was breakfast, morning tea or lunch, there were always 'guests' in the food tent. At dinner time, I sometimes found it hard to get a plate or a steak for myself.

Sponsorship acquisition and retention is something people tell me I did very well. I'm not so certain. I've been very fortunate over the years to connect with certain people who have become my guardian angels but, on the flip side, my personality hasn't made it easy to accept or forgive people in my life who have fallen into that zone of dismissal from which there's no return. I know it's a character flaw and I could do a lot better in life if I tried a bit harder to be inclusive, but I just can't do it. I'm extremely fortunate that there are professionals out there willing to share or at least condone my way of doing business and living life.

When the guy from Ampol slapped his sticker on the Mustang at its first meeting and then didn't follow through with a deal, I wrote off Australia's biggest domestic oil company. How stupid is that? Fortunately, John Pryce, a wonderful Englishman and doyen of the commercialisation of Australian motor sport, turned up and offered me fuel and lubricant in return for a modest BP sticker on the front guard. When you're travelling all over the countryside in a fuel- and oil-burning International truck, free fuel and oil is a gift beyond measure.

But John brought far more than that. His R&D department would devise lubricants purpose-built for my race cars, each one with a different requirement. The Mustang used the first synthetic gearbox oil ever introduced into Australia, and I installed it without a qualm, not only because I trusted BP but because I trusted John Pryce.

John was also able to pour oil on troubled waters. My relationship with the sport's controlling body, CAMS, was never easy. Its chief executive Donald Thomson, who liked to refer to himself as secretary general in the French way, was an autocrat and a martinet. It was his way or the highway. At a time when I was desperately trying to attract commercial support, he was working to push it away in the most pretentious of ways. 'It's easy to foresee motor sport following football, golf, tennis, cycling, even cricket into the cold wasteland of commercialism and meaningless titles,' he wrote. 'So much money and publicity has forced its way into the door that sporting concepts have largely had to fly out the window.'

Thomson did a lot of good things for motor sport, but his opposition to its commercialisation was not one of them. He wasn't a huge fan when the FIA, the world governing body with which CAMS was affiliated, allowed sponsors' signage on cars in late 1968. It was that landmark moment that had led to my Coke sponsorship.

Fortunately, John Pryce was in the CAMS inner circle and was able to mollify Thomson's more vehement outbursts, so that at least some sponsors, his own BP included, did not feel alienated. At one tedious CAMS dinner, in a mahogany and oak dining room of course, Holden's John Bagshaw walked out after copping another Thomson tirade.

I used to hate dealing with CAMS, with their stuffy, gentlemen's-club pretentions, and their assumption that the 'sport' was only for those who could afford to play it. I disliked their duplicitous attitude. On the one hand they set the agenda for an even playing field with a set of standards so high it was as if they came from the Sermon on the Mount.

'Sport is simulated battle,' Thomson said. 'A sublimation of the innate desire of humans to excel against others. It should be carried out in mutual respect and honour in a fashion that leaves both the opponents as persons and the sport as an abstraction better than before.'

But on the other hand, he fed the competitors—like the gladiators of ancient Rome—to the lions and let the promoters prosper.

It was about the time Ford pulled out of motor sport that CAMS, prompted by people like John Pryce, started to wake up. They instituted a program called Get Up and Go, and for the first time they started to refer to motor racing as an 'industry'. But it was all words. They called a symposium and invited speakers to give their views, recognising, but not really meaning, that 'it would have to be destructive to be constructive'.

There were seven speakers and I represented the drivers.

'Every driver believes CAMS has the means to coax the promoters into some form of bilateral consultations, and many of us will be tempted to conclude that CAMS is not really very serious about protecting our interests if all we continue to see is the promoters' interests fostered,' I said.

'The introduction of commercialism into our sport in 1969 was meant to be beneficial to both segments of the sport—not just one.

'You cannot continually take out more than you put in. We need far-sighted thinking and planning that will produce a blueprint for integration and give the driver–promoter–sponsor relationship a whole new dimension.'

Nothing came of it. The promoters' response was that they would set up a bureau to help sponsors get full value out of their involvement (it never happened), and 'they would install telex machines to speed up the distribution of news from race circuits'. (Much later it was left to the team owners to establish TEGA, the Touring Car Entrants Group, to begin its own negotiations. I was on that board. And much later still it took a brash, abrasive, rock-and-roll impresario—Tony Cochrane— to shake the establishment to its roots, forming what is now Supercars Australia.)

John Pryce was a World War II hero. As a Red Beret commando he flew a glider behind enemy lines into France on D-Day, crash landing and knocking himself unconscious, but later he was still able to play his part in the battle. He stood up to Thomson but was also his friend. He was my friend too, a genuine mentor. When he succumbed to a virulent cancer in 1984 it was Pauline who regularly drove his wife Marie to and from the hospital. One of the saddest memories I have is of John struggling for breath in his hospital artificial lung.

At the end of the Ford works team, my sponsorship with Coca-Cola also dried up. It was a perfect storm. In fact, some of the sponsorships that had publicly been my most successful and given me a reputation as some sort of commercial svengali, complete with divining rod, had been close to disastrous.

Max Ward from Ford had christened me Marvin the Magician for my sponsorship pulling power, and it was a nickname that would stick with me all my career, although it was shortened to just Marvin and usually used in a derogatory sense.

Coke was one of the disasters. Coke was such a big brand name, and appearing on the Mustang right at the start of allowable-commercial exposure, it had seized media attention way beyond its cash value to me. They were getting a really good deal. I was getting piecemeal payments in the hundreds, not the thousands.

We were both before our time. Another decade or so later, when Coke came under national ownership and had some marketing clout, things would have been different. I was being screwed by state bottlers who were getting the reward without the investment, and those who were paying were equally being worked over by their colleagues. One of my prime contacts took this dilemma to Coke's global head office in Atlanta, presenting a reasoned case for them to provide concerted support for my efforts. But his proposal didn't get to first base. I don't think I was his only issue with the company but he was so disillusioned he resigned on the spot. Not good for him, and not good for me, because my three-year contract was at an end and there was no sign of a new one from the dysfunctional Coke structure in Australia.

Despite the frustration, that Coke involvement meant more to me than I could ever express. No one from Coke was pressing me to do it, but I'd always make sure I was photographed with a Coke can or bottle in my hand, and I'd always try to carry one onto the winners' podium. Today my drink of choice is always Coke Zero.

Pan Am was another of my early partners. Paul Casey was its regional marketing manager, and without him and his enthusiasm for my racing program we would have been sunk. Money never changed hands. Like BP, it was all in kind. That said, Paul also used me for reputational support—speeches, advertisements and the like, and that attracted additional dollars. But when you consider how much airfreight we had to move around the world, and how much maintenance of my own global contacts meant to me, having a Pan Am ticket available on call was of immense importance. Pan Am flew the first-ever jumbo jet into Australia in 1969 and they were so much a part of the trans-Pacific link to the USA. But even as I was experiencing my perfect storm, they were facing theirs.

The 1973 global oil crisis hit Pan Am hard and it was a body blow from which they'd not recover. Ultimately they declared bankruptcy and disappeared from the skies.

I'd already had one small scare, driving home the importance of vigilance in maintenance of any relationship. Pan Am's supply of tickets was seemingly never-ending, but they were graded by travel class. I got to travel up the front while my crew was further back, although not so far back that they couldn't see the pilot.

One day, when I wasn't with them, one of the boys, a senior operator, decided to impersonate me and demanded his seat in the pointy end. If I'm kind, it was just a lark, but it's the sort of unintended arrogance that can bring an entire relationship crashing around your ears. It took a bit of talking, and Paul's understanding, to smooth it over. The guy didn't fly at all for a while.

By far the most enduring commercial association I could rely on as I contemplated my future was that of Goodyear. Larry Truesdale, Goodyear's global racing boss, and his Number Two Mike Babich were more than sponsors, they were close friends. We formed a bond that was enduring. There's a popular legend among the inner circle that I once saved Larry's life. I'd been staying at his home when he collapsed and, with no immediate help forthcoming, I took the initiative and drove him pretty quickly to hospital where, indeed, his life was saved. I was praised for quick action, but saved his life? It's a bit far-fetched. On the other hand, Larry and Mike had saved my racing life with tyre supplies on more than one occasion. When Al Turner had determined the Ford GTHOs needed to be on race tyres at Bathurst in 1969, it was my contact with Mike Babich that smoothed the way and made it possible. The strength of our relationship was the only thing that got us through Ford's public rebuke of Goodyear after their effort imploded. I vowed then I'd never again put my integrity on the line for a third party, even if its name was Ford.

Mike came to every Bathurst after that. I can't say for sure that he wasn't simply guarding his own ass, but his involvement in my race efforts was a hallmark. I simply couldn't do it without him.

And then there were the friends. The people I'd come to rely on for the sort of support I truly didn't think I deserved. I'm not outgoing, not full of effusive praise. Even when Ford was still in the game, and especially when they pulled out, I just couldn't bring myself to work the corridors of power, glad-handing. I wouldn't have visited Lot Six more than half-a-dozen times. My job was at the race track. I would have walked through Ford's Broadmeadow headquarters even less. If I had a meeting there, I went to the meeting. But I didn't push myself into areas where I hadn't been invited. Was that the right thing to do? It's hard to say. I was being myself, no one else, and surely that's better than manipulating, or being perceived to manipulate, for your own advantage.

When we were going to race meetings there was a Ford guy who had management responsibility for the race team. He used to carry a small black briefcase, seemingly permanently, and inside it were accreditation and entry passes that he would hand out on an as-needed basis. Occasionally I'd ask him for additional passes for sponsors and even friends, people who'd helped along the way. Invariably he'd refuse: 'Sorry Allan, these are for Ford VIPs,' he'd say. At the end of any day, he'd have bundles left over. It was a power play and privately it infuriated me.

Keith Horner was a friend. It wasn't a case of being elitist or exclusive. He adopted us and we welcomed him. Later, when I was getting down to the next phase in my career, a guy with a similar view would turn up. His name was Edsel Ford, Henry II's son and Henry I's great-grandson, and he'd been sent to Australia to gain a little knowledge. He was and is a great guy, wary of people who cosy up to him because his name is on the hub caps. We shared a common shyness and we had a good time together, even if it was perhaps a little different from that enjoyed by most mortals.

In the late 1970s I had a big win in the Macau Grand Prix Touring Car race and decided to reward myself with a gold Rolex, bought in Hong Kong with a price negotiated by a very influential local. It was a spectacularly good deal. Back in Melbourne we were at dinner with Edsel and his wife Cynthia when Edsel asked for a look. He promptly took off his own and weighed the two, one in each hand. 'Yours is heavier than mine,' he said. I'd obviously gotten an even better deal than I thought.

Much later Fred Gibson and I were visiting Dearborn and we decided we'd seek out our old friend. We'd talked and wheedled our way onto an executive level of Ford's Glasshouse headquarters and were trying without much success to move through the next series of castle gates when Edsel walked out of an office and greeted us like the old mates we were. It stunned his minders in that rarefied atmosphere, but it's an indication of just what that small microcosm of racing in Australia meant.

The friends were few but important. Guys like Bill Gibson, who worked for a freight company and parlayed that into becoming an international freight forwarder of renown. Later he'd have squadrons of jumbo jets at his disposal and a contract with Formula One management to move F1 cars around the world. He lent me his company's utility. And on one occasion, when we couldn't afford to pay the freight on a Trans Am engine that had been confiscated after we'd brought it into the country, he tracked it through Customs and ensured we bought it back at the customs auction for a fraction of the money it would have cost us originally.

Andrew Wilson walked into 711 as a university student and a dab hand at graphic art. He devised the Allan Moffat Racing logo that was to endure throughout my career and was also instrumental in finding more commercial partners, like the Hilton Hotel group. Pauline and I would become godparents to his son Ben. June Bingham, sister of Gordon, my university and VW cadet friend, did my books part time and, as importantly, fed me on milk and chips when my diet options were limited. These were the people who mattered to me in 1974 as I faced the sheer size of the task ahead.

I was a small businessman, an owner of what they'd call today an SME. The only product I was producing was race wins. The car, or cars if I got it right, were simply my tools of trade. I had debts up to my ears, but also assets. My policy was always to clear debts as quickly as possible, so I was already well advanced in my repayments of 711 and Sydney Street. If Armageddon struck, I'd probably walk away about dead even, back to ground zero. The only downside I could see was that my business was registered in a milk bar.

Before we'd bought 711, we'd decided we needed a prestigious address. A milk bar up the road had a small post office attached so we'd secured PO Box No. 1, Armadale. It looked good on paper, but not something you'd want prospective partners to visit.

Looking to the future, I decided there were two paths to follow and I'd step them both in parallel. I was a pretty handy gun for hire and I knew there were drives out there that would suit me, advance my career, and be lucrative to boot. But to be truly successful I'd also need to take control of my own destiny and build a car, or cars, and a race team that would blow the opposition out of the water.

10

PROJECT B52 AND PROJECT PHOENIX

WHAT'S THE BEST KNOWN, MOST SUCCESSFUL, STRIKE FORCE MILITARY aircraft of the 1960s and '70s? The Boeing B52 Stratofortress.

At the time Ford pulled out of motor racing in Australia, America was also looking for a way out of the ill-executed Vietnam War, but while it was on, the B52 was the star act, the linchpin in a campaign they called Operation Rolling Thunder.

There are many reasons to consider both the Vietnam War and the Cold War as anything other than laudable. Who can forget Peter Sellers' wonderful parody of the whole disaster, Dr Strangelove, as the disabled B52 ploughed relentlessly on into Russian airspace to the driving anthem of the American Civil War, 'When Johnny Comes Marching Home'?

Vietnam was front-page news every day, and if ever you were looking for a symbol of might and power, you'd need search no further than the B52. So that's what I called my 1974 Bathurst campaign—Operation B52.

It was like nothing that had ever been attempted in Australia before. Sure, Al Turner had called on Ford in the States for help with the GTHO, but no one had made the decision to purpose build a car for Bathurst—not in Australia, but in the USA.

That's what I did. I called on every contact I had in the States. I shipped an XB Falcon to DeKon Engineering, a firm that would loom large in my future. It was run by Horst Kwech, my old teammate and adversary in the Bud Moore Trans Am campaign, and Lee Dykstra, the brilliant chassis engineer with whom I'd worked at Kar Kraft and who was one of those responsible for the design of my Trans Am Mustang. DeKon stood for Dykstra and Kwech, intermingled with the words Design and Construction.

At 711 we built two sensational engines, both based on the understanding we had of the development of the Mustang, which was by then running successfully as a sports sedan. Both engines went to the States for testing. We were deadly serious. We tested on a huge, flat skid-pan in Mid-Ohio, doing amazing things to the car in a very scientific process aimed at rooting out the gremlins we knew could strike at Bathurst, among them the oil surge that was the scourge of all touring cars of the time. You could pitch into a corner and gravity would sweep all the oil in the engine away from the moving parts and cause them to detonate. Goodyear got in on the act, as I knew and hoped they would. We went to Akron and developed tyres to work with the chassis that Lee had effectively designed. There was a lot of anticipation about the B52.

Back in Australia I still had a touring-car championship to run, alongside the Mustang's sports-sedan campaign, and I was doing it tough, even with Brut 33 on board.

As part of our annulment, Ford had given me the remnants of their 1973 works team so, with my car a wreck after the Phillip Island crash, I had Fred Gibson's Falcon ready to go for the first round of my title defence at Symmons Plains. Trouble is, I didn't have enough money to get there. It took a Tasmanian Ford dealer, Harry Cumstey at Fairford in Burnie, to spring for the boat trip. By the time I got the money and the ticket there was a dock strike, so I arrived at the circuit too late for practice but in time to come third in a preliminary event, briefly lead the main and ultimately place second to Brock. It was going to be one of those seasons.

At round two, Calder, Peter Brock and the Holden Dealer Team changed the world. They turned up with Marlboro emblazoned across the front of their car. It was the first time, domestically, that anyone had secured tobacco sponsorship. A bit like the Vietnam War, you look back on it now and tut-tut. At the time attitudes were different. Cigarette advertising was allowed, in fact encouraged. There was a huge economy built around tobacco companies' vast war chests of money. And the Holden Dealer Team had just opened the doors to that money flowing into motor racing. As much as I hate to say it, it was good to see Brock win that day. Nothing keeps a sponsor more motivated than winning.

But I could only allow him the one shot. On the long, fast, open surface of Sandown, I blew him away, closely followed home by Murray Carter, who was just half a second behind. The next race at Amaroo was a disaster. My engine blew on the warm-up lap after I'd set the fastest-ever pole at the tight Sydney circuit. Fred Gibson leapt out of his car and gave it to me, even though we were no longer strictly teammates. From the back of the grid, I passed six cars on the first run up the hill, but at Amaroo there weren't many places for passing and I was stuck there, out of the championship points, for the rest of the race.

And that, to me, made the championship chase look pointless. I'd tentatively accepted the offer to lead a tourist trip to the Indy 500 and I confirmed it, effectively giving up on the title. Of course it was the wrong decision. I won the next round at Oran Park after an initial battle with Brock and I was back in points contention, but I'd run out of rounds.

My priority was to go the USA, visit Indy and spend most of the time at DeKon working on Project B52.

Brock debuted the new V8 Holden, the SLR 5000, at Surfers Paradise and ran away with the race, as he did also at the final round at Adelaide, to win his first ATCC. It was a turning point in his career. He was growing increasingly frustrated with Harry Firth's management of the Holden Dealer Team, and he was letting his contacts at Holden know that there was a better way—his way. It was an uncomfortable situation, not the last Peter would engineer in his life.

I came back for the 1974 Sandown 400.

The B52 was still in the States undergoing final testing so I ran the touring-car championship car. It was to be my first clash with the Holden Dealer Team V8s and I was looking forward to testing my preparedness against them. It never happened. I won the race from flag to flag while the Holdens dropped away with oil-pump failures. The dreaded oil surge I'd been working so hard to correct on the B52 had hit them. These were happy days.

In testing in Ohio, the B52 had been performing so well it even caught the eye of the great Mark Donohue. He was at a test complex undertaking long-distance performance on a flat track, and he approached me and asked for a drive. 'Sure,' I said, and then finally had to stand on the track waving my arms to bring him back in because he was enjoying it so much.

DeKon fixed me up with a noted co-driver, Germany's Dieter Glemser, a recent winner of the European Touring Car Championship and the Spa 24 Hour race. Our paths had crossed in a parallel universe when we'd both raced and won in the fabulous Ford Capri 2600RS at the Macau Grand Prix in the early 1970s.

Two weeks before Bathurst we held a media conference to reveal the best-looking car I'd ever taken to the mountain. It was painted electric blue with huge NASCAR-type numbers incorporating the sponsor's name on each door (Brut 33). When we arrived in Bathurst, we got two huge shocks. For a start the scrutineers told me to take the numbers off the car. They didn't comply with CAMS regulations. I said the numbers stayed or we didn't race. We were both bluffing, but I won.

'We want you to race,' they said. It was just stupid, petty bureaucracy—but it actually set up our belly-to-belly posture, maybe positively, for shock number two.

Harry Firth entered a fifteen-point protest on the B52. It was the weekend of the race. He'd had weeks before to question my eligibility and to have me respond, but left it until the eve of the race in a deliberate ploy to unsettle me. There were two options—run under protest with the car to be pulled down post-race, or submit to inspection then and there. I chose to pull it down immediately.

To this day, I can't say it was the right call, but I was damned if I was going to have my integrity and that of some of the best engineers in the business brought into question on race day.

I like to think I'm beyond mind games, but Harry was a master. My response, quoted at the time was: 'It's the greatest insult I've ever received in Australia and it shows the level of sportsmanship of the opposition.' Obviously he'd gotten to me. The scrutineers, who wanted me to race, went through the Falcon item by item and found nothing. Harry only needed one ball bearing to be illegal to get me, and he failed.

But so did I. By the time my car got back from its off-site inspection at a garage in Bathurst we'd missed a full session of practice with a car that had done lots of testing miles but had never been driven in race conditions. A journalist later wrote: 'With the precious little time available to sort out the car for the Mt Panorama circuit now completely gone, you only have to look into Moffat's eyes as he sits in the passenger seat of his giant motor-home to know that he lost the race on Saturday.'

The best we could muster was a fifteenth place on the grid. On the morning of the race I went for a walk up the grid to talk to the drivers in front of me. It's an old ploy. You aren't so arrogant as to say 'please get out of my way when I come through', but that's the implication. I didn't speak to the Holden Dealer Team.

The race just went from fifteenth to retirement.

Everything that could go wrong did.

Lee Dykstra had come over to run my pit and we'd put together a crew that was absolutely committed to our mutual success. Without them we wouldn't have gotten as far as lap 112 of the 163-lap race before we retired.

In that time we replaced an electrical coil, a distributor, a front-wheel bearing, a front spring—and then the clutch blew. They were all things that might not have gone wrong if we hadn't had our unscheduled strip down.

I pulled up on Pit Straight, opposite the crew. We exchanged glances that conveyed our dismay and I drove one more slow lap and retired. In a race day plagued by wet weather, I walked up the pit row to where John Goss was watching co-driver Kevin Bartlett battle manfully for the lead in his now elderly Falcon coupe. The car had already been off the track once, cracking a wheel and limping to the pits. Goss was on Bridgestones but I had several sets of the best wet-weather tyres in the business, my purpose-built Goodyears, and I gave them to him. He used them to win the race.

My only consolation was that the Holden Dealer Team failed too. Both cars had oil leaks, causing Peter Brock to retire and Colin Bond to limp, smoking, to fourth.

I was to drive the Brut 33 car once more that year because there was still a mathematical chance I'd clinch the five-round Australian Manufacturers' Championship points score. At Phillip Island a tiny stone pierced my radiator, a fan belt came off, the engine overheated and blew. So much for the title.

After Bathurst, in the maelstrom of Holden politics that were being played out, Harry Firth had shifted most of his team's attention to Colin Bond to the detriment of Brock. It was Bond who won the last two rounds of the series while Brock retired.

That was enough for Peter. He made his run on the bank, offering, somewhat forcefully, to General Motors to take over the Holden Dealer Team from a man he and Bond regarded as 'going senile'.

But Harry had just delivered Holden its second Manufacturers' Championship in succession. A corporation doesn't mess with success. Not for the last time Peter had misjudged his ultimate value to General Motors and he joined me in the ranks of the privateers.

Neither of us was well funded. Brut 33 had sent me a letter saying they had great promotional plans for the next year, but they didn't include me.

Colin was elevated to Holden Dealer Team leadership, and he was to win the ATCC in 1975 and contribute mightily to Holden's third straight win in the Manufacturers' title.

Brock upset the applecart at Bathurst, thumbing his nose at the factory with a fine win in a privately entered Torana.

For me, domestically, 1975 was a gap year. To understand that, there's a need for perspective.

I was in demand overseas and racing successfully there, and I was still driving the Mustang in Australian sports sedans, earning money. And I was in conversation with DeKon about exciting prospects. Things weren't all bad.

Sponsorship was limited largely to in-kind support. International Harvester, a long-time partner, had provided me with the best transporter in the championship and some assistance as well.

The ATCC started badly when the B52, now painted International Harvester red with a gold GT stripe, crashed with Allan Grice's Torana and spun back to fifth. In the two following races I was also crashed out.

At Bathurst I teamed with Pete Geoghegan and, from second place on the grid, alongside Colin Bond, we led for quite a while until oil leaks, a gearbox change and ultimately a suspension collapse caused our retirement. My frustration was showing. 'That's the idiocy of having such fast, heavy cars running on standard suspension,' I told several million television viewers, ignoring the fact I was already many laps in arrears.

I won only one domestic touring-car race that year, the Surfers Paradise Rothmans 300, starting from pole and putting pressure on Allan Grice all race long until he spun his Torana into deep mud and bogged.

The following season, things started to look up. Salvation, if you can call it that, arrived in the shape of a Ford executive named Doug Jacobi. Doug had been a finance man so, naturally, he'd been promoted to a position way outside his area of expertise: he was in charge of spare parts and a division called Motorcraft.

No matter how it sounds, that's not a demotion. In any car company the real profit lies at the back end of the business— service and parts. Retaining customers and ensuring they service their car at your dealership with your parts is an essential part of the business. It's in everyone's best interests. The customer has their car kept in good condition, attracting better resale value, and the dealer not only gets the business but is in a position to make another sale.

Doug wanted me to be the motivator for his dealers.

Holden was running the Holden Dealer Team and, while there were some very serious Holden dealers on the motor-racing committee, most people accepted it was a front for Holden money coming through the back door.

When the Ford Dealer Team appeared on my newly liveried car most people figured Ford had followed suit, but it wasn't so. Every month a man from Doug's department would turn up at 711 with a cheque, and every month, as well as racing, I'd be available to schmooze dealers and headline Ford's parts campaigns. Corporate hospitality might have been rudimentary but it was enthusiastic. Doug lopped the top off a double-decker bus, painted it in Motorcraft colours and brought it to local races. There was no subterfuge at all.

That money was the incentive and support I needed to win my second ATCC. CAMS had combined the touring-car title—a drivers' championship—with the Manufacturers' Championship, so there were eleven rounds. In an incredibly hard-fought season, I was to win just three of them. Consistent points scoring, though, would get me over the line in the championship. That year there were six different race winners. Colin Bond would take three wins, like me, and come second. Peter Brock, who, like me, was picking up international drives to supplement his income, scored two towards the end of the season.

But my season was the most dramatic.

I'd won two out of the first five rounds and claimed a second by the time we headed for Adelaide International Raceway.

My big International Harvester transporter had left 711 heading for the circuit and I flew to Adelaide.

Off the plane, the police were waiting. 'We have bad news,' they said.

Not stolen again, I thought, referencing my 1973 theft. Nope.

'Your transporter has been burnt to the ground with the car inside.'

The fire had occurred at Murray Bridge, about 80 kilometres out of the city. It was so intense it had fused the wheels of the truck into the bitumen road surface. The two drivers had failed to extract the B52, but they had managed to salvage their own suitcases. I suggested they use them for the long hitchhike back to Melbourne.

And that's when John Goss came to the fore. In those early GTHO years, John had resented Fred Gibson and myself. We were the works drivers. He was the private entrant, usually with the help of Sydney dealer Max McLeod, but he could never quite crack the code to get right inside our Ford tent. By the time he won Bathurst in 1974 the tent had folded—unfortunately for him. He was running a very ambitious program, like all of us short on funds and big on ambition. As well as his Falcon race car, he was the proud owner of a Matich A53 F5000 open wheeler. I truly envied him. I'd always wanted to try my hand at open-wheeler racing but I'd always fallen back to my default position before it came to pass.

Goss was a true talent, not only a good engineer but a brave driver. He made himself famous in the sport, not just for his on-track performance but his off-circuit persona. He was the only man I ever knew to wear his race suit to the airport and the only one who could, straight-faced, refer to his transporter as a 'ground-based facility'.

John wasn't doing the championship, preferring to concentrate his funds on his open-wheeler campaign. He offered me his Bathurst-winning Falcon and it was hurriedly brought across from Sydney. With a little bit of tweaking, I managed to put it on the front row of the grid and then win both heats to extend my title lead. It was a good car. My major discomfort came from wearing Goss's race suit and helmet, since mine had been destroyed in the fire.

Project B52 became Project Phoenix, not particularly inventive, but an apt description of the task ahead.

I'd set the Sandown Hang Ten 400 in three months as the deadline to build a new car out of the ashes. Peter Molloy, a noted Sydney engine-builder and team manager was on board, and we had our sights set not only on the touring-car title but also Bathurst.

I kept the Goss car for the next round to finish second to Colin Bond, for whom I was gaining incredible respect, then we headed for Sandown to race Brock as well at the Hang Ten 400.

It was a big ask with essentially a brand-new car.

I was to finish second to Peter who, as usual, did a sensational job on his return drive in Australia to win the Hang Ten by a full lap.

At that same race meeting John Goss won the Australian Grand Prix in his Matich in an absolute cliffhanger, from South Australian international Vern Schuppan. They fought wheel to wheel in one of the best open-wheeler duels I've ever seen.

Bathurst was looming and I'd already made a call to Britain to secure a co-driver of note. Coincidentally it was Vern Schuppan, who was making a strong name for himself in motor sport. He'd been Rookie of the Year at Indy, and earlier in 1976 he'd won the Rothmans Tasman series in Australia. He was already racing at Le Mans, mainly for wealthy American teams, and finishing as high as fifth, and would later win the 24-hour classic for Porsche.

'Allan called me out of the blue,' Vern said. 'We'd never met but I knew his reputation. The idea really appealed to me. I'd never driven a touring car before. I knew Molloy through open-wheeler racing and I really admired his skills. None of us was making much money. The most you made from a race was prize money and you picked up a living where you could, driving prototypes in test programs. So Allan's offer wasn't about the money.'

But Vern did have a small reservation about me: 'I'm told you don't want to be at the wheel of his car if something goes wrong, even if it isn't your fault. You'll get the blame.' Oh, really?

Vern loved the car. He got to see it and drive it for the first time in practice and he was truly impressed—so much so that I had to call him in. 'You have to get on the brakes earlier,' I told him. 'You're coming over the second hump of Conrod Straight and I can see air under your tyres. It's like a Pan Am 747.'

Publicity is important. It's good for business. But that year Brock and I, modestly the local stars of Bathurst, were both gazumped. Promoters contrived to enter Jack Brabham and Stirling Moss together in an L34 Torana. Bringing Stirling back to competition, fourteen years after his near-fatal crash at Goodwood, was a world-beating coup. Not in their wildest dreams were these two veterans going to win but they secured every column inch of available coverage.

Brock and I engaged in a huge battle for pole position, swapping fastest laps until I took the honour. At the start, Peter bogged down and I seized the lead, but few saw it, because spectator attention was still focused at the start line. Way back in the field, Jack had got his gear selection wrong and compounded the problem by not sticking up his hand as a warning. He was hit from behind at serious speed and, although his pit crew got the car going again so Stirling could get in some ego-laps, it was all over.

Up front things ultimately didn't go well for either Brock or myself. It just takes one mistake, one error of analysis to wreck your day. For Brock it was a faulty fuel pick up, which led him to believe he'd snapped a throttle linkage. He pulled to the side of the track on Conrod and got bogged, losing two laps.

For me it was a faulty bonnet-catch that brought Vern in for an unscheduled stop. I'm there, jumping up and down, screaming at Peter Molloy to fix it. Heat of the moment stuff. And then shortly afterwards it was all over. The car broke a crankshaft pulley that slipped the fan belt and fried a head gasket. Simple things with big consequences. Did I blame Vern?

Well I didn't invite him back again the following year, but I don't recall the two being related. 'I would have come back if he'd asked me,' Vern said. 'The following year I was asked to co-drive with Dick Johnson and I leapt at the chance. It was curious though, as compared to Allan's car, Dick's didn't handle nearly as well. Dick's kind of wobbled around. The implication was obvious but honestly I thought Allan was straight up.'

I won the ATCC at the Surfers Paradise 300 held after Bathurst with a second to Brock, even after my pit-stop protocols let me down. It was a disaster. I had one scheduled stop and then had to come back in twice more, once to get the bonnet properly shut and then to remove an air hose that had wrapped around the rear axle.

One thing I knew for sure was that, the next year, I'd have the best-drilled pit crew in the business.

At the end of 1976 I pulled off the motor-racing coup of the decade. I swooped on Colin Bond and stole him away from Holden. It was quite deliberate on several fronts. Colin was mightily impressive as a front runner. After Peter Brock he was the best of the rest.

It was only years later that people asked me: 'Why not approach Brock, instead of Bond?'

It's not something I ever considered. Brock to me was a genuine icon—far removed, in my mind, from any possibility of joining my team. Honestly, I would not have known how to approach him.

Colin, on the other hand, was in my stratosphere. And what a catch! As well as winning the ATCC, winning Bathurst on debut, winning Sandown and being the rock for Holden's northern motor-racing operations, he'd also won three Australian Rally Championships for Holden. Harry Firth would probably never have admitted it publicly but compared to the volatile, mercurial Brock, Bond was just about the best team player he could ever have exploited.

They were rough-and-tumble days, played to cowboy rules.

Brock and Bond had the best drives in the country, but they were also on call to 'H' to do spanner duty in the workshop. They were paid menial wages while their labour was charged back to Holden at far greater mark-up. Far greater. They knew that but were powerless to do anything about it.

The deal was they got the prize money but, when they went to pick it up from circuit promoters, they sometimes found the purse was minus the entry fee, because Harry hadn't paid it. In the case of one circuit, they discovered the team had taken up-front appearance money instead of prize money and they didn't share in that at all.

Initially they received no salary. It was only when Robyn Bond, Colin's wife, alerted a surprised Holden executive to that fact ('We didn't know,' he said) that a back-door deal was arranged with sponsor Castrol to pay Peter and Colin with Holden money. Why that circuitous route?

According to Colin, 'GM's global policy was still no motor

racing so Holden couldn't pay us directly'. Rallying, however, was okay, which legitimised the workshop. 'Whenever a visiting executive wanted to have a look at the team, there'd be a mad scramble on the shop floor to put rally lights on the race cars.'

No wonder Peter left, and no wonder Colin was open to a reasonable offer.

'I went for the money,' Colin said. 'Moffat offered me a signing on fee well beyond anything I'd ever earned and a split of the prize money which was reasonable in the circumstances. I knew I wasn't going to be winning unless he crashed or broke down, but that was okay.'

Colin's motivations ran a bit deeper. His first love had always been rallying, and moving to me was also a move to Ford, which didn't have an Australian rally team. Within a year, in a separate deal well away from me, he was preparing and running a Ford Escort rally team. In 1978 he'd win the national championship for them with Greg Carr at the wheel. Greg would also win the televised and highly popular Castrol International Rally in Canberra four years in succession for Colin's Ford team. Colin was instrumental in bringing out world champions like Ari Vatanen to drive in his team, a huge publicity-getter for Ford. He even secured Vatanen's world championship co-driver, young Dave Richards, who would go on to start giant motor-racing company Prodrive, run an F1 team and become chairman of Aston Martin.

Colin's defection was big news. 'There were lots of letters from fans, lots of people saying they can't sleep at night, crying, dog-died, that sort of stuff,' Colin said.

But I maintain to this day that we shook up the establishment, made motor racing more relevant to a larger audience and, by the way, made it more professional.

I'd brought in Carroll Smith from the States to run the team. He'd worked with the Ford GT40 team that won Le Mans in 1966 and 1967, and he'd just published the seminal motor-racing textbook *Prepare To Win*, still the handbook for any team owner. He went on to write *Tune To Win* and *Drive To Win*, among others, but far from being an academic, he was simply a very well-organised bloke who knew the rules and could apply the strategies. He ran the best pit operation I'd ever experienced.

In something of a personal win, in time for Bathurst I'd brought a cigarette company on board. R.J. Reynolds would go on to sponsor Team Lotus in Formula One with their Camel brand but they started out with me in Australia.

Their Joe Camel logo would later become controversial, with allegations that it was purpose-designed to exploit children. It was also one of the images most brought under attack by the successful anti-smoking legislators.

I was pleased to have them as backers. I have never been a smoker—can't stand it—but I figure the world is full of free choice and as long as I felt I was operating within the standards of the day, then I was okay with the decision to accept them on the car. Honestly, at the time, it was not a consideration.

In 1977 we blew the doors off Holden.

I won the first five rounds of the ATCC with Colin second on four of those occasions. At the next round Colin snuck by me and I was so engrossed in a huge battle for second with Brock that there was no opportunity to redress the winning position.

By that point in the championship we'd, predictably, been accused of cheating. That's the stance everyone takes when somebody is consistently better. It doesn't matter what the sport is. There was a fourteen-point protest pending against us. I was called before a CAMS Board of Enquiry to answer questions ranging from my construction of a mounting system for the rear-brake calliper to my use of twin fanbelts on the car. To each protest CAMS determined: 'The points in question are a matter of interpretation and that specifications laid down in the National Competition Rule do not clearly define whether the components Moffat used could be deemed ineligible.'

Green light.

Was I cheating? No way. Was I doing what Harry Firth had done for years? You bet. Only better. And did I derive some satisfaction from beating the system? A race report from the season described my victory speech after round four as 'cocky and sarcastic'. Humility was something I knew I had to work on.

Peter Brock won the next round when I blew the engine. He would have won anyway because I was off the pace after a crash in practice.

At the Sandown 500 I blew another engine in practice, and Peter won again this time in the new Torana A9X—the best Holden supercar ever built. We both got a standing ovation from the huge grandstand crowd because we'd put on a monstrous battle towards race end, even though I was only trying to unlap myself. I still finished third.

At Bathurst, Colin and I staged our 1–2 formation finish, creating one of the most memorable moments in Australian motor sport. Looking back now, I feel it probably wasn't my most satisfying victory. It wasn't clean. In fact, it was contrived. But as a point in time when everything aligned in my favour, it's a standout.

Although it wasn't my intention, that famous shot of us crossing the line was a big boost for Ford (intended) and humiliation for Holden (unintended).

I went on from Bathurst to win two of the remaining three rounds of the long, exhausting and exhilarating season, and then elected not to go to Phillip Island's finale because I didn't need the points. Colin went because he had to wrap up second place in the series, and he achieved that despite getting a flat tyre five laps from home.

At the end of the year Harry Firth was out of Holden.

John Bagshaw, General Motors-Holden's sales director and the man who had stage-managed the Holden Dealer Team since its inception, made two momentous recommendations and sold them successfully to his board. The first was that the Holden Dealer Team had to be better managed. The second was that Brock was good for Holden and Holden was good for Brock.

Peter was back in, reportedly at an annual salary of $40,000 plus bonuses, which at the time made him the highest-paid racing driver in Australia. John Sheppard, formerly Pete Geoghegan's main man, took the 'H' role.

I was under more than a bit of stress. Ford was sending me signals. The small bonus they paid me after our best-ever year was one of them.

They possibly were not happy that my teammate and employee was pursuing me over a prize money dispute—something they definitely knew about since he was also running their rally team. In the factional world of Ford, there were strong dealers who were in Colin's camp.

I was exposed. My greatest supporter at Ford, Keith Horner, had retired midway through 1976 so I was without the executive suite back-up that I'd never taken for granted but certainly relied upon. Max Gransden, the new sales director, was not a fan, and Bill Dix, who controlled finance, seemed not to understand the value of motor racing even though it was presenting him with success.

At the end of Ford's most successful season and Holden's worst, it was as if there'd been a complete flip-flop. Holden, led by Bagshaw, was fired up and fighting back. Ford wasn't actually refusing to fight. They just didn't know what to fight for.

That's when Edsel Ford came into our lives. Edsel was 30 years old, sent to Australia by his dad to learn the ropes. He came with his own security team and his own sense of entitlement as befits a man whose father and great-grandfather were both named Henry Ford. Coincidentally he was in the Sydney Hilton Hotel the night a bomb went off at the hotel's entrance. If you want proof of security efficiency, that was the night. Even as police and emergency crews were still arriving, Edsel's team had him out of the place and on his private plane back to Melbourne.

Edsel was on a fast track. He'd been to Babson College where future leaders graduate, and then moved on to Harvard. He was being groomed for the very top.

Pauline and I liked Edsel and his wife Cynthia. They were good people and we socialised a bit. Edsel understood what a performance image could do for his company. In 1979 he made quite a name for himself with the factory and the dealers when he came up with a plan to clear 400 XC Falcon two doors that just weren't moving out the door at the end of the model's run-out. Australians were over their love affair with big coupes. Edsel painted them white, put blue stripes down them and called them Cobras in homage to the Shelby image in the States. He made them special and they sold like hotcakes.

But Edsel's life wasn't easy in Australia. In a way, it wasn't meant to be. His dad wanted him to be roughed up a bit. Like me, he found Gransden to be fractious and, according to Ford's official history, Edsel lobbied hard for his dismissal. But Sir Brian Inglis refused and Henry II backed his managing director, not his son.

Edsel came to a few races in 1978 and I think his presence and interest probably staved off what would be Ford's eventual decision to pull out of motor sport—again.

Without a budget to speak of, in 1978 I won just one race of the eight-round sprint series and finished second to Colin Bond in a reverse 1–2 finish at Adelaide. This time it was the '2' car that led the Number One over the line. Peter Brock claimed the championship, his second.

The highlight of that year came in the Queen's Birthday honours. I was granted the Order of the British Empire, an OBE, in recognition of my contribution to motor sport. It was a year after Brian Inglis had been knighted and, although I never knew how either came about, I always assumed they were in some way linked through the same recommendation system. I treasure that honour although I've never formally worn it. It's in a very safe place.

I brought Jacky Ickx back for the 1978 Bathurst and put my old friend and partner Fred Gibson with Colin Bond in the Number Two car. But it was not to be. Holden had a saying around that time: 'When you're hot, you're hot.' We were not.

Engine failure took both cars out before halfway.

Ford, even with Edsel as its deputy managing director, ceased supporting domestic motor racing at the end of what had been Holden's exceptional year.

That meant Colin was out of a drive. Strangely, despite the ongoing tension over the Bathurst prize money, we'd been getting on all right. I thought there was respect there, both ways. It was his connections who were causing the trouble.

The 1979 ATCC was dismal.

Among my other commitments, I managed to pull together enough support to compete in just three rounds, in which I failed to finish two and came fifth in the other.

As always I threw everything at Bathurst, importing the 1976 co-winner Englishman John Fitzpatrick to drive with me in a car largely supported by Federation Insurance with help from Camel Filters. I'd blown the engine at Sandown and came to Bathurst with two new ones. In practice one of them started dropping oil so badly and so quickly that I spread oil over the racing line, an uncharacteristic lack of professionalism for which

I apologised. Putting oil on the track is about the worst sin you can commit. It's not only dangerous, it can wreck a fast lap time.

More controversy followed.

Hardie's Heroes, the one-lap dash for pole position reserved for the fastest ten drivers in practice, carried an $8000 purse that I sorely needed. But I was outside the top ten and unqualified until the organisers made the decision to include me and exclude the Holden Number Two car of John Harvey. Having me in the shoot-out was obviously good for the race promotion and I swear I did nothing to lobby for my place. But when the organisers flung Harvey, they ensured my popularity ratings plummeted.

I threw in a new motor and had a go. It was all for nothing. I qualified fourth, way behind a dominant Brock, and got no money.

In the race, the oil leak came back. We were among the front-runners, using a prodigious amount of oil at each pit stop, until on lap 136, tantalisingly close to the finish, John Fitzpatrick pulled to a halt on pit straight. I will never forget him climbing from the car and giving a mournful thumbs down. It was over and I just turned and walked back to the truck and, I suppose, sulked.

That was the year Peter Brock won by six laps.

There were no words of consolation from Ford, certainly no money.

In 1980 I took one of the new four-door Falcon XDs to Bathurst with John Fitzpatrick once again. We blew a motor in practice, starting from ninth on the grid, and managed just three laps before the new motor gave up as well. I'd cross-entered my team with 1976 winner Bob Morris and on his lap 70 he put me in his car, only to pull me out again sixteen laps later because I wasn't matching his lap times. There was a reason for that. When scheduled co-driver Bill O'Brien took over the car, it blew one lap later.

Leading the race, Dick Johnson, not yet a star but working on it, jinked his Falcon to the right up through the Cutting to avoid one of those incredibly dangerous quick-lift trucks that used to go out during the race to pick up stranded cars. But in the right-hand lane was a 50-kilogram rock that had been dislodged by a spectator. Dick hit it full on with both left wheels, tearing them from the car.

The sight of a disconsolate Johnson sitting on the safety fence tore the hearts out of race-goers and sent television ratings soaring. No one has a more expressively morose face than Dick. Channel Seven were always on the lookout for a good drama, so when Dick let viewers know his life savings were in that car, Seven started an instant telethon and was well on the way to raising $30,000—an incredible amount—when Sydney *Daily Telegraph* journalist Wayne Webster called Edsel Ford in Melbourne. Edsel pledged a dollar-for-dollar contribution.

By the end of the day Dick had $72,000 and Ford had a new hero.

I never drove a Ford Falcon at Bathurst again.

11

MAZDA MAN

IT WAS IN 1979, ON THE NIGHT OF MY 40TH BIRTHDAY, THAT I LEARNED MY big ace-in-the-hole had gone forever.

For almost a year, with Ford's support so obviously already drawing to an unhappy ending, I'd been courting BMW. I had won for them at the 1975 Sebring 12 Hour in one of my overseas driving assignments and that had given me entree at a reasonably credible level. The fact that my old VW colleague Gordon Bingham was now head of BMW in the USA was another factor in my favour.

Pauline threw a suitably discreet party for my 40th. I'm not one for big bashes. At any function I'm the one in the corner searching for a plausible excuse to leave. But this was looking good.

Gordon had flown in from the USA, especially for my birthday, and other BMW heavies were in the room. I'd done a lot of work on the proposal and I was feeling positive. So positive in fact that Gordon was embarrassed, because he'd just learned of the Australian division's decision. He couldn't face me, and he couldn't accept my hospitality without coming clean. He took Pauline aside and confided in her that BMW had decided to run an Australian race team, but under the management of Frank Gardner.

JPS BMW would go on to be a huge success, first in sports sedans and then in touring-car racing.

When Frank had returned from his very successful international racing career, he had treated us all like a bunch of colonial cowboys. Strange, I know, coming from a Canadian but I kind of resented his attitude. I felt he lorded over us. Frank talked the talk. He'd learned to do that in the big ponds of America and Europe, where your survival and success both depend in equal measure on visible self-belief, and he did it very successfully.

But he did put a downer on my birthday.

Turning 40 is a big deal, especially for a racing driver. For most people it's the entry point into middle age. For a racing driver it's a time of great re-evaluation, a milestone moment when you question your motivation and your reflexes, both of which are absolutely critical to outright speed. In recent times Australia's Mark Weber walked away at 40. Jack Brabham famously appeared on the grid with a fake beard and walking stick, poking fun at his age, only to go on to win the race. But he then pulled out at 43 anyway, under family pressure. He spent the rest of his life bemoaning his early retirement.

I guess, without giving it too much conscious thought, I was also a victim, but for different reasons. As a late starter in motor racing, I had no doubt about my commitment or my ability: I reckoned I was still improving. I had already set myself a target for retirement, for when I expected to be not totally on my game, but it was another decade off. Right now my problem was more fiscal than physical.

I was a race team without a race car, a project management organisation without a project. I could go on racing for other people and perhaps even field a car of my own, but I was geared up for more than that. Allan Moffat Racing needed to be a manufacturer's representative, developing a car to support an entire marketing campaign based on motor-racing success. And, above all, to be winning.

Happily BMW was not my only ace, although I admit it was my preferred choice, simply because of its ready suitability.

By far the greater challenge lay with Toyo Kogyo, the holding company of Mazda, and a 70 per cent shareholder in its Australian distribution network.

I'm not so certain whether I jumped ship or whether I clambered into the only available lifeboat. Either way my soon-to-be relationship with Mazda was to be one of the most satisfying, and rewarding, of my motor-racing career.

With them, I took international class victories, won my fourth ATCC, twice won the Australian Endurance Championship and claimed three Bathurst podiums out of four attempts, although frustratingly not a victory.

The Mazda association started with a massive battle within CAMS, and ended pretty much the same way.

Mazda had been in Australia since 1959 but, unlike Toyota and Nissan, it had never taken any great steps towards becoming a local manufacturer.

It was satisfied with its role of bringing in fully built-up models, a task it performed so well that by the mid-1970s it had become the country's largest exclusive importer. Motor racing had played some part in that success. Like the other Japanese, Mazda had played in the tiddler categories, gaining a solid reputation by winning the small-car class at Bathurst on three occasions between 1971 and 1979. While they paddled in the shallow end, the big boys weren't too worried.

But when you look at the Australian automotive market, Ford and Holden had growing cause for concern. In 1970, around when I joined Ford, the pair jointly accounted for well over half of all car and truck sales. A decade later their share was down to 42 per cent. The trend was pretty obvious. While demand for cars in Australia was expanding, the two big local manufacturers weren't keeping pace. In spite of government tariff protection, they were losing out to the Japanese importers, a situation heightened by various fuel and oil crises that brought attention to the frugal habits of most of the imports along with their obviously superior build quality.

In 1978 Mazda launched the rotary engine RX7—and the game completely changed.

The RX7 was a weapon and, if allowed to race, could seriously unsettle the V8 status quo. Getting it homologated for racing in Australia took a three-year battle, strongly opposed by the factories and their 'privateer' teams.

Mazda was a pioneer of rotary engines. Rotary technology is a way of extracting far greater power from a smaller engine size by not using a conventional piston set-up. In its early days it was notoriously unreliable.

Mazda had a technical tie-up with NSU in Germany, and NSU RO80 drivers became famous for holding up fingers to each other as they passed in traffic, each finger indicating the number of engine changes they'd had so far.

Comparatively, Mazda got it right. Apart from engine-seal problems and very high fuel consumption, the RX7s were pretty much bulletproof. But that lack of fuel economy almost brought the entire company undone. They had bet the farm on the rotary and, when the world fuel crisis of the 1970s captured the thirsty RX series in its net, Mazda was stuck with heaps of unsold stock and was heading for bankruptcy.

It took a monster effort of will by Mazda and its suppliers, as only the Japanese team mentality can achieve, to come through the dark days but still, in 1979, the company allowed Ford to take a 7 per cent 'technology' share in the company as part of the bailout. In that respect, I was to be back in the Ford fold.

The RX7 was Mazda's coming-of-age celebration—a recognition that the rotary would no longer be a mainstream technology but that in certain places, like sports-car performance, it had a really exciting role to perform. The RX7 was to be the halo car for the whole brand.

There were several stages of tune for this rotary engine, the wildest being peripheral porting: a way of altering the combustion chamber of the standard car to extract almost double the horsepower from the same cubic capacity. It was this modification that made it so difficult for regulators, especially in Australia, to get their heads around. Mazda was proud of its RX7. They took it racing in North America and in Europe. In Australia, they offered the car to race teams at a hugely preferential rate, and even offered free freight back to Japan so Australians could compete in domestic Japanese series. But they got no takers. The problem was that the RX7 was a sports car, ineligible, it seemed, for the ATCC.

I wasn't so sure.

My first contact with Mazda Australia was in December 1978, right at the end of my contract with Ford. Distribution was a bit fragmented. Malcolm Gough was managing director of Mazda Australia, which sold the brand in Victoria and Tasmania. Ray Baxter was in charge of Great Western Australia (GWA), which accounted for Queensland, New South Wales and Western Australia. In the 1980s it was the biggest importer of fully assembled vehicles in the country. Their resolve to go racing was absolute.

The problem was this: how to crack the code for entry into touring cars? It was a double-edged sword. On the surface, there was no factory support from Holden and Ford, not like there had been in the days of the GTHOs. But with Ford's interest seemingly fast diminishing, there was good marketing sense in Holden, as 'unofficial' as they might be, having a new factory to beat. But what if they were beaten? This wasn't going to be an easy problem to solve.

As was my way, I took matters into my own hands. With an introduction from Mazda Australia, I flew to Japan to meet with the Mazda top brass. The guy I connected with was certainly that. He was Kenichi Yamamoto, universally recognised as the father of the Mazda rotary and later to become managing director of the company. Yamamoto san pointed me towards the teams already racing in the USA. I hooked up with Seattle-based Jerry Wright, and in April 1979 we did several days of testing, covering more than 700 race-speed kilometres.

The RX7 was an impressive car. Its cubic capacity was listed at just 1.2 litres but, with peripheral porting, it put out power the equivalent of a 5-litre V8. The claim was around 270 hp. But it was more the way it was delivered: all up, around 9000 rpm, and in a chassis that was so nimble and responsive.

I was determined to have one . . . or two.

The local lobby program ramped up in earnest. Allan Horsley, who had been a supporter throughout my career, was now a critical part of my future. Apart from running Sydney's Oran Park he was CAMS official measurer for the ATCC. While the world said the RX7 was a sports car, I needed Allan to prove it was also a touring car. There was no subterfuge; no incentives were offered.

Allan was the straightest shooter in motor racing. Whether he was a supporter of mine or not, when it came to the dimensions examination his ruler would rule. A small dip in the back seat made all the difference. By the merest fraction of a centimetre, the interior dimensions of the RX7 squeezed within regulations for local touring-car compliance.

On 10 December 1979, a year after my meeting with Mazda, the national council of CAMS approved the RX7, but with a huge caveat.

Unwilling to offend anyone, CAMS called its decision 'tentative' and opened it to comment from interested parties. It seemed the rules themselves were not enough. Other participants or potential participants in the touring-car series were now able to sit in judgement. Given the chance, both Holden and, strangely, Toyota loudly objected.

Simultaneously I took off for the Daytona 24 Hour race to drive for Mazda. My testing with Jerry Wright had led to an offer I was not going to refuse, a full-on drive in the race I knew quite well. Besides, it was another way of gaining confidence in the car.

For 440 laps along with my co-drivers, Mazda stalwarts Amos Johnson and Stu Fisher, I pounded around the Florida track, contesting the GTU class victory, staying on the pace by driving at ten-tenths while also remaining clear of the much faster cars that were leading the race outright.

It's a juggling act demanding extreme concentration—one eye forward and one always in the mirrors. I'd been used to nursing an engine, especially at Daytona. The year before, 46 of the 68 Daytona starters had failed to finish, most through mechanical failure, but this car was sweet. It was set and forget—as long as you didn't over-rev it. One rpm too much and you were gone, but that's what being a race driver is all about: precision. We were looking so good, then one of my co-drivers hit a wall and we were out. We'd amassed so many laps we were still classified 24th outright and ninth in class.

I had a brilliant idea. Why not borrow the race car, bring it back to Australia, and let its detractors determine for themselves whether it should be allowed to race? What was there to lose?

I set up a test day at Sandown and issued invitations but only Peter Brock showed up. The others decided to maintain their objections through a veil of ignorance. To his eternal credit, Peter was supportive. The laps he did in the car convinced him that it could be competitive, but his knowledge of his own machinery, I think, also convinced him I was beatable.

Way beyond commercial considerations, Peter was a sportsman, and the last thing he wanted was to win races in anything but a meaningful way. Otherwise the titles would be shallow. His support swayed CAMS a lot, but still they vacillated, backwards and forwards as the winds of protest and opportunity swept them about. Committee members came and went and the controversy continued. God knows why.

I decided to get on with life, anticipating a positive outcome. To Mazda I put the proposition that they should own all the equipment, even my workshop tools, and they should contract me to build the cars and run the race team. It seemed a good deal at the time—one I would later regret but would correct when I did the opposite deal in the next phase of my career.

Mazda was happy with the idea. They said, fine, as long as they could insert an appropriate manager. We agreed on one. Allan Horsley had grown tired of race promotion and, just as he was about to take a severe career correction by becoming a partner in a real estate agency, he instead became Mazda's man in Allan Moffat Racing. Naturally, given his role in my homologation by CAMS, there were whispers, none of them with any foundation, and Allan went on to see out an illustrious 35-year career with Mazda.

The cigarette wars were at their height in the 1980s. Brock had Marlboro. Gardner had JPS. I had had Camel but no longer, and not for the right money. I went to Rothmans with a strong proposition and found myself addressing a proud South African.

Sometimes good luck just hits you in the face.

I was able to conduct the entire presentation in Afrikaans and walked out with the Peter Stuyvesant account. It was to be one of the best sponsorships of my life—all because I'd listened in the schoolyard, even if I'd failed the exam.

Yamamoto san came to Australia to visit his fast-growing band of retail troops and, also, to have a look at my workshop. While he was there Pauline and I presented him with a glorious sheepskin jacket. He was most impressed. Then I asked him for two body shells and two engines.

A short time later no fewer than six engines showed up, along with the body shells.

We built those race cars on the magic surface plate that Ford had given me all those years before. Some people used jigs—effectively rotisseries—where the car could be turned through 360 degrees to enable accurate welding. I was much more concerned with getting the weight right on every corner of the car. You can always fix a weld, but you can't easily correct a basic flaw in design. The whole idea of the plate is that it helps to finely balance the car. With the big V8s, you could never get it right. It was always a compromise. But, right from the start of construction, the RX7 put 25 per cent of its weight evenly on each corner: perfect.

The whole thing was being done under a cloak of secrecy. I had raced in a Porsche at Le Mans in 1980 but I went back in 1981 as a spectator, to support the Mazda team. I had guys from Mazda Australia and Rothmans with me, and we were discovered by Australian journalists.

'Watch this space' is all I could say as I retreated into the hospitality zone.

Back in Australia we did most of our testing at what is now the Australian Automotive Research Centre, but which was then International Harvester's test track at Anglesea outside Melbourne. Some might have said there wasn't a lot of testing to do, but I disagreed. You can never do too much. Yamamoto san's engines remained uncracked—that is, we never went inside them—but suspension tuning to get them absolutely right was a never-ending quest.

Thanks to the CAMS equivocation we forewent the ATCC in 1981, but we were ready for the Hang Ten 400, the Sandown prelude to Bathurst.

A short time before, dressed in a tuxedo, I had the absolute pleasure of unveiling the latest entrant in the title race at a gala black-tie affair at the Melbourne Hilton Hotel. The beautiful blue-and-white car carried the race number 43: that's 4 + 3 = 7, a very lucky number.

Bathurst was the goal; the Hang Ten was just a work-out. The Mazda cruised around to sixth place, five laps down on Brock's Commodore, but happily one lap up on Allan Grice's Frank Gardner-entered BMW 635CSi. You can't help but be competitive.

I'd thought of having Jacky Ickx as a Bathurst co-driver but settled for his Le Mans-winning partner, Derek Bell.

F1 driver, sports-car expert and more Australian than most Australians with his laid-back attitude, Englishman Derek was in Australia for the Melbourne Motor Show in March when I asked him if he'd drive at Bathurst with me. He had won Le Mans with Ickx in 1975, two years before Ickx won Bathurst with me, and he was aware of my team's potential. He said yes, which was something of a surprise, made more so when he kept his promise even after winning Le Mans again with Jacky in June.

Suddenly, unexpectedly, I had the current Le Mans champion on my team and we were even more in the spotlight.

Watching Derek work the RX7 up to maximum performance across the top of Mount Panorama was a delight. We knew we'd be slow up the 600-metre climb to the top of the mountain but, once there, we were relying on corner speed to establish an edge. Derek took just three laps to work out how to hold the Mazda flat from Reid Park all the way through the constant left-hand dips to the top of Skyline. First lap—a definite back-off; second lap—a hesitant lift; third lap—flat, with the RX7's rasping wail creating a whole new audio backdrop to practice.

We were contesting the six-cylinder rotary class, a butcher's picnic comprised of any cars that effectively weren't V8s. I wasn't very interested in that. An outright win was my only concern.

We put the RX7 on fifth grid position among a phalanx of Fords, Holdens and Camaros and significantly ahead of Grice's six-cylinder BMW, co-driven by another British Le Mans racer, David Hobbs.

A hundred and twenty laps later, a little over two-thirds race distance, we were in third place and primed for a win when previous winner Bob Morris collided with Christine Gibson at McPhillamy Park, both Falcons triggering a chain reaction that eliminated another four cars and blocked the track. CAMS general secretary John Keeffe consulted the rule book and informed race secretary Ivan Stibbard that the race had gone the distance required for a full result to be declared. Stibbard consulted host broadcaster Channel Seven's head honcho Geoff Healy about the impact on television time and together the three wise men stopped the race and, by backdating the results a lap as required by the regulations, ordained Dick Johnson the winner even though his Falcon was haemorrhaging oil and unlikely to finish, with Bob Morris second even though his Falcon was a wreck in the middle of the track. My Mazda was in perfect condition, needing just one more quick pit stop, and could have won Bathurst on debut. Instead Derek and I were given third. It was gut wrenching.

A month later I won the last race of the season, the Surfers Paradise 300, in circumstances that absolutely highlighted why the RX7 was so special. Newly crowned Australian champion Dick Johnson and Peter Brock went head to head, swapping the lead constantly while the Mazda settled into third. I always said the Mazda's chief attribute was reliability.

Johnson lost his brakes and rolled into a ditch—no rock this time but another opportunity to put on his morose face. Brock survived a dangerous driving charge for passing a slower car under yellow warning flags, then incurred a minute's penalty for push-starting the Commodore in the pits when it wouldn't fire up on the starter.

Wherever you looked there was carnage. A Holden had dropped its sump full of oil under the Dunlop Bridge, the fastest corner in Australian motor racing, and had gone off slamming the tyre barriers. Others followed him, including Allan Grice and John Goss. Later Peter Williamson thumped his Celica, and even Mazda privateer Peter McLeod managed to roll. The infield was a mass of mangled metal.

Brock took the chequered flag first but, with his penalty, I was declared the winner by just 2.5 seconds.

It wasn't the way to win a motor race and I guess my face reflected it. What I'd witnessed was the desperation that characterised Australian motor racing. What I'd experienced was a better way.

When I signed on with Mazda Australia the responsibility to perform well in Australia was paramount but Mazda, more than any of the domestic brands, also provided me with international opportunity.

In 1982 I was part of Mazda's class-winning crew at the Daytona 24 Hour, and later was in the first Mazda home at the Le Mans 24 Hour. Other people have to give up their local ambitions to even compete in those races. For me, it was part of my development program.

I tested hard in Japan with the works team. They rewarded me with race drives.

At Daytona in January, Mazda won both the GTO (over 2.5-litre) and GTU (under 2.5-litre) classes and came fourth, sixth and seventh outright. It was the company's best-ever result.

I was hooked up with US Mazda specialist and International Motor Sports Association champ Lee Mueller, and with America's best female driver of the time, Kathy Rude. We won the GTU class and came sixth. I did most of the night stints, survived an in-field clash with an outright Porsche and managed to keep the car straight on the steep Daytona speed bowl in spite of a chronic lack of vision from the extremely weak headlights. Kathy had a short night stint, although she had never practised in the dark, and brought the car home in the last 45 minutes to become the first American woman—she's Canadian, actually—to win a major sports-car race. Our teammate Yoshimi Katayama guided the GTO RX7 home in fourth and indicated he would quite like to come to Bathurst in October. (He had last been there in 1977 when he barrel-rolled an RX3 eight times at Murray's Corner.)

The ATCC was really a secondary consideration for me. Bathurst is the main prize. That's why, when I told Mazda and Rothmans that I'd prefer not to race in the Calder round, they were surprised and thankfully supportive. Bob Jane owned Calder. He owed me money and he had been an enemy of the Mazda effort. On both counts, I was determined not to show up. Despite that, and also not doing the long haul to Wanneroo in Western Australia, I still managed to claim third in the title behind Dick Johnson.

In 1982 there was so much legal action about eligibility of the V8 teams, and so much animosity among the competitors, that the touring-car title was a toxic place to be. I crossed the line first in three rounds but my win at Oran Park was disallowed for an alleged jump-start, which I hotly but unsuccessfully contested, ultimately accepting eighth place. The other two wins—at Lakeside and Surfers Paradise—stuck. When Allan Grice, now back in Holden, accepted his second-place trophy at Surfers, he claimed to have won the touring-car race while, he said, I'd won the sports-car division. It was childish. I couldn't wait to get out of there and go to Le Mans.

'I regard this as the most significant drive of my career,' I said when my entry alongside Mazda works drivers Yojiro Terada and Takashi Yorino was announced. That was a big call and probably a bit overstated. But Le Mans is larger than life, and to be there in a works team was not something any quasi-Australian had accomplished up to that point. (Geoff Brabham and Vern Schuppan would later go on to win outright for Peugeot and Porsche.)

A repeat of Daytona was not to be. My two Bathurst teammates, Ickx and Bell, won again. We finished fourteenth, just 1000 kilometres behind them after a 45-minute gearbox change.

You don't lose from experiences like that. Once again, I'd been chosen to do a lot of the night driving and at one point I was put in the car early to undertake a sprint stint—quite an honour in an otherwise all-Japanese outfit.

Terada, Yorino and myself were in the first Mazda ever to finish the Le Mans race. Nine years later they'd win it outright with the rotary-engined 787B. To this day Mazda is still the only Japanese car, and the only one without conventional pistons, to claim victory at the Circuit de la Sarthe.

Back in Australia, I was met with a torrent of abuse. 'Jap crap' had become the rallying cry for supporters of homegrown V8s. Only five years ago I'd been Ford's hero, a front-page sensation, the standard bearer for the Blue Oval. Now they were burning effigies of me in the spectator areas. There were some who claimed the signs that were being brandished at race meetings had been professionally produced. Team manager Allan Horsley said he had proof it was Holden. Well, not Holden, exactly, but its highly effective skunk-works PR organisation.

It fired me up.

The Australian Endurance Championship, in effect a manu-facturers' trophy, was important to Mazda and, in the lead-up to Bathurst, I set out to win it. I failed at the jump. Oran Park was the first round and I spent four days there, relentlessly testing, to put myself in contention. I captured pole position and in a 260-kilometre race that would require a pit stop for everyone, I'd moved to second after my stop when the throttle cable broke. I limped back to the pits and finished fourteenth.

The Castrol 400 at Sandown was my chance to make up. There's a term in rallying—maximum attack—and that's what

Horsley and I decided was the only strategy. I needed to go fast everywhere.

The Sandown pit lane is long and narrow. At the time there was no pit speed limit, but there was a local rule, imposed for that race. That said you could be penalised for going too fast in the lane—but that speed was undefined and nebulous at best. And nobody, least of all CAMS, knew about it. My first time down the lane people were waving me to slow down. A cameraman got in the way and it was alleged by his producer, a bumptious bloke, that I'd hit him and, worse still, damaged the camera.

Officials said they had imposed a one-minute penalty, but Horsley said he never received notification. Next pit stop and this time there's a sea of people waving their arms. A pit board suddenly appears in my path as some sort of roadblock and it smashes sideways. Once more a one-minute penalty is allegedly announced over the PA, but not delivered to my team.

A black flag is hung out for me, ordering me to the pits. Naturally I obey, but when I get there no one from the organisers is in my garage to tell me what I'd done or what to do next. Horsley orders me back out. For another two laps, they hang out the black flag. Each time I ignore it. The PA then announces I've been excluded from the race. But I'm still racing, in the lead with Allan Grice a lap behind me, Peter Brock well out with mechanical problems.

On lap 110 I cross the finish line. Behind me Grice starts lap 109 and they give him the chequered flag.

I park in front of Sandown's magnificent grandstand and climb on the Mazda's roof to claim victory, roundly booed by the crowd. The officials give the trophy to Grice.

It was a shambles that took months to sort out.

First the organisers gave me back second place, claiming that penalties would still apply. Then a court of appeal found against the race organisers, because they had not informed CAMS of pit-lane speed restrictions, and I was finally named as the winner.

I went on to win the final two rounds of the Endurance Championship as well—at Surfers Paradise and Adelaide International Raceway, enough to secure the drivers' trophy for me, but not enough to capture the manufacturers' title for Mazda. That honour would go to Nissan, which had just that year re-entered the touring-car title on Mazda's coat-tails, managed by none other than Howard Marsden.

In the middle of the Endurance Championship, we went to Bathurst.

It was so good to be in an international works team with so much equipment and so many components at your disposal.

For Bathurst, I wanted a left-hand drive car. Mount Panorama is an anticlockwise circuit and, if you want to drive at ten-tenths and place your car exactly, then you need to be able to brush the apex with precision. With a left-hand drive car you can reach out and touch the walls with your little finger.

I asked Mazda for a car in that configuration. They gave me two, and as co-driver, Yoshimi Katayama, the guy they rated as their grand master. The little veteran, one year my junior, was a small-capacity motorcycle Grand Prix ace. He'd claimed second for Suzuki in the now defunct 50 cc motorcycle world title and then he'd moved up to the 125s where he scored four Grand Prix victories. This was a person who knew how to maintain pace in the absence of power.

I matched Yoshi with a motorcycle ace of my own. Queenslander Gregg Hansford had won ten world-championship Grands Prix for Kawasaki. He had won the 1973 500 cc and Unlimited TTs at Bathurst, but he was best remembered, just like me, for the Bathurst race he had lost. In 1974 he and Warren Willing staged an epic duel at the Mountain on the new TZ700 Yamaha superbikes, mono-wheeling over the second hump at 280 km/h. Willing won by a slight margin and their battle went into legend, just like mine with Pete Geoghegan two years earlier. I had to have Gregg for my team.

I had tried to get him in 1977 to co-drive with Colin Bond in the second Falcon but a mixture of international commitments and race injuries kept him away. Now he was back, retired from bikes. According to others I was taking a huge risk by giving him his first-ever competitive four-wheel drive in Australia's biggest motor race. But I wasn't worried. I tested him and he confirmed what I suspected—he was as good and talented and right-minded as any driver I've ever known.

His co-driver, though, was another matter. Pauline had this thing for Lucio Cesario, a Melbourne fireball of an open-wheeler driver. She convinced me to hire him. Allan Horsley saw trouble coming in testing. Lucio was quick but undisciplined, at one stage charging under me in a corner when I was on a testing lap. In practice at Bathurst he got it totally wrong at McPhillamy Park and damaged the second car beyond immediate repair. I sent him home and started the race with one car.

Maybe I should have gone home too. We were banking on fewer and faster pit stops to match the V8 pace, but it was not to be. After Sandown, we'd homologated a new front-brake package, strategising that it would get us through without a pad change, but it didn't. At three-quarters race distance Yoshi came in with the brakes so worn that changing them took thirteen minutes of fiddling. We came sixth, the first Japanese car home, one lap down on the BMW now driven by Jim Richards, who had decamped from Holden. It was the worst result our Mazda would ever have at Bathurst.

The next year I won the 1983 ATCC, my fourth. It meant having to drive at Calder and there's a photograph that shows circuit-owner Bob Jane shaking my hand as he gave me the winner's silverware. The sinews on his brawny arm are standing out as he clutches me in a death grip and won't let go. My face tells it all—I'm struggling not to give in, but I'm looking downwards and you can tell I'm about to collapse to the ground. It was a magic moment in motor sport.

I won four rounds of the title and claimed victory by just six points in 160, beating neither a Ford nor a Holden but a Nissan Bluebird. Nissan's George Fury didn't win a race that season but the speed and consistency of the turbo-charged Bluebird sent another message that change was coming. The dinosaurs were under attack.

You had to be smart to win. Speed alone wasn't enough. Tactics created some of the best racing I've enjoyed, especially against Brock.

At Wanneroo I knew the Mazda was significantly disadvantaged. Serious strategy was required.

Allan Horsley had just watched a European Grand Prix where Ferrari surprised the F1 field by diving in for a mid-race fuel stop at a time when everyone started and finished on one tank. He figured we could do the same thing. We started on light tanks and I was bothering Brock the whole way, finally getting through him and moving away. On the sixteenth lap, I peeled off for the pits and Brock saw me do it as he went past, taking the lead and presuming I was out of the race.

Our stop was lightning fast; so rushed that, in his haste, one of the mechanics smashed the side rear-window with the fuel filler. But we were out in seconds and when Brock looked in his mirrors three laps later, there I was again.

Talk about magic moments. The look of surprise will stay with me forever, as will the fact that the man they call Peter Perfect was so distracted he missed his braking marker and went off into the sand trap.

Mind games were played by everyone. Brock was convinced I had more pace than I did—in fact, he was telling people I was backing off in the straights so he could keep up, thereby disguising the speed of my car.

Some people were convinced I was running funny-nitro fuel. It was a fallacy but one I encouraged. Every time I finished a race, before I got out, my mechanic Mick Webb would come to the car and appear to fiddle with something behind the driver's seat. It was nothing, but it created so much speculation. Finally we painted an old fire-extinguisher black and labelled it NG, the chemical symbol for nitro, just so it would be found.

This year there was to be no Le Mans for me. The final round of the touring-car championship at Lakeside clashed with Le Mans, and Mazda Australia rightly pointed out local victory was my priority.

I needed Lakeside to clinch the title, although I'd pretty much wrapped it up the race before at Oran Park. That was a good-news, bad-news day. Mazda earlier that year had developed a new rotary motor. The engine I'd been using was termed the 12A. The new one would be a 13B. The 12 stood for 1.2 litres, the 13, naturally, for 1.3. It doesn't sound like much but, with all the other developments, it led to a claimed increase of 30 horsepower to more than 300 hp. I had begun lobbying for its use immediately. I was one of only several interested parties pushing CAMS for rule updates. Some, BMW especially, had decided the rules we raced under were archaic and were petitioning for adoption of a global set of regulations called Group A.

At Oran Park CAMS did one of the most extraordinary things I've ever experienced. Even while the race was proceeding they announced on the national broadcaster, the ABC, that they would adopt Group A rules in eighteen months' time at the start of the 1985 season and, in the meantime, they would approve use of my 13B engine to give me parity. Talk about giving with one hand and taking away with the other. They'd provided me with a short-term solution and guaranteed me a long-term shutdown. There was no way Mazda could meet the Group A regulations, which were so Eurocentric they were purpose built for a few specialist race-car teams.

When the word spread along pit lane after the race, which incidentally I'd won after a kamikaze move on Brock, there was nothing but shock and awe. Even though I knew I'd just been given a Bathurst-winning gift, I could see this phase of my career flashing before my eyes. The Nissan team were so distressed they boycotted the final round at Lakeside, handing me my title without a final fight.

I left it to Sandown to debut the 13B engine, and it won. Amid all sorts of accusations and wrong-footed commentary and claims that CAMS was ruining the sport, I qualified fifth, dropped to tenth at the start, then worked my way back up to take the lead 21 laps into a 129-lap race with another kamikaze run, this time on Grice. There were only two glitches in an otherwise perfect day. I was forced to change the rear track of my car after a Holden protest because I was judged to have too wide a footprint on the road (true), and I only just made it across the line after a fuel-economy run in the closing stages when I realised the 13B was running a bit thirsty. I'd have to watch that at Bathurst.

I set the 13B up for the Bathurst race, not for practice or qualifying. When I didn't make the top ten cut for the Hardie's Heroes dash for cash, the annual one-lap madness that puts race cars at risk the day before the main event, everyone said I was foxing. I wasn't. I drove the car mighty hard in its race set-up to qualify fourteenth. Gregg Hansford in the second car, powered by the 12A engine, was twelfth. People said I must have been galled by that. I wasn't.

In Hardie's Heroes, when Dick Johnson sped off into the trees at Forrest's Elbow, necessitating the building of essentially a new car overnight, he proved my point.

Honestly, I would have liked to have been faster. I tried every Bathurst trick in the book, taping up the panel gaps to get more aerodynamic advantage, even shooting down the escape road at the bottom of Conrod Straight, and then powering back onto the track to cross the start line faster on your next flying lap than you could if you'd taken the corner. Everything. But my time was what it was. The race would tell.

By lap eight I was up to seventh when race leader Peter Brock blew up. It was like a gift from God. But on lap 20, when the second Marlboro Holden Dealer Team car pulled to the pits for its scheduled stop, driver John Harvey saw not Phil Brock waiting to jump in but Phil's brother Peter. Brock had cross-entered himself and he was back in the race.

On lap 40, I was in the lead, but when I handed over to Yoshi Katayama, who'd joined me again, he had a problem. The race reports said he couldn't get a gear. That wasn't true. For some reason, at the driver change the driver's door had jammed shut after Yoshi got in and the crew couldn't help him do up his belts. He shuddered out of the pits, then stopped on Mountain Straight to properly secure himself. For the rest of the race we entered and exited through the passenger's door, clambering over the transmission tunnel, losing valuable time—probably not enough to cost us the race, but enough to create immense frustration. I could feel this one slipping away.

It came down to horsepower. There was a time mid-race when Brock lapped the Mazda and we staged a duel for several laps before the lap was regained on pit stops.

On his last stop, Brock was two minutes ahead of me, or around 20 seconds behind on the road. When he got to his pit he stayed in the car, although Harvey was waiting to take over. People said the look in his eyes was intense, and Harvey's frustration and disappointment was on show. Then he charged, reeling me in, until finally he slammed past to put himself a lap up. It was a purposeful act of bastardry.

After a year when Brock had been frustrated by my car, when he'd gone out of his way to tell people I was deliberately slowing down to disguise my true pace, when he'd felt the mantle of perfection slipping away, this was his way of redressing it all.

I had to admire him for it.

In his position, I would have done the same thing. That's the difference between being a driver and a racer. Second was as close as I'd ever come again to winning Bathurst.

On the victory dais Prime Minister Bob Hawke asked Brock why the crowd was booing him. After all he was a Labor prime minister and the essentially blue-collar members of the crowd were his people.

'They're not booing you, Bob,' Brock grinned. 'They're booing him'—pointing at me.

Mazda won the Endurance Championship that year, tied with Holden. Privateer Peter McLeod, not me, was crowned the endurance drivers' champion.

Nineteen-eighty-four, my last year with Mazda, was going to be my best yet. I had a good car, a fast-developing teammate in Gregg, and a willingness to sweep all before me. With Allan Horsley, I'd also started on another of my secret projects, a plan to build a GPA Mazda based on the 929 saloon car with V8 components under the skin.

To say things didn't go as planned is an understatement.

Four races into my title defence, I had one win under my belt and one deplorable failure to finish with which to contend, and I was lying on my back in a hospital bed with my season in tatters.

Everyone expected a blinder from me at the opening round at Sandown. I finished third, struggling with an engine-oil problem that was to be a critical feature of the 13B engine. Brock and Johnson, who beat me, seemed as pleased with that as they did with their own two positions.

Getting the engine temperature just right for the start is essential in the Mazda. We developed a car-bra, a wrap-around car cover for the front of the car that masked the radiators and brought the temperature up quickly on the warm-up lap. Then you'd take it off for the race. We had maybe half-a-dozen Peter Stuyvesant grid girls at each race meeting. Brock had a similar number of Marlboro girls. They were a distraction. At the second round of the title at Symmons Plains, the distraction proved too much for the mechanic charged with removing the car-bra. He forgot about it, left it on, and I blew the engine before the end of the first lap. He got to walk home and wasn't with us when we won next time out at Wanneroo.

I took pole at Surfers Paradise and was lying in fourth mid-race with rain increasingly falling when a back marker, Garry Willmington, squeezed me on the fastest corner in Australian motor sport, under the Dunlop Bridge. There's something about Willmington. He'd taken me out a year before and he'd done the same to Gregg. I was well aware of the danger of this corner. There's a wide grass strip and then an earth barrier, behind which lies a deep culvert and then Nerang Road. A decade before, open-wheeler driver Warwick Brown had crashed there on the warm-up lap of the Tasman series and gone missing, with near-fatal consequences, over the mound and into the ditch. It was only through good fortune his life was saved.

I was determined not to get to the mound, but on wet grass you experience unintended acceleration so I needed something to slow me down. As much as I could I aimed for an innoc-uous-looking bush, anything to scrub off speed. What I found instead was an immovable stump camouflaged by its shrubby exterior. It stopped the Mazda, and me, instantly. I broke my hand and, for the second time in my racing career, my sternum. Before they took me off to hospital, I let circuit manager David Harding know what I thought of his gardening. My touring-car title and my race car were over and out.

The Endurance Championship and Bathurst were going to be my last hurrah in the Mazda. The 929 project was just not working out. It was too big a step away from what Mazda wanted to achieve and, even though the mechanical fit was pretty perfect, with the gear lever emerging within the car in just the right place as if we'd planned it that way, it just wasn't going to happen.

I missed the first race at Amaroo but Gregg and I turned up in the one car at Oran Park for the Valvoline 250, each of us driving half distance to beat home Dick Johnson. At Sandown Brock and Larry Perkins ganged up on us and took first place by one lap.

The Bathurst 1000 was a round of the endurance title and I went for a novel and radical approach. We entered two cars but only two drivers.

Gregg and I were each entered as the lead driver in one of our two cars, with the other cross-entered as co-driver. In other words we intended to start the race with two cars and finish with just one. It was the first time this strategy had been attempted.

It caused some controversy, especially as we both snuck into the top ten Hardie's Heroes, qualifying with no real intention that both cars would finish the race, although both would start.

Bathurst was billed as the last race for the 'Big Bangers'—the last under the current Group C regulations. It was a muddled affair. Organisers let a heap of Group A cars into the race as well, presumably to promote the next year. Instead it just promoted confusion. I'd improved four seconds a lap on my previous year's times and I was hopeful . . . ever hopeful.

The start dashed those hopes. I was squeezed up onto the wall by a Falcon while behind me a melee erupted as Tom Walkinshaw's Jaguar lost its drive line and was tagged by a following Camaro. With the track blocked, the race was stopped. For me it was a relief.

It took the entire adjournment to get the Mazda tracking straight again after its heavy contact with the wall.

Half an hour later we got under way, but I was able to go only fifteen laps before the 13B seized. Instead of bringing Gregg up to the faster car, my fate was now to go back to the slower one. And that was us—stuck in third place behind the two Marlboro Holden Dealer Team cars of Brock and Harvey, unable to catch them.

The final round of the Endurance Championship, at Surfers Paradise, gave me the chance to end the Mazda era with a title win for me and a title win for my manufacturer. Brock saw a similar opportunity for himself. For the first time ever I allowed myself to imagine a race more important than Bathurst.

Gregg and I held a narrow points margin over Brock and Larry Perkins. But it wasn't winner take all. To assure ourselves of first in both titles, we could afford to let Brock win, but we had to come second and third. And that's exactly how it worked out. Sometimes it just comes together. Driving rain with accompanying thunder and lightning arrived just as we got the chequered flag. It was quite a celebration.

I scored a 3.5-point victory over Brock with Gregg in second, just half a point clear of Peter. And Mazda claimed the manufacturers' title just three points clear of Holden.

It was a shame, really, that we'd all left our best for last. The racing with Peter, when we were both at our best, was something I'd hoped would just go on and on.

As a thank you, Mazda Australia and Rothmans let us mount an all-Aussie effort at the Daytona 24 Hour in January 1985. It was a big media affair—television, journalists, the lot. I took Gregg, who'd raced there, bravely, on bikes, as well as Kevin Bartlett. Mazda brought along Peter McLeod both as a reward for his contribution to its success and because he was an influential dealer. I wasn't keen on McLeod driving. There's a power of difference between domestic racing and an international event like Daytona. As it turned out, he wasn't keen either once he'd seen what was involved but, by the time we'd worked our way up into the top ten outright, Mazda put the pressure right on and I relented. Regrettably, perhaps even predictably, he crashed. By the time we'd fixed the car and then had a subsequent mechanical failure, we finished 24th.

Back home I had a workshop full of Mazdas.

Allan Horsley made the call. 'We need to collect them all, you understand,' he said apologetically. They sent a truck to take them all away. There was an auction in Sydney and they sold everything—cars, engines, spares—for a fraction of their real cost.

Sometimes accountants shouldn't be allowed near motor racing.

12

BROCK

PETER BROCK HAD A DREAM. ONE OF MANY REALLY.

He'd determined that he wanted his Holden Dealer Team to win the inaugural World Touring Car Championship in 1987, taking on the factory teams of BMW, Ford, Rover and any other comers.

Peter's ambition rescued me from a motor-sport graveyard. With my Mazda days over and absolutely nothing on the horizon, I joined forces with my most serious adversary at the most tumultuous time of his life.

It was a ride I'll never forget.

As it turned out, the world title was a massive, costly and embarrassing debacle, to be disbanded as soon as its first and only winner was determined in motor sport's highest court of law many months after the racing finished.

Blunders in the enforcement of technical regulations would result in the works teams of both BMW and Ford being excluded from critical heat wins. Because of those disqualifications Peter and I both claimed unexpected victories. They promoted me to being the winner of the first-ever World Touring Car race and gave Peter his ninth, and last, Bathurst 1000 win.

Peter Brock had a huge ego and huge ambition, and was one of the few people I knew who was capable of living up to the immense pressures placed on him by both.

I admired him as a driver and as a man. Truth be known I was a bit in awe of him. He had style and grace and an easy-going public persona—something with which I struggled. His ability behind the wheel was not perfect but pretty close to benchmark, although in this area I felt then, and still do, that I conceded nothing to him.

For two decades we were the gold standard of Australian touring-car racing, and while that seems a terribly self-centred claim, the statistics speak for themselves.

In an eleven-year period from 1973, either Peter or I claimed the Australian Touring Car Championship seven times.

Over eighteen years we won the Bathurst 1000—and its 500-mile predecessor—thirteen times between us.

Over twenty years we won the Sandown 500 in its various forms no fewer than fifteen times, including a stretch of twelve straight years where either one of us claimed victory.

By 1985, at the end of my Mazda era, Peter and I had won 46 per cent of all Bathurst races ever held and, incredibly, we'd won 43 per cent of all ATCC rounds ever contested, including all those before we had even begun racing.

The Brock-and-Moffat show was the star act of Australian motor sport, not by design but by an act of extreme good fortune that simply placed us both in the same arena at the same time.

In 1977 when Holden was in its own motor-sport wilderness, with Brock off racing his own cars and me winning everything, a couple of Holden guys asked me: 'What can we do to beat you?' I told them: 'Simple—re-employ Brock.'

We were a promoter's dream and also their nightmare. Brock and Moffat, combined, guaranteed a huge crowd and gate receipts bigger than Scrooge McDuck's money bin. One of us without the other meant smaller crowds and lower earnings. Keeping us together was the key to the promoters' success. They were cleaning up at the expense of the teams and the drivers and we, collectively, were too stupid to understand our role in the money-making machine.

In 1980 when I was out of a Ford drive and lost in the motor-sport desert, the Light Car Club of Australia, promoters of the Sandown 500, hatched a plot to have me drive Peter's second Commodore in their race. It was audacious. 'Moffat joins the Holden Dealer Team'—and, by extension, the tantalising proposition of whether I could beat Peter in his own car on equal terms. It was a licence to print money.

Peter and I were initially aghast. For a decade we'd operated out of two bunkers in Melbourne, mine at 711 Malvern Road and his at various locations in the inner city. We were both big on security. Intellectual property wasn't a term widely used at the time, but it applied precisely to how we both felt about letting one of us near the other's car. We weren't frequent house-guests of each other. Peter would have been welcome any time at 711, but only if the dust covers were on the cars.

In this case, the risk was all Peter's. He was planning a big Bathurst assault and it was known I was going again with another Falcon attempt, as it turned out my last, with John Fitzpatrick, although in truth it was pretty clear it wasn't going to be my best-funded or most ambitious project.

Peter was under immense pressure to do the Sandown deal, putting me in John Harvey's second Holden Dealer Team car, and it was said he agreed only if I would stand down from my Bathurst entry, thereby neutralising the knowledge I would gain from driving his car. I have no recollection of making such a deal, and I went on to do Bathurst in the Falcon, lasting just a desultory three laps before the engine blew.

Peter won Sandown and I came third, let down by terrible pit work that sent me on my way with the wheel nuts still not tightened, requiring a second stop. For the last fifteen laps Peter and I staged a huge duel, although we were separated by a lap, and it brought the screaming grandstand crowd to its feet.

It was as real as a dogfight can get. When Peter slipped by me with a couple of laps to go, people said it was a deliberate move by him to humiliate me, but that wasn't the case. I knew my place in that dog-and-pony act, especially since I was a lap in arrears, and if there were going to be two Holden Dealer Team cars getting the chequered flag in close proximity, then it had to be Brock first, Moffat second.

As a one-off it was a bit of fun and it did teach me a fair bit about their cars and operations that I was able to put to good use when Mazda came on the scene.

But that was 1980. In 1985 I was sitting in a darkened workshop with the ghost cars of victories past winking at me through the gloom. The Mazdas had all been taken away and the phone wasn't ringing. It was about as lonely and soul-destroying as it gets.

And then Peter's secretary called: 'When would it be convenient for me to have coffee with Peter at his workshop?' I told her I'd catch a cab because I wasn't exactly certain where their place of business was located.

I arrived in a taxi and went home in a brand-new HDT Commodore, my new company car.

Coffee had turned into lunch and an agreement with Peter's top brass in his remarkable mini-corporation. He'd outlined his plans to me.

He was, as I knew, developing special vehicles for the Holden dealer network, taking them off-line from Holden's production facility, modifying them, and selling them as premium products through Holden dealerships complete with factory warranty. It was all happening with Holden's financial and total support. He was, truly, a business partner of General Motors.

Peter was on his way to becoming a millionaire—in the true sense of the word—while the rest of us were just journeymen. His success, though, was still based on his on-track activities and, I think, more than that, his own sense of self was tied to regular sightings of the chequered flag.

The upcoming World Touring Car Championship provided him with the opportunity to achieve many goals both for his race team and for his business empire. It would give him exposure on the world stage. Peter was a visionary. Australia was not enough. He wanted to take his Holden Special Vehicles to global markets.

Sitting with Peter at that point in time was like, I imagine, being in the presence of Bill Gates or Steve Jobs. Here was a guy I'd known as an on-track rival but I'd never been inside his business or exposed to his aspirations. While I was kicking dust in an empty workshop, he was taking on the world. It was motivating and demoralising all at the same time. Now he was asking me to be a part of it.

My role would be to work with him on the international assault. We would contest selected rounds of the FIA touring-car title in Europe in 1986, effectively a dress rehearsal for the following year's world championship, as well as Australia and New Zealand's long-distance races. Then we'd take on the world in the WTCC in 1987.

Could we work together, having been rivals for so long? The first two races in New Zealand would be sort of a litmus test before we headed to Europe.

It all came about because of John Harvey. The former Speedway champion, winner of the Australian 1.5-litre open-wheeler championship, twice Australian sports-car champion, 1983 Bathurst winner and Brock's right-hand man at the Holden Dealer Team, had recommended me.

The Harveys and the Moffats were off-track friends. When I came to after my Surfers Paradise Mazda crash in 1984, it was John who was cradling me in his arms, making sure I was okay. We'd been friends for a while but that sealed the deal. We tried not to talk business at our social engagements. Apart from

Howard Marsden and I seldom saw eye-to-eye, but he was my Ford team boss and I had to listen.

In 1974 I was testing the B52 Falcon in Ohio, and the great Mark Donohue asked for a drive. It was hard to get him out of the car.

The black-tie launch of the B52 Falcon at Melbourne's Southern Cross Hotel in 1974. Somebody came up with the dopey idea of putting Falcon in reverse on the windscreen so it would be right way around in competitors' rear-view mirrors. The NASCAR-type numbers on the doors, a tribute to sponsor Brut 33, caused immense problems at scrutineering.

One of the most enduring sponsors of my career was International Harvester. When the transporter they gave me burnt to the ground en route to Adelaide in 1976, they simply built another. At the time this was an absolute state-of-the-art race truck.

It's obviously a set-up shot, but I always saw myself as a desk jockey as well as a race driver. When there wasn't a race meeting it was very important to keep up appearances and be constantly on it. This is my home office in Monaro Crescent.

Out front at 711 Malvern Road in 1976 with three of my most successful cars—the Mustang, the Ford Cologne Capri and the Chevy Monza. We were still selling petrol—BP, of course.

I used both the Chevy Monza and the Ford Cologne Capri to win the 1976 Australian Sports Sedan Series. Even against far more powerful competition, the Capri was a jackrabbit off the start.

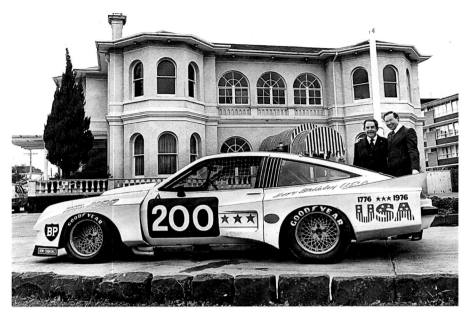

When the United States celebrated its bicentenary in 1976, the US consul to Melbourne dressed my Dekon Monza in special livery to celebrate the occasion, not taking into account that my drawl originated across the border in Canada.

The Chevvy Monza heads Bob Jane's monster Monaro—right on the limit and using the chassis to good advantage, 1976.

Signing Colin Bond to the Moffat Ford Dealer Team, 1976—it was a huge coup and it split the Ford and Holden camps.

I took the then Prime Minister Malcolm Fraser for a guest ride at Sandown, 1976. Our helmets were monogrammed AM and PM, respectively.

John Fitzpatrick paired successfully with Bob Morris to win Bathurst in 1976. Our co-driving efforts were less successful, but it was John who led me to race a Porsche 935 at Le Mans.

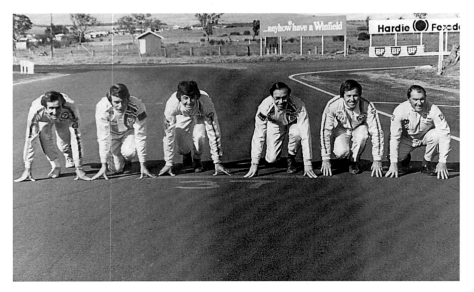

An early Hardie-Ferodo 1000 publicity shot—winners, all of us, c. 1977. Left to right: Bob Morris, Colin Bond, Peter Brock, me, John Goss and Bruce McPhee.

In 1977 I brought Carroll Smith (left) out to run my team along with local guns. It worked.

The 1–2 finish at Bathurst, 1977. So many pictures have been taken from so many angles. I just love this one. It's iconic. Ray Berghouse

Hardie-Ferodo victory podium, 1977. Left to right: Jacky Ickx, me, Colin Bond and Alan Hamilton. The guy holding the trophy at far left is the then Prime Minister Malcolm Fraser.

The day in 1978 I received my OBE, with my mum (far left) and the governor of Victoria, Sir Henry Winneke AC.

At Sydney's Amaroo Park, 1979—the day I drove and won in Bob Morris's (centre) Torana. With legendary commentator Evan Green, the man who killed Supercars at Bathurst.

This is the magic surface plate which allowed millimetre-fine accuracy, helping me to build stronger and straighter cars than anyone else, 1979.

In 1980 Alan Hamilton hired me to drive his Porsche 934 to win the Australian Sports Car Championship, which I did with a round to go. My major competitor, and the guy who was favourite to win the title, was the late Peter Hopwood in a 1.6-litre Lotus Elan.

On a handling circuit the peripheral-ported Mazda RX7 was seriously competitive, but never unbeatable. No matter where I took it, I had to work hard to win, although my competitors, including Peter Brock, said otherwise.

Firstborn son Andrew, already in race suit and cap, with his proud parents, 1983.

Look at the windscreen banner—Brock and Moffat, 1986. It says everything about the respect we held for each other, and what could have been had we teamed up earlier.

In 1986, I thought I was about to become Australia's first astronaut. In Peter Brock's car I hit the wall at Bathurst's Skyline at just on 200 km/h—and then I had to go and face the boss.

The Moffat/Harvey assault on the Spa 24 Hour race with John (right), 1987. Probably one of the most satisfying races of my career.

Bathurst 1988, and the race we should have won. The ANZ Sierra leads Tony Longhurst's Sierra on another lap up Mountain Straight.

Teammates Gregg Hansford (left) and Colin Bond (right)—both true champions in their own right.

With Sue at a charity ball at the Grand Hyatt, 1993.

When I became an Australian citizen in 2004, Peter Brock honoured me by reading the citation. It was good to have Peter as a friend.

It's a generational thing. When son James unveiled his new Norton Falcon Supercar in 2012, we used a specially made car cover, designed to replicate my Falcon GTHO.

Edsel Ford was, and is, the man with his name on the hubcaps. He was a good ally and friend during his time in Australia. In 2016 I caught up with him at an historic race meeting at Laguna Seca.

In the United States in 2015 I knew I'd be catching up with my old Ford mentor Peter Quenet, so I had special Ford English Line caps made for the occasion. Peter was most appreciative.

Three Moffat generations, 2017—and Max at his first race meeting when he was just three weeks old. Left to right: me, Sue, Leah and Max, James. Andy Pearson – AJP Photography

anything else, John's boss would have been horrified to think he was fraternising with the enemy,

Brock was initially taken aback. You don't bury years of intense rivalry in a moment. But when he thought about it, he could see sense in the proposition. I was a safe pair of hands. In all our years of close racing we'd scraped paint only the once, and then not seriously.

He knew my work ethic, which in reality was a step up on his own. While he was busy visualising, usually with a mug of tea in his hand, I was forever doing the hard yards of testing.

I was well connected internationally, which could do no harm in a European campaign, and I knew how to run a team, which, although that wasn't my role, at least pointed to the fact that I understood discipline and rigour.

At our meeting, he never once mentioned his energy polariser, the technically unsupportable device that he truly believed enhanced vehicle performance and that would soon be the cause of his entire empire crumbling around him.

It turns out that it was the polariser that obliquely got me my job. Former Australian F1 driver Larry Perkins had been working for Peter, running his dynamometer, a rolling-road test-bed, but they had fallen out over the contribution the polariser might make. Larry was the logical in-house choice to go with Peter to Europe, but a few months before my offer came, Larry had walked into the workshop to find a polariser suspended over the dyno. In subsequent meetings, apparently quite heated, they agreed to part company.

Peter and I went to New Zealand and won on debut.

I said to Brock, 'Why didn't we do this ten years ago?' He agreed. In the course of one race meeting, great rivals had become great teammates.

It took some adjustment. For the first time in Australia, I had a team leader. It was his role to set the pace and do the qualifying. Now it was my job to hold it together in the middle stages. That takes a certain kind of mindset adjustment and I was surprised how easily I fell into the pattern. Our first race was the 1986 Wellington 500, an incredibly tight and dangerous public road, and for the entire 40-minute session of first practice I sat on the pit counter while Peter sorted the car, shades of Jacky Ickx with me at Bathurst in 1977.

When I finally got a lap, I was way off Peter's pace, and was happy to have him qualify third. In the race he moved to first just before it rained and my stint was completed on a succession of dry tyres and intermediates—a hybrid of wet and dry compounds and tread patterns—with the car slipping and sliding and at one stage half-spinning, and I dropped to second. Peter brought us back up to first when the leader's suspension collapsed. Some would say it was a lucky victory; I say that's motor racing.

The victory celebration was a festival of mutual congratulation—Brock was full of praise for my controlled drive in the wet. I admired his ability to drive so hard in the dry. 'You only have to look at him to see how difficult this track is. He's buggered,' I said.

At New Zealand's second race, on the purpose-built Pukekohe track outside Auckland, we blew up but our team car, driven by John Harvey and New Zealander Neal Lowe, won.

Two for two—against at least some of the European opposition, who had come out to test themselves before the start of their own championship and given us a strong work-out, but we'd prevailed.

From inside the Holden Dealer Team tent I was discovering a lot of similarity between Peter and me. He was as secretive as I was about technical developments and I guess also about plans in general. Like me, he was demanding on his staff. In both the Moffat and Brock camps it must have taken a sheer act of willpower on the part of our blokes not to occasionally strike back when we got on our high horse.

Peter wasn't as perfect in the privacy of his workshop. His tirades were legendary.

I had, according to my blokes, two personalities, and they gave each of them names. 'Arthur', coincidentally my father's name, was the harsh disciplinarian. 'Allan' was the public face. Before they entered my pit or my workshop people used to ask who was in the house today—Arthur or Allan.

There were differences, too. Peter drank copious cups of tea to calm himself. I drank Coke to power myself up. Peter surrounded himself with gurus and people who could help his off- and on-track psychology. I remained a lone wolf with my demons tightly locked inside my head.

We were gaining confidence for the European assault. It would be the first time an Australian touring car had raced in Europe—a historic moment.

My contribution was to take a flat in London. It was a basement affair, quite close to the CBD, and it would serve as a good base for the people who'd come and go to run and support our team. Although the European series was over fourteen rounds, our plan was to do just four of them, enough to test the water and establish our credentials for the 1987 assault.

John Harvey was to stay back in Australia and run the Holden Dealer Team in the ATCC.

Peter's contribution was to be Peter. When we returned from New Zealand his first job was to be King of Moomba, leading Australia's most famous street parade, dressed in gown and crown, perched on the top of a Holden with his kids Robert and Alexandra peering out from the windows beneath. It was a huge honour for Peter and for motor racing. This bloke transcended our sport. He was a genuine Aussie hero and it didn't matter that he used a steering wheel instead of a bat, ball or Speedos.

He absolutely could do no wrong.

At the end of 1984, just as I was losing Mazda and, along with them, Peter Stuyvesant, Peter had made the genius decision to replace his principal sponsor Marlboro with Mobil. It was an inspired move. The anti-smoking lobby was hitting its straps and a cigarette sponsor wasn't necessarily a good look, especially alongside Peter's race number 05, which was designed to promote the national blood-alcohol driving limit.

As I understand it, Mobil came to him, seeking to enter the sport. It was sheer coincidence that Brock, a man who enjoyed a drink and a smoke, had given up both on the advice of his chiropractor, Eric Dowker. Dr Dowker was so much more to Peter than a pair of hands to keep his body supple. He had morphed into a close confidant, guiding Peter's sometimes optimistic ambitions in what I like to think was intended as a positive way.

As only Peter could, he became an enthusiastic non-smoking devotee—an advocate—and Mobil gave him the opportunity to achieve his goal of losing the smoking connection without cost penalty.

For all that though, it was increasingly obvious that Peter was a man under pressure. It was impossible to imagine how he could hold it all together. He had taken on so much: the Special Vehicles division, the Australian motor-racing program, the international assault, and his special project—the energy polariser. I tried to isolate myself from it. I knew my job description and addressed it. My job was to test, to perform well, and potentially to win in Europe.

But it wasn't possible to remain in the silo.

In England Peter borrowed a Vauxhall as our road transport. It was to be my first experience, knowingly, with the energy polariser. Peter and Eric Dowker had begun what I believe was a quite innocent investigation into the impact of magnetism on matter. Eric had used 'energy healing' as part of his chiropractic treatment of Peter, and Peter was convinced it had worked.

Surely the concept could be expanded. And so the idea of magnetism and crystal placement to enhance car performance grew and grew and grew. I'm not being supercilious at all when I say I have no idea whether it was science or wishful thinking. All I know is that, as only Peter could, he was obsessed with the concept. He truly, passionately, believed in it. And it cost him his business.

The story has it that I evaluated the polariser for Peter, but that's not true. In England I was in the back seat while he threw the Vauxhall around on the public roads, pointing out to me how much better and more responsive it was because he and Eric had fitted a polariser.

Sheer politeness led me to nod in agreement, although in truth I was in no position to make any reasoned judgement. In Australia I had received a major criticism of my Brock company car. It was tram-tracking in a straight line, so I gave it to Peter to fix. When it came back, it drove straight as an arrow. He told me the only difference was the fitting of a polariser. Later I was told the workshop had performed a complete front-end replacement on it: new shocks, springs and anti-roll bar. I honestly don't know if that's true.

What I do know is that in order to promote the value of the polariser, without my agreement Peter used comments I had allegedly made. He'd joined unintended dots to make it appear that I was an expert witness.

To my discredit, and now regret, I never really took it up with him. In the grand scheme of what was going on at the time, it was easier just to let it slide by.

My job was to go motor racing and win the world touring-car title with the best team in Australia. Perhaps if I had raised the matter—forcefully and loud—my voice, along with others, might have swayed him from the disastrous path he'd set for himself.

By early 1987 he would become the only man I'll ever know who'd fired General Motors. But this was 1986 and we were at Monza, north of Milan, the home of Italian thoroughbreds.

Along with fellow Australian Allan Grice, who was also out to prove a point with his own Holden team, we were about to attack the Europeans on their home ground.

Suddenly the cars we'd been able to trounce in New Zealand just two months before had grown horns. They were faster and stronger.

Predictably team leader Peter was quicker than me, and unpredictably Grice was faster than us both. During practice I walked down to the first chicane at the end of a straight so long and wide that you could land a 747 on it to find out why. Both of them were bouncing over the kerbs, attacking the concrete blocks with their wheels and suspension in a way that would guarantee neither car could possibly finish the 500-kilometre race. That made me mad and I confronted Peter on it: 'Al,' he said (he was the only person ever to call me Al and get away with it), 'It was just the once, honest.' Oh yeah?

I think that one incident cemented our relationship. He had a co-driver who'd stand up to him and someone who'd obviously demonstrated his commitment to the team's success.

At Monza that hardly mattered. We were just six laps into the race when the rear axle broke—the first such failure the team had suffered in five years. I never got to drive.

The next round was at Donington in England just two weeks later. Peter chose not to stick around between races. He flew to the USA, where I presumed he didn't have a lot of contacts until I became more aware of the General Motors network, several of whom had been in Australia. His mission, it appears, was to sell his polariser directly into head office. I was left to test and prepare for the race. Like I said, keeping my focus. When he got back, the trip and its outcome weren't mentioned.

Donington was the coldest, bleakest, wettest race I've ever contested. People were being treated for early onset frostbite. In morning warm-up I turned into the first corner at zero speed and still went straight on into the sand trap, the tyres so cold they simply could not function. Not my finest moment.

With local knowledge, though, we could have won. Both Peter and Allan Grice used Holden power to push to the lead ahead of the Europeans but, when heavy rain struck, they pulled to the pits for wet-weather tyres. Tom Walkinshaw, the leading European—who ironically would one day own the Holden Dealer Team—stayed out, knowing the rain would soon clear. Grice's car ultimately ended up in a sand trap courtesy of his cashed-up co-driver, and Peter dropped a lap that I was able to make up in my stint, bringing us home fifth. One stop fewer and we would have been on the podium's top step.

I'll never forget the one rain-soaked fan, waving a bedraggled Australian flag every time I charged down the main straight. It seemed like he was the only spectator in the whole place.

Hockenheim in Germany is a track that carries some emotion for me. It was there in 1968 that Jim Clark, for whom I was water boy at Indy in 1965, was killed when his F2 Lotus went off into the trees. Jim died instantly, an indelible loss to the sport. There's a small memorial to him, difficult to find, and I made a private pilgrimage.

The third round of the 1986 touring-car series ran on a somewhat different layout to the one on which Clark died and we again were fifth, a promising effort in a race that was almost as cold as Donington. The Holden Dealer Team car developed an oil leak early in the race. Peter did the opening and closing stints. I took the mid-race run and together we nursed the car home against mechanical odds. That's what professionals do.

We both put on a brave face. With three months to go before the next race of our 1986 experiment at Spa we were leaving our opposition to race on, continually developing. It wasn't ideal. 'The Europeans have a tyre advantage on us,' Peter told the media. 'But we now know what we have to do. We'll have to screw more horses out of it.'

I, too, had the glass half-full: 'There is a different set of guidelines in Europe. Now that we know what they are we can do something about it.'

The Spa 24 Hour race in Belgium's Ardennes mountains is like doing four Bathursts back to back. Peter had been before. I was seeing it for the first time and, while I respect Mount Panorama immensely, my comment at the time was 'this makes Bathurst look like a kindergarten'.

Eau Rouge, the right-hand uphill sweeper after the pits, is one of the most demanding corners in motor sport, later made famous in Australia when Mark Webber pulled his passing move on Fernando Alonso in their 2011 F1 clash, Mark completing the manoeuvre with millimetre precision. This was a circuit not built for amateurs, and there were a few in the field. You needed to be doubly careful because any one of them could take you out.

Peter was putting maximum effort into this attack. There were two cars: one for us, one for his New Zealand connection run by Neal Lowe. John Harvey was our third driver, Eric Dowker was our team chiropractor (Peter even lending him to Tom Walkinshaw to fix his sore back), and there was accountant Greg Chambers, who, given the amount of money we were going through, was probably the most essential team member of all.

A head gasket blew our chances. Less than two hours into 24, we were to spend two frustrating hours in the pits fixing a blown gasket and, despite soldiering on, we were to come home 22nd, four places behind our team car.

Midway through that very long night Peter Brock retired from motor racing—effective immediately. I was in the car at the time, so it is hearsay, but I believe it occurred. The ebullient, never-say-die Brock had put his heart into this effort, and he was unusually down. He called his confidants together and said he was pulling the pin, from that moment on, but that John and I could stay out there and have some fun.

It didn't last. He was back in the car in the early hours, and it was never mentioned again, at least not to me.

Our consolation at Spa was that, along with Allan Grice, our three Holdens won the King's Cup team trophy. In all my motor-racing career, I've believed it's a good thing to bring home some success to show the sponsors. This was one of those times. It wasn't a particularly significant trophy—but it was still something.

Peter wasn't there, though, to collect the cup. He had departed the circuit early to get to the airport. I was left to drive the last stint, stage a formation finish—something of an art form for me—and seize the silverware.

I can only imagine what was going through Peter's mind in the second half of that year. His business interests, way beyond my need-to-know, were imploding as he continued to fight for something in which he believed passionately but for which support was diminishing. The polariser had become his holy grail and his soon-to-be-released HDT Holden Director was the steed he would use to ride into battle.

We raced together at the 1986 Sandown 500 and were soundly beaten by the new breed of turbo-charged Nissan Skylines. A flat tyre put us in fourth behind Grice's Commodore.

At Bathurst I let the side down mightily and Brock rose to new heights in my estimation. This was the race enthusiasts were waiting to see: Peter and I in the same car with the opposition stacking up against us, all on Australia's most testing circuit.

In practice on Friday I was following another Commodore so closely over the top of the mountain that the only forward vision I had was through its windscreen. Across McPhillamy Park my right rear tyre just kissed a small amount of dirt that had found its way onto the track surface. The car immediately snapped 90 degrees sideways at full speed—something like 200 km/h—and I mounted the concrete wall.

I thought I was about to become Australia's first astronaut. I could see only sky as I climbed ever upwards, but then the rear axle caught on the lip of the fence and instead of launching I slid, sideways, along the top before crashing back down trackside.

I was devastated. Not only had I crashed the race favourite, but I had to face the boss—a new experience for me.

'Don't be concerned, Al,' he said, tea in hand. 'It's only a car. We can fix it.' Peter's partner Bev was equally gracious, concerned only for me, not for the car or their race chances. They took me to their tent behind the pits, fed me tea and calmed my nerves, even as mayhem, caused by me, was breaking out all around us.

In my mind, this response typified those two. No matter what you might say about Peter's business decisions or even the stories you hear of his lifestyle, at that point in time they were something very special. They genuinely cared, not just for the people with whom they were involved and relied on; that would be too easy, too self-centred. They cared for humanity as a whole. They had a holistic view on life and their contribution to it was nothing short of extraordinary. In their community, they helped the underprivileged. Peter would never stint on giving his time and energy to other people's causes.

The fix to our Bathurst car was described by one journalist as 'the most extraordinary rescue operation the Great Race has ever seen'.

Holden's production plant in Melbourne had been shut for the weekend, and they opened it so senior engineers, brought in specially, could cherry-pick parts to build a whole new front-end assembly, all without official paperwork or security clearance. They raced the parts to Tullamarine and flew them to Sydney, where a truck was waiting to bring them to Bathurst. A display car in Bathurst was driven under police escort to the track to cannibalise its body parts. We were back in business—starting outside the top ten but in with a chance.

Peter had the car up to second, behind Allan Grice's ultimately victorious Commodore, and then coming into the pits I managed to hit a ripple strip, cracking an oil cooler, with the repair dropping us to seventh, from which we salvaged fifth. John Harvey was a glorious second in the other team car. Some say it was the best 1000 he had ever driven.

That was the day Mike Burgmann, the race's accountant and member of the negotiating team for the following year's round of the world touring-car title, was killed when his car slammed into the bridge supports on Conrod Straight. He was the first fatality of the great race and his passing put everything else into perspective.

In January 1987, in preparation for the World Touring Car Championship, the Holden Dealer Team headed once more for New Zealand. Again Peter and I won, this time with John Harvey and Neal Lowe second. It couldn't get better. At Pukekohe we were third and fifth.

But the world title attack was a big, black hole. Peter wasn't being forthcoming. It's one thing to keep your plans to yourself, but this was seriously unsettling. So much was going on in Peter's world that you could only trust him in a blind-faith sort of way.

The Pukekohe race was on 1 February. The following Friday, 6 February, Peter used one of his sponsoring radio stations, in Adelaide, to announce that our bid for the World Touring Car Championship was cancelled because of lack of funds. That was news to me, and to John Harvey, who was still actively seeking commercial support. In a budget of above $2 million he was around $400,000 short. In my world that's not insurmountable. With enough money in the bank to start the campaign and with faith in yourself, you'd be inclined to get underway and keep selling and accumulating throughout the year.

But for Peter, burdened with other concerns, it was obviously a bridge too far. An announcement like that is also a sure-fire way to kill any further support, so effectively the campaign was over because of a few ill-chosen words.

That February was a horror for Peter. Holden, which had so much respect for and faith in him, had tried every avenue to get him to play by their rules. They'd sent the polariser to Detroit for testing at considerable expense but found no performance gain. Even faced with the maths, Peter had rejected their findings.

On top of that he was about to launch a new Special Vehicles model, the Director, but apparently had not had it homologated to Holden's rigorous standards. He left them with no option but to withdraw their support. Think of the liability implications if they had let a Holden-badged car go to market without their approval.

I'll say it now and I felt it then. I have been through the corporate wringer myself. I have railed against bureaucracy and been frustrated by people who simply won't be reasonable and do things my way. I have, in my view, been severely let down by people I've trusted—although possibly they don't share that opinion.

But if I'd been in a position where I had General Motors in my hip pocket, I would never, never, never have put myself above them. That's not corporate cowardice; it's just common sense. Peter could have lived to fight another day. Who knows? In some parallel universe he might even have got the polariser up.

John Harvey, the last man standing, resigned. I went with him. There seemed nothing, really, to hang around for.

Ten months later Peter won Bathurst, again.

Despite all that had gone down, he had accomplished a rise from the ashes that made my Project Phoenix all those years ago look paltry.

Mobil had made a big commitment to Peter and they kept it. Whatever mistakes he'd made, whatever position he'd taken, whatever indiscretions he'd committed, he was still Peter Brock, King of Moomba and, for the right sponsor, he was money in the bank.

Peter's Bathurst win came at the expense of the two works Ford Sierras of Swiss entrant Rudi Eggenberger. In a world championship plagued with scrutineering inaccuracies, the initially winning Sierras were found to have a wheel arch that was marginally too wide, and, after protests, hearings and legal action in both Australia and Europe, they were excluded from their Bathurst win and their world-title victory. Peter was again King not only of Moomba but of the Mountain.

We never drove together again, mainly because my retirement, unknown to anyone, was imminent. But through it all we maintained a relationship and a mutual respect.

We weren't close friends, but we would meet once a year for dinner with friends who came out from Europe, and of course we'd see each other at functions and race meetings. I went to his 60th birthday party at his home at Hurstbridge, north-east of Melbourne.

My mother had passed away just two weeks after the 9/11 attack in 2011. She'd been on a seniors' bus trip to New York City, and getting through all the security to repatriate her body was enough for me to grow disenchanted with North America. I determined at her funeral that Australia should remain my home. I still had family in Canada but there was no real appeal in returning.

Some time before I'd begun the process of applying for citizenship but somehow the paperwork got lost. It took the Australian Grand Prix Corporation to sort it out. They surprised me in 2004, when I finally became an Australian citizen, by having Peter deliver my citation in a well-publicised ceremony in their headquarters. It was a great honour.

Peter and I discussed retirement. My view was absolute. Quit while you're ahead. His view was typically optimistic—the best was yet to come.

He'd had several goes at retiring, the first at Bathurst in 1997. He came back of course, even winning the 2003 Bathurst 12-hour race in a monstrous 7-litre Monaro, and he remained, typically, forever restless.

He and Bev started a foundation especially aimed at helping young people. In what would be the last year of his life, he left Bev for Julie, a long-time friend, and, while that has been the subject of controversy and ongoing whispers, the one thing I can say is that Peter found a certain pride in his new independence. 'Al, I actually know how to book an airline ticket,' he told me.

For so many years he'd had such a support system around him that even the simplest of actions were foreign to him. I guess there are many retired senior executives in business who can relate to that.

It was no surprise that Peter took an old FJ 'humpy' Holden to the Goodwood Revival meeting in Britain, perhaps the world's greatest celebration of our sport. It was no surprise either that he won the Spirit of Goodwood Trophy for the way he conducted himself at the 2006 event. He embodied the motor-sport ethos.

But it did surprise me that he came home and, without sufficient rest or preparation, went straight to a damned car rally in Western Australia. But why not?

In his own mind, Peter was invincible. He'd rallied before, winning the Repco Round Australia Trial in 1979, leading home a Holden 1–2–3. He'd competed in rallycross and he'd recently developed a taste for closed-road tarmac rallies like Targa Tasmania where, I think, he relied a bit too much on the innate skill and timing of a race driver in situations where specialist rally drivers may have been a bit more circumspect. Trees and culverts on rally courses are a lot less forgiving than catch fences and sand traps on race tracks.

I'd driven 200 kilometres north of Melbourne to Winton Raceway, testing a Porsche with my son Andrew, when the news came through on 8 September 2006—a prominent Australian racing driver had been badly injured in a road accident. The rest of my family thought it could have been me and made urgent calls. But then there was clarification. It was Peter, and he'd not survived.

He'd left the road on a timed special stage of Targa West and, in one of those millimetre-each-way strokes of misfortune, he'd hit a tree right where the car was at its most vulnerable, where his head and body were exposed.

I fielded 55 media calls that afternoon and answered none of them. With the help of a friend, I drafted a statement the next day that I could read, once, to get the media off my back. A day later I was scheduled to work at a BMW drive day and because a television station wanted me in a studio to talk, live, about Peter at the same time, the PR for BMW rescheduled my commitment. I didn't go to the studio.

I went to Peter's funeral and to his wake, and said nothing. I couldn't.

In order to requite the huge outpouring of grief from fans, Sandown Raceway convened a memorial service on the main straight, in front of the grandstand where the crowd had roared for us both. I accepted the invitation to speak. Five times ATCC Mark Skaife, a Brock protégé, did also. As we were introduced to the crowd Skaife said to me: 'Don't you dare cry.'

I let him down.

13

ANZ: BANKING ON SUCCESS

EUROPE WAS BECKONING. I AM, FIRST AND FOREMOST, A RACING DRIVER and I was committed to not letting the experience of my European training with Peter Brock go to waste.

Quickly I put together a plan, calling on my contacts, and my bank manager for support.

After he'd lost General Motors, Peter had been forced to hold a fire sale to cover his immediate obligations. Everything had to go. In the corner of his workshop was a brand-new rolling chassis—a built-up car without an engine. It was the VL Commodore destined for the 1987 world title, a car capable of winning the championship.

I knew he'd never sell it to me, or to John Harvey. The wounds were too raw, the despair too great. So I called on a nominee.

I'll let John tell the story.

'With everything going on, I'd forgotten the car was still there. It wasn't top of my mind. One day [before the closure of Holden Special Vehicles but after the announcement] three men in suits turned up to look at the shell. Peter came down from his office and asked them what interest they had in motor sport and what they would plan to do with the car. He was, as always, suspicious and protective.

'They told him they had no direct interest in the sport, but they were huge Peter Brock fans and they wanted this car as a memento of all that he stood for.

'That did the trick. It hit him straight in the ego. He still drove a hard bargain but they bought the car.'

The shell was taken straight to 711 Malvern Road.

Some said it was a dirty trick. If I'd gone about it another way maybe I could have brought Peter along for the ride. But you had to be there. It was a time of great turmoil, especially for Peter, and decisions were being taken so quickly, in such a short space of time, that only hindsight now leads you to wonder what if . . . ?

Could I have taken Peter to Europe with me? If I'd stayed, could I have won Bathurst with him? They're all hypotheticals. At the time the only thing that mattered was the here and now.

I'd begun a relationship with the ANZ bank and they'd advanced me $125,000 to fund the purchase of Peter's car and a partial assault on the world title. I would take John Harvey with me.

Rothmans and I had mothballed our relationship on good terms after the Mazda era came to an end and now we dusted it off, not in Australia, but in Britain, where there were sufficient funds to cover an opening salvo at Monza 1987, one or two other races and perhaps, with some more help, another shot at Spa—in other words, the previous year all over again, but with a fresh car.

•

The world title was a farce. As everyone struggled with the new regulations, it was all too easy to liberally misinterpret the rules and end up excluded. The turbo-charged Ford Sierras suffered that fate before the first round at Monza when their fuel-injection systems were found to be non-compliant. Their disqualification before the starter's flag even dropped compressed the field somewhat.

For John Harvey and myself it was a godsend. We raced hard all day around the flat-out Monza track. The Commodore was a dream—so much better than the car the previous year. We were well pleased to finish seventh behind the works BMW team and three of BMW's privateer entries. We'd won the popularity stakes. The fans loved the sound of our car—a big raw V8 that roared on the straight, still held corner speed and was pretty much a match for the Europeans.

Part of the championship's problem was that post-race technical checking was, to put it mildly, cursory.

When we went to scrutineering, the BMWs were already on their transporters and officials took just a passing glance at our car before clearing us, too. After all, we'd finished seventh. No one is interested in being too precise about a car that finished that far off the podium.

But then hell broke loose. One of the BMW privateers, a leading German BMW dealer, took exception to the works cars running bits he hadn't been given. It was that typical 'works team gets the best parts scenario', just as we'd experienced with the Falcon GTHOs at Bathurst in the 1970s.

This guy went on the rev limiter. He demanded officials have a closer look, so the BMWs came off their trailers for a second inspection. In normal circumstances the factory might have applied better control over its supported privateers but in this case they didn't, perhaps deferring to the guy's status as one of their best dealers.

John Harvey knew all about that. One of the underlying unsubstantiated legends of Bathurst is that, in 1976, his works Holden actually covered more laps than that of Bob Morris, who was named the winner. But rather than protesting, Holden quietly suppressed the lap recount in deference to their star dealer, Ron Hodgson, who was Bob's team owner.

But not so at Monza. It was all out there on public view.

The turn up was that all six BMWs were examined and excluded, a huge scandal. They'd been running lightweight body parts, equal to about the same weight as a fat official. They had carbon-fibre roofs, bonnets and mudguards, and a whole heap of underbody parts made of titanium. It wasn't a minor indiscretion. It was a huge cheat.

By protesting the works cars, the privateer had been caught in the same web and brought down the entire marque.

John and I were already back at our cheap-and-cheerful hotel while all this was going on, heating up an evening meal the host had left out for us. We weren't staying anywhere opulent.

It took a late-arriving fellow competitor to alert us to the fact something big might be happening.

We didn't believe it. Those sorts of things just don't go on. Not at that level.

Next morning we came down to breakfast to applause. The newspaper confirmed it: the BMWs had been disqualified and we had won the first-ever World Touring Car Championship race.

BMW didn't bother to appeal. They knew they'd been caught.

It was a win beyond any expectation. Sure, we might have been the last team standing, but our modest one-car entry from far-flung Australia had achieved something truly miraculous. The promoters of the Bathurst 1000 were rapturous. Bathurst would be a World Touring Car Championship round and, the week after Mount Panorama, another 500-kilometre round would be run at Calder. Our win had made both races big-ticket drawcards for local fans.

It was too much to hope that it would last.

We failed to finish in Spain after a wheel fell off, and we blew an engine at the following round in France. In two race meetings we fell from heroes to near zeroes.

But then at Spa 1987, we were nothing short of magnificent.

ANZ had bought a bank in Europe, Grindlays, but awareness of ANZ on the Continent was very low. Somehow they figured an involvement with me in the Spa 24 Hour race would be a relatively inexpensive way of raising their profile.

For Spa, Rothmans remained prominent but across the bonnet was the new sponsor name: ANZ—a promise for the future. After years of working with soft drink and cigarette companies, and battling with my bank manager, I was starting to adopt an entirely new and very positive opinion about the financial institutions.

It still wasn't a lot of money and we'd drafted an Australian privateer, Tony Mulvihill, into the team to help out. Poor Tony never got a drive. Constant rain absolutely destroyed practice for him and he failed to qualify.

I said to John, 'That's bad news—we have to do the whole 24-hour race on our own.'

He said, 'That's good news.'

We'd both had Spa experience the year before and, with the greatest of respect to Tony, his withdrawal removed one additional risk. I ended up driving fourteen hours, the longest I've done in any race. John did the other ten.

The conditions were horrible that weekend. Spa has a downhill pit area and cars were arriving at their pits and sliding right past on torrents of water, requiring them to go all the way around again.

A group of high-ranking CAMS and Bathurst officials, over to suss out the place for the Bathurst round of the WTCC, pitched in and ran our pit. One was Frank Lowndes, father of V8 Supercar ace Craig, who was already advancing from bright-eyed pit pest to go-kart champion. They kept us going, mechanically, physically and mentally. The strain of a 24-hour race on a team of just two drivers is immense, but we did have one ace up our sleeves. We may not have had a team of nutritionists and masseurs, but Rothmans had sent their giant hospitality coach across from Britain, so our on-site accommodation was the equal of anyone's.

At the end of a twice-around-the-clock race, we rewarded every one of our supporters by coming fourth, one off the podium, a huge achievement in a packed European field.

Peter Brock was there too. He'd mustered sufficient support to do just one round of the WTCC with wealthy automotive dealer and importer Neville Crichton as one of his able co-drivers. While we started from nineteenth grid position and finished fourth, they started from eighteenth but got to only just over half-distance before their effort ceased.

We'd finished surrounded by BMWs. The turbo-charged Ford Sierra Cosworths that had started the season with so much promise were fading, but there was a new model coming—the purpose-built RS500—and it was capturing everyone's imagination. Just 500 were being built by British specialist tuner Tickford, under orders from the Ford Motor Company, and they were said to eliminate every shortcoming of the Cosworth and add 100 horsepower as well.

King of the European Ford push was Swiss tuner Rudi Eggenberger. His team had dominated Spa. With the 'standard' car, they'd claimed pole position and were a lap clear when a blown head gasket sidelined them at the twenty-hour mark. Close behind in the tuner stakes was British ace Andy Rouse.

From the next round, both would have the RS500 model, which would dominate the second half of the title.

I was convinced a Commodore could not win Bathurst 1987. The weapon to have was the RS500.

There was no way I could secure and prepare one in time, but I could lease the best in the business. I came to an arrangement with Andy Rouse, the 1985 British saloon-car champion, to bring his team to Australia to run under my colours.

317

ANZ were mightily on board. Only once in a lifetime do you get a commercial supporter like ANZ's chief executive Will Bailey. I'd not met him until just before my Monza race. When I initially sought ANZ's assistance, it was at a much lower level, but suddenly I found myself at Friday night drinks at their Melbourne headquarters, in deep and enthusiastic conversation with this red-headed dynamo of a man who turned out to be the boss.

Some people call it president's prerogative, the ability of the chief executive to determine exactly how his company should be represented to the public. My good fortune was that Will wasn't into tennis or golf. He was a rev head.

The first motor race he ever saw was the 1956 Australian Grand Prix at Albert Park when Stirling Moss and Jean Behra were first and second in the works Maserati 250Fs, sliding the cars around one-handed and giving everyone else a driving lesson.

It was extraordinary that Will was there that day. He was a rising athletic star and the Olympics were on at the MCG across town, but he and his dad opted for the car races.

In his days as a regional bank manager in central Victoria, Will hectored his local Ford dealer into a first drive of the original gold Falcon GT, the 1967 Bathurst winner, and his company car was the 1967 1/2 Fairlane with the 289 Pony motor. Later Nissan chief Ivan Deveson would arrange for him to own the third-ever Nissan R32 GT-R brought to the country. When you're a big cheese at a big bank, you can do that.

He'd already checked me out. Will was a great exponent of the expression 'Winning isn't everything, it's the only thing', and he reckoned motor racing epitomised that. Long before we met he'd hired planes and flown to Bathurst with a few of his key executives to watch the world's most famous motivational cliché come to life. He wouldn't take a corporate box, but went and stood on the hill, among the punters. He saw me race the Mazda there, saw me fail to win, and saw my expression and read my body language in the hard times. He thought I might be right for his bank. He made enquiries of friends in exulted circles—men like Lindsay Fox, the trucking magnate—who gave me if not a clean bill of health, at least a reference to which Will could relate—along the lines of 'driven' and 'uncompromising'.

In 1987, on the back of Spa's fourth place, he funded my Bathurst WTCC assault.

Rouse turned up with allegedly his best Sierra and with co-driver Thierry Tassin, already two wins into his excellent record of four Spa 24 Hour victories.

I have to say the RS500 was a beautiful car to drive. Some people said it was brutish, difficult and unforgiving. I found it just the opposite: 500-plus horsepower of eager anticipation. It would go where you pointed it and do exactly as you asked. It was also delicate and in need of tender care. I was so positive about this Bathurst race.

Rouse put us on the front row of the grid but a long way off the pole time of Eggenberger's works car, driven by Klaus Niedzwiedz and Klaus Ludwig.

Rouse and Eggenberger were fierce competitors. Both held Ford works contracts, Rouse for Great Britain and Eggenberger for the Continent. So, in the intense heat of this battle on Mount Panorama I expected the world from Rouse.

He gave me just 31 laps of a race distance of 161 laps, and I didn't even get to drive.

From the outset that weekend I recognised that Rouse owned the car and he understood it better than anyone else, so it was natural he should take prime position behind the wheel. I was happy with that. Winning, after all, is everything.

But for reasons that totally escape logic or common sense, the Rouse team brought the Sierra fitted with the gearbox that had done the full Spa 24 Hour race, and they'd not told me or anybody that it was in the car. It just wasn't up to the task and it broke. If I'd known, if I'd been given a full equipment life-list, I would have stood up to them, but I got nothing.

By the time the gearbox broke, Rouse was already in trouble. He'd started losing turbo pressure midway into his first stint and was dropping back. Even before he came to a halt I could see my latest, glorious effort slipping away.

The race, as it turned out, was a scrutineering nightmare. The Eggenberger cars that won, fair and square, were disqualified on a technicality, and a quarter of a year later a legal determination in Geneva elevated Peter Brock to his ninth Bathurst victory.

The following weekend we went to the bumpy Calder circuit where, in order to make up a championship-length course, two flat and totally unsuitable corners had been devised to link its race track to its NASCAR-type Thunderdome. It was makeshift at best.

And again we failed—just one stint, with Rouse at the wheel, and the head gasket blew.

It was a completely unprofessional effort from the Rouse team and I made my opinion felt. I've no idea what they were thinking. For them the WTCC was already unattainable: we knew that. Did they think they could come to Australia just to put on a show, or were they on a mission to pick up a considerable amount of money—mine as it turned out—for doing very little?

It astounded me when Peter Brock went the same route with Rouse in 1989, and got the same result.

I thought I was a shot duck. Surely my ANZ money would disappear. After all I was driving for an uncompromising master. Will Bailey had no truck with failure. 'Allan,' he said. 'Get a decent car.'

I was still in business.

The team that had fully impressed me was that of Rudi Eggenberger. The German-speaking Swiss's Sierras had won at both Bathurst and Calder, only to be rubbed out of the results and ultimately the championship by a scrutineering decision that their wheel arches were marginally too wide. It was another example of the idiocy of the regulatory system of the championship. Sure, it had delivered me a win in the first heat, but the underweight BMWs were blatant.

The wheel-arch decision, in my view, was down to interpretation. It was CAMS that pushed the matter, ultimately ending up in a court of appeal in Europe on Australia Day 1988—our Bicentennial celebration—to sink Ford's claim to the title and incidentally elevate BMW to the winning position by just one point.

The outcome was massively divisive. I thought it was petty bureaucracy at its egotistical worst. Others thought the 'Kraut had been caught' and good riddance.

Either way, I thought, *if you want to race a Sierra and win, you needed one from Eggenberger.*

It took a lot of persuasion. Understandably, Rudi was somewhat peeved with Australia. And he didn't build customer cars anyway. His job was to work with Ford to win championships. But I wore him down and he agreed to make me a car. From start to finish it was only a couple of months but it was a long-enough delay that I missed the first three rounds of the 1988 ATCC.

It was a frustrating wait. The Holden Commodore and Ford Falcon had suddenly, miraculously, disappeared from the championship—with the exception of lone ranger Larry Perkins in a VL Commodore. With the RS500 the obvious weapon of choice, most people had taken delivery of their cars. Only Peter Brock had gone the BMW route, which he would soon learn was a dead-end street.

Dick Johnson was on top of the Sierra better than anyone else. His 1988 touring-car title would prove to be a repeat of my 1977 effort with the Falcon—resulting in almost complete domination.

My return to Ford at championship level had opened all sorts of commercial possibilities. Most Ford dealers at the time accessed their finance through Esanda, an ANZ financial subsidiary, so this was much more than a brand-awareness exercise and Esanda would feature prominently on my car. And when I say my car, I mean *mine*. Will had made it very clear from the outset: he was not in the business of motor racing. ANZ did not want a race car on its books. I would own the car and the equipment. He would sponsor it. Simple. After the recent repossession of 'my' Mazdas, that was music to my ears.

Promoters of the fourth round of the title at Wanneroo Raceway in Western Australia made a big deal about my entry. 'The Boss is Back', they shouted on their billboards and television commercials. In truth it wasn't a bad comeback. I scored sixth place on the grid, hit a sand trap when it started raining hard enough to stop the race and I was running with the pack on the restart when sand in my gearbox caused me to stop.

I'd been hugely impressed with the progressive power of the Sierra, loved the way it pointed, but couldn't understand why in qualifying I was 1.5 seconds off Johnson's car. This was an Eggenberger machine, a world-championship contender. It looked good, in fact great, and was beautifully engineered. My expectation, not unreasonably, was that I'd be on the pace right out of the box—even against people who had had more time with their cars.

At the next four rounds I was seventh, third, fourth and sixth. It was pretty clear I wasn't going to make a late run for the title.

At the last round at Oran Park, I took the opportunity to give my chosen long-distance co-driver Gregg Hansford time in the car. We turned a sprint race into two halves with me handing over to Gregg, dropping us to a contrived fourteenth position. At least we were using the time productively.

I was thinking deeply about all this. I'd bought a customer car from a works team. What had I expected to happen? The realisation was blindingly obvious and a real kick in the tail.

Of course I wouldn't get works-car treatment. I'd get a car that was well built, bulletproof and not likely to cause a 'warranty' complaint. But I wouldn't get a car that could win.

I was on a plane to Switzerland to confront the gnome in his home. Even though I had an appointment, Rudi kept me waiting a mighty long time. If ever you want to feel like a total inconvenience, just turn up in Switzerland with a complaint.

I have to say the meeting was convivial. I left not with a box of parts or a blueprint of how to rebuild the turbo-charger. I left with a computer chip.

A new reality was confronting me. I was an analogue man in a digital world. While I'd been used to manually tuning my cars, and I'd even been introduced to the early concept of engine mapping, this whole process of plugging in a Pac-Man game to alter performance was foreign to me.

I came though Customs feeling no compulsion to declare what I was carrying in my briefcase. I installed it in my Sierra, and won the 1988 Sandown 500.

Gregg Hansford had again become my co-driver. He'd had a fairly unfortunate season with Dick Johnson the year before and it was my good luck and his loss that he was cast adrift just as Dick entered his winning streak. Dick had, apparently, earlier suffered the same Sierra fate as me and his confrontation with his car builder in England, Rouse, had been ugly, resulting in

Dick's Shell team developing its own in-car electronics. And it was certainly working.

He took pole at Sandown and all I could muster was seventh. I was ready to spit chips.

But Rudi hadn't let me down. He'd given me a fast car that was bulletproof for 500 kilometres. Gregg and I steadily worked our way through the field and took over the lead at the quarter-distance, losing it only during the pit stops. There's an old adage: 'He who wins Sandown never wins Bathurst'. I'd proved that wrong as early as 1970 and, standing on the victory dais at Sandown, I was pretty certain the curse would not be on me this year.

One amazing outcome of my trip to Switzerland was that I persuaded Rudi Eggenberger to return to Australia. Not only that, he agreed to bring half of his 1987 winning-driver combination—Klaus Niedzwiedz—with him, along with some pretty decent mechanics. Klaus also performed the role of interpreter. Although his English is pretty good, Rudi had built a wall around himself for this return, and for all intents and purposes the only way to communicate with him was in German. CAMS officials were well advised to steer clear.

Rudi turned up with a laptop computer. Compared to what we see today it was, pardon the pun, rudimentary. But for me it was eye-opening. Rudi and his computer were seldom separated, even when he was speaking with Klaus who, it was pretty obvious, was to be the lead driver in my team.

I don't think I'd ever felt under as much pressure as in that race. For a start it was an event that almost didn't happen.

The massive infrastructure improvements the Australian Racing Drivers' Club had been forced to make to accommodate the WTCC the year before had bankrupted the club, forcing CAMS and telecaster Channel Seven to institute a bail out.

The worst casualty was long-time sponsor and supporter James Hardie Industries. Here was a sponsor as excellent as ANZ. For every dollar you saw of their money, they invested another three quietly behind the scenes. But people who didn't understand that had arrogantly demanded Hardie stump up with heaps more sponsorship dollars and the company, quietly outraged, declined. I'd been close to both Hardie and the Australian Racing Drivers' Club. As much as I tried to separate myself from politics, it was impossible.

The new sponsor was brewer Tooheys and they introduced a new sharpness to naming rights investment. Woe betide anyone who brought, and especially tried to sell, an opposition product on site. Perhaps a bit naively, and not completely understanding the ramifications of my actions, I'd accepted a personal endorsement from rival Fosters that involved me always wearing their cap. It could have been worth a lot of money on the victory dais but it proved just another distraction and one that didn't go down well with the new sponsors.

ANZ organised a film crew to produce a major documentary on our race. You don't want race day to start with a camera at your motel door and you certainly don't want them to do the long walk with you to the track. It's a habit of mine. I'm not a physical fitness person—not like you have to be now—but I do recognise you need your endorphins raised and your metabolism active when you step into the car, so I like to walk to the track from my accommodation. And it's 'alone time' that gets my head together.

I declined the opportunity to let them come with me, but agreed to a re-enactment. 'It's just like being a senior executive at ANZ,' I said a bit pretentiously. 'If you're preparing for a big meeting its quite legitimate to say, "No calls and no callers." Forty-five minutes out from the start of a race I don't want interruptions.'

The pits were abuzz with protest. Tom Walkinshaw, who had taken over the Holden Racing Team from Peter Brock, issued a blanket protest on the Sierras. Walkinshaw was late in his development of his Holdens so, to create a playing field more suited to him, he was after the locals. Dick Johnson fired a protest straight back, pinging Walkinshaw's cars on several key points.

The race was being run in the courtroom, not on the track, and it was difficult to keep your head when all around you were losing theirs.

Klaus and Rudi were obviously a close team. When you're setting a car up for a race, you don't want a multitude of development drivers. The fewer inputs, the better. Klaus was on a wavelength with Rudi that I could never achieve and they worked together to bring our times down and build us a race package. Gregg and I watched, truthfully a bit in awe. My respect for Klaus grew by the session, and that led to an association that would last for years.

Klaus was on it from the start, setting the fastest time in the opening session. By qualifying, he'd slipped to fourth but then came the Saturday afternoon lap dash, which traditionally decided pole but this year would only be for show and the promise of a healthy $15,000 prize purse. With only the money to gain and everything else to lose, Klaus let rip and blew the field away.

Watching on the monitors, I found it heart-stopping stuff.

If he got it wrong, we were sunk. Into the downhill wheel-lifting Dipper, where I am always so super cautious, he took an aggressive first gear and missed it. For a split second, it could have been wall-time, but he got the gear and blasted home first.

He had shocked me by taking first gear there. I eased through in second, maintaining pace but not putting the car under so much stress.

When he was on a flyer, Klaus was so physical in the car that he taped up his hands under his gloves to ensure strong grip on wheel and gear shift. This was motor racing at the top European level and, as much as I wanted to believe we were on the same page, we weren't.

On Saturday night after the lap dash, we pulled out the practice motor and installed the race motor. It was F1 stuff being played out on a country road just over the Blue Mountains.

For the first time in my Bathurst career—and Bathurst was my life—I would not face the starter. That had to be Klaus. In fact we considered letting him double stint, going as long and as fast as he could to create a gap. There was no thought of not winning.

It was the first time the Bathurst 1000 featured a flying start. If the Sierras had an Achilles' heel, it was their drive train, and officials had succumbed to pressure not to impose an axle-breaking standing start—although it was sold by all as a safety precaution, referencing my wild ride up the wall in the Mazda those few years before.

Dick Johnson took the lead, but Klaus was in second. As the inevitable casualties and pit stops occurred, he flirted with first until he handed over to me. I didn't know it then—they were to be my last race laps at Bathurst.

We kept the lead, or close to it, through two more stints and then Gregg got in the car more than a lap ahead of the field.

This was looking so good, and yet I had a premonition.

Initially I'd planned to take the last stint myself, to see the chequered flag and claim my fifth Bathurst crown. But it didn't feel right. Something was gnawing at me. It surprised me when I asked Klaus if he would be prepared to take a third stint, with Gregg and I having only one each. If it worked out, I would win my fifth Bathurst having covered just 29 laps, a long way from my solo victories back in 1970 and 1971. But it would still be a win.

The use of pace cars is quite different now from the way it was then. Back then, you'd have 'clearing' interruptions to the race so broken-down cars and debris could be collected from the track at random periods with the field bunched behind the pace car.

They pulled one on Gregg and he fell into line, third in the queue behind lapped cars. You want the safety car to go as fast as it can so you can manage your temperatures, both tyre and engine. In a turbo-charged car like the Sierra, temperature is critical. You need to gap the car in front to give yourself clear air.

When the race went green, Gregg brought himself back up to pace, but it wasn't there, not as sweet as before. He called in, warned us, and I told him to get it to the pits where Klaus was waiting to get in the car, but even then we knew it was over. 'I felt it going as I came across the top of the mountain,' Gregg told me.

Rudi had the bonnet up, then he had the spark plugs out, but nothing will re-start a car when its head gasket has blown.

Tony Longhurst flashed by in the winning car—a Sierra—while we were still working in front of the pits, before we pushed the car away.

In hindsight, we all knew Gregg could have managed the safety-car period better. But we had radio contact and maybe Rudi could have offered advice. Maybe I should have listened to my premonition, but I didn't want to talk across Rudi. Or maybe pigs could have flown that day.

It was a racing incident. My Mazda car-bra at Symmons Plains and my fake-tyre failure at Bathurst in the GTHO had been heartbreaking but this was devastation on a scale I'd never felt before.

I couldn't help thinking: what if I'd been in the car? What if the main thing I'd brought to my team that day had been twenty years of experience at the Mountain? Because at Bathurst you're not racing 60 other cars or whatever the field size is, you're fighting the mountain. That's your only task—to take on the mountain and beat it. And nothing beats it like experience.

Will Bailey was in the pit. God knows what he was thinking. 'I will never forget the look on Allan's face,' Will later said. 'It was full of horror and dismay. But he handled it well, with great dignity. He was, and is, a far more impressive person in a total sense than others I've known who've raced cars.'

That night Will walked up to Rudi. This was the bollocking that we knew had to come. How could Will face his board, some of whom, to put it mildly, weren't as supportive of the motor racing idea as him? How could he, personally, handle this crushing, avoidable, loss?

'Next year,' he said to Rudi, 'bring two cars.'

Will had picked it in one. Our fault had been that we'd bet it all on the black. We had the resources, the ability and the will to win, but we had spread it all too thin. We had left ourselves with no contingency. And Will, at the time of our greatest despair, was giving us a chance to redress it.

That reprieve was both a blessing and a curse. I was tired, deflated and conflicted. For a quarter of a century I'd been pursuing my dream at top speed. I'd seldom stopped to look around me. It had all been maximum attack and that depletes you mentally.

In 1989 I would turn 50. These days people say 50 is the new 40, but for me it was a ceiling I'd set for myself a long while ago.

Way back at Indianapolis, more than two decades before, I'd seen old men walking Gasoline Alley looking, almost begging, for a drive. I'd seen a past hero lifted into his race car and then have his fire-mangled hands wrapped around the steering wheel where they'd stay until someone prised them loose. I'd promised myself that wouldn't be me.

I was dealing with private turmoil, changes in my marital status and with my family that, if I'm honest, I'd put on hold for too long. It was difficult to see a clear future. My focus, once so finely tuned, was becoming blurred.

But when a sponsor says 'Try again', you pick yourself up and do just that. Everything I'd held dear in life—competition and winning—was still on offer and that became the engine room that drove all other considerations to one side.

The 1989 Australian Touring Car Championship, however, proved beyond doubt that you cannot race without a clear mind. We were just never in the hunt.

I drove six of the eight rounds and Gregg did the other two. The best either of us could muster was a fifth.

It was generally regarded by the pit pundits and our fellow competitors that we had the best chassis on the grid, but the weakest engine. I think I had the weakest mind. The touring-car title requires a sprint-race mentality. You've got to be on it every second. Yet that season I allowed myself to be forced wide by a mid-fielder and I beached the car in a sand trap because of slippery conditions. I knew in my own 'I'm my own worst critic' mind that it just wasn't good enough.

At the Sandown Enduro, which Gregg and I had so convincingly won the year before, we had engine problems and started from sixteenth grid position. Within three laps I'd charged up to eleventh and then *bang*. I coasted to a halt on the old pit straight with water pooling on the cabin floor from what was left of the car's cooling system.

I wasn't much into making myself definitive promises at that moment, but I was so despondent that I thought it was highly unlikely I'd be an active part of the two-car Bathurst team—a participant, yes, but from the pit, not on the track.

And that's the way it turned out. Rudi came back this time not only with a new car to supplement mine but with no fewer than three of his works drivers—Klaus, of course; Frank Biela, a 25-year-old member of Ford's Youngster team who'd go on to win Le Mans five times for Audi; and Pierre Dieudonné, disqualified winner of the 1987 Bathurst. My contribution was Gregg Hansford, who deserved redemption.

A lot had changed in a year. In 1987 and 1988 it was fair to say the Europeans held the upper hand. They were state of the art in their development processes, spurred on by the intensity of competition and the demands of the vast European market.

But Australians are a resilient bunch. Air travel might be readily available and comparatively cheap but, if the Europeans aren't going to freely share their technology when you get there, you may as well do it yourself.

Pretty much every counter-measure for performance deficiencies in the Sierras—things like engine overheating and weak axles—had been developed by local engineers and tested to destruction in the cauldron of the local touring-car title.

Some of the fixes were novel indeed. All of our cars carry on-board fire extinguishers with under-bonnet nozzles ready to snuff out engine flames. It was alleged, but never proved, that one of those nozzles, carefully aimed, could spray cooling Halon gas onto the Sierra's turbo-charger intercooler, thus reducing engine-destroying overheating. Surely not. But Brock did receive a $5000 fine for a 'moral infringement of the rules'.

When Rudi turned up, he was faced with an entirely different prospect from that which he'd experienced in the previous two years. No doubt his new car was stronger and better than anything he'd built before, and my current car would receive near to similar upgrades, but he was up against cars that were purpose-built for Bathurst.

Our plan was to run our cars as a hare and a tortoise, or at least as much as you can in a race that was fast becoming a 1000-kilometre sprint.

Niedzwiedz and Biela would be the hare while the two blond-haired team members, Pierre and Gregg, would stay in close proximity as back up. It came as a bit of a shock when Klaus was comprehensively beaten in the top ten shoot-out, fourth behind Peter Brock, Dick Johnson and Tony Longhurst. The other car was just outside the top ten, perfectly positioned.

Fifty-five cars gridded up on that hot October morning and officials took their own sweet time in getting the race underway. In finely tuned machines, it doesn't take long for engine temperatures to rise, and the two-minute delay suffered by those at the front, waiting for those at the back to grid up, would be responsible for a string of retirements in the opening hour.

It was disgraceful. Officials have a duty of care and that day they were in dereliction.

Midway through Pierre's first stint, Rudi saw the warning signs on his telemetry. The car-to-pit electronic monitoring connection that so changed the face of motor sport had issued an alert.

Rudi pulled him to the pits for an early stop—under-bonnet inspection and water top-up. But when Gregg went out in the car, he lasted just two laps and it was all over. Overheating had done its damage.

A failure twice in two years was just horrible, a blow to both your confidence and your self-belief. Gregg was the epitome of the laid-back Queenslander—some said he was too laconic to be a race driver—but I knew that what he wasn't showing externally he was feeling inside.

Klaus and Frank just powered on. Dick Johnson and co-driver John Bowe had taken the lead on the first lap and, as it turned out, they'd hold it to the chequered flag, but not without extreme pressure from our ANZ car. At one stage Klaus was within seven seconds of the Johnson car. The last stint was shaping up as a sprint. In a down-and-out battle my money was on Klaus, especially as pit-lane rumour maintained the Johnson car was losing turbo power.

Just 35 seconds separated the leaders on the final stop. Bowe, the fastest of his team at race pace, stayed in for a second stint. Klaus, fresh, took over from Frank.

Twenty-nine laps remained. On the surface, our pit crew had done a superb job at the last stop. While no time was gained, none was lost either. Klaus needed to pull back just over a second a lap and then get by the leader. No problem.

But three laps later, Klaus was in the pits. In the stop, a wheel had been incorrectly seated on its spline. If it pulled loose we'd have been out of the race. Worse, Klaus could be in a wall. He had no option but to get it properly fixed.

By the time he rejoined the track, Bowe was charging up pit straight behind him. We'd surrendered almost a lap, and while we were still to finish second, it was bittersweet to stand on the podium.

'Go again,' said Will.

I couldn't tell him what I was thinking.

As an end-of-year treat, a celebration of our expected great Bathurst victory, I'd accepted an invitation for Klaus and myself to enter the Fuji Intertec 500, the final round of Japan's touring-car title. Klaus had won the race the previous two years. It was to be held on the weekend of 10–12 November 1989, my 50th birthday. I requested the racing number 39, the year of my birth. It was a nuance lost on just about everyone and I wasn't making it known.

Mount Fuji Raceway is one of the fastest and, for some, most fearsome circuits in the world. Certainly it is among the top ten. It sits beneath Japan's tallest mountain, Fuji san, at 3776 metres a perfectly symmetrical cone-shaped active volcano whose peak is under snow most of the year.

The race track was built in 1963, initially to attract NASCAR-style racing to Japan. They built a banked corner, the Daiichi Banking, and it had a habit of killing people.

After the final double fatality of several, they abandoned it, although even today you can walk over the back of the track behind turn one and stand on its near-vertical ellipse, just as you do at Monza.

In 1976 James Hunt and Niki Lauda determined the outcome of the world F1 championship on a dangerous rain-swept Fuji track, Lauda's cautious retirement and Hunt's inherited victory immortalised in Ron Howard's film *Rush*. Less remembered is that a year later Gilles Villeneuve, perhaps the bravest of all F1 drivers, crashed there, killing two spectators. As a consequence, Formula One moved to the equally fearsome figure-eight Suzuka Circuit, and Fuji became the domain of sports and touring cars.

Fuji is renowned for two things: the never-ending right-hand corner onto the main straight, 300R, where 300 stands for the radius of the corner in metres—an extraordinary length; and the straight itself, which is an engine-bursting 1.5 kilometres long.

Just as Mount Fuji is one of Japan's sacred mountains—in Shinto mythology the permanent residence of the primordial God of the Universe—so Fuji Raceway is a place to be approached with reverence.

The six-heat Japanese championship had been decided by the final round. Masahiro Hasemi, who'd come tenth in the 1976 Japanese Grand Prix in the short-lived Kojima F1 car owned by a local banana-importing baron, had already claimed the first of ultimately three touring-car titles in a Nissan Skyline GT-R.

So there was nothing to play for, except glory. The Japanese pushed their Skylines and Supras well past their limit. By three-quarter distance Hasemi had blown up and so had pole-man Kazuyoshi Hoshino.

Klaus and I pummelled our way to the lead, establishing an almost one-minute gap on the Toyota Supra of Masanori Sekiya, who a few years later would become the first Japanese to win

Le Mans. (He loves the place so much that he flew his fiancée over there so they could be married at the track.)

You cannot discount these fellows. They are fast, talented and fearless. The guy running third, Keiichi Tsuchiya, has now, in his sixties, re-established himself as the Drift King, the undisputed global superstar of tyre-shredding sideways racing.

Sekiya and Tsuchiya got caught up in their own battle for second, which gave us some relief.

Late that afternoon, we took the chequered flag in first place at an average speed of 156.9 km/h.

When you stand on the podium, peeking just around the corner of the grandstand, opposite your left is Mount Fuji. It's a surreal sight.

I told no one, made no announcements and blew no trumpets. But that day, the anniversary of my 50th year on this earth, I retired from professional race driving.

14

GUN FOR HIRE

IT IS LATE AT NIGHT, POURING WITH RAIN, THERE IS NEXT TO ZERO VISIBILITY and I am driving an 800 hp Porsche for the very first time. I am on the 6-kilometre long Mulsanne Straight at Le Mans. In a slow car, it's flat the whole way. In a quick one, there's a kink that needs to be taken with precision otherwise you're off into the trees. People have died there.

There are distance markers—300, 200, 100—and my first time through, I cannot distinguish them and I give myself a huge scare as I power in, virtually unsighted. I admit it: it's the first and only time I've ever been truly frightened behind the wheel of a racing car.

Next time through, I use a mixture of judgement and luck, and turn in where I think the kink might be. Just as I turn I notice the 300-metre marker, and I nail the apex exactly. It's a huge relief.

Back in the pits, I ask the team how fast I was going through the kink. They say 240.

I think, 'That's not too bad. I've gone faster than that at Bathurst.'

Then they tell me that is *miles* per hour. I was doing 380 km/h—the fastest I've ever been.

That race meeting, 1980, at the Le Mans 24 Hour, remains to this day the epitome of my racing career. That's a big call, but for me it was Mount Everest. There are no doubt harder mountains to climb, but there is only one pinnacle of the world.

I lived my motor-racing career in two parallel paths. There was the Allan Moffat Racing stream where I ran the most precarious business in the world, backing myself at every moment that I could balance the demands of running the team with the onerous requirement of being its lead driver. The second stream was gun for hire, where people would employ me for nothing more than my driving skill and, for a small period of time, I'd be relieved of any other responsibility except to go fast.

Those opportunities came as early as my formative years in the USA, but in those days I didn't recognise them as separate. Everything was a struggle, and there were no distinctions in my overwhelming and sometimes blinding ambition. Edsel Ford once called me the 'most driven white man he'd ever met'. I don't get the distinction between white and black, but that reputation has stuck with me all my career so I guess there's something others see in me that I don't myself.

It was 1971, when I'd won Bathurst for the second time, that I was given the chance to race in the Macau Grand Prix. The 6.6-kilometre street circuit around the Portuguese protectorate, equidistant from Hong Kong and mainland China, is one of the world's great once-a-year race tracks. It has one of the longest and fastest straights anywhere and the slowest hairpin—so tight that, if you get it wrong, you have to back and fill.

The track is surrounded by steel fences erected especially for the race meeting. For 50 per cent of its distance, it climbs through a canyon of high-rise buildings that allow you almost no defined braking points. If you're not careful you can get lost—or at least lose perspective of where you are.

For the rest of the year, and even on the morning of the race, it's a public road, covered with the detritus of high-volume traffic—road grime, diesel spill—you name it, it's there.

Ford wanted to support its local dealer who, incidentally, would soon become the company's highest-volume seller in the world, and they decided I should race a Falcon GTHO there. Coincidentally Holden sent Peter Brock with a Torana XU1. His car arrived on time and he got to practise. Mine arrived on the morning of the race and I started from the rear of the grid.

There's a huge straight away from the starting line, a bit like Mulsanne with a right-hand kink, although more defined. At the end of the straight you brake hard and turn 90 degrees right and up the hill towards the hospital, past one of the original Macau casinos, the Lisboa.

I arrived way too hot. I'd already made my way up through the pack, using the only V8 in the field to simply blow them away.

At the very moment I knew I wasn't going to make the corner, I spied a gap in the fence and went for it. Suddenly I was in the porte-cochere of the Lisboa Hotel complete with a liveried concierge who jumped neatly out of my way as I drove straight through, popped out the other side and went on to finish sixth.

Macau was a great experience. The local Ford concessionaire was Bob Harper, whose grandfather had imported the first Model T into China and who would go on to sell his franchise for a fortune to the trading company Sime Darby. Dieter Glemser was there for the German Ford team, driving one of the very special Capri RS2600s and winning outright from a local Alfa GTAM with Brock third.

Dieter and I enjoyed Bob Harper's hospitality, a lot, and I was to go back several times, winning outright in 1973 in the RS2600.

Macau opened my eyes to international opportunity. You could build a reputation, make a bit of money and have a good time to boot. Good times have never been part of my employment framework, so to be able to occasionally kick back and enjoy myself was a bonus.

Macau is where I learned to gamble. It is now the gambling capital of the region, rivalling in many respects Las Vegas and Monaco, at least in reputation.

Back then it was still developing. One of its tsars was Teddy Yip, a desperately keen motor-sport enthusiast who was one of the driving forces behind the race meeting. Teddy was a reasonable hand at the wheel and his name appears on several of the early trophies won before the event, like motor racing, became too professional. Teddy lived in a grand mansion on the track edge and his parties were legendary. He went on to fund Theodore Racing in Formula One and nurtured the career of some of Australia's leading open-wheeler drivers, including F1 champion Alan Jones.

To set the record straight: I'm not a gambler, but I enjoyed it on rare occasions. I'm not the ugg-boot-wearing, slot-machine style of punter. But at the top end, albeit for small stakes, I enjoy the ambience of the gaming rooms. Success, however, evades me.

In Macau I had to borrow from Kevin Bartlett when my own funds ran out before my ambition subsided. I used the loan to good effect and early in the morning I was able to return the initial capital with substantial interest.

Talk about a 007 moment.

At the end of 1974 I was licking my wounds after a dismal season, third in the ATCC with just two wins, and a failure to finish at Bathurst—with Dieter Glemser—when the clutch fell out of the car. Two weeks after Bathurst I'd received that letter from my post-Ford sponsor, Brut 33, telling me that although they were broadening their avenues of support in 1975 I 'unfortunately would not be part of this expansion'. I felt so insulted I didn't bother to reply.

Then I got a telegram from America. It was from BMW.

Ronnie Peterson, the great Swedish F1 driver who was later to die, aged 34, as a result of a horrible crash at Monza, had just signed with Team Lotus to partner Emerson Fittipaldi in the 1975 world championship. Would I be available to take his seat in their works team for the Sebring 12 Hour race, a round of the International Motor Sports Association series?

I'd be joining their firebrand lead driver, 24-year-old Hans-Joachim Stuck, Brian Redman and Sam Posey in a two-car assault on the once-around-the-clock race. *Why me?* I wondered. I'd had experience at the track in my Trans Am days so that was a plus, but surely with the world's best from which to choose it was an unusual call to get. It took me several enquiries to confirm it wasn't a hoax. Turns out it was my old colleague Gordon Bingham, now with BMW USA, who had made the recommendation.

If you discount the TR3, this was to be my first drive, ever, in a car not branded a Ford or built by Ford.

It was a last-minute call-up and, when I got to Florida, Peterson's name was still on the car, but I was in it, and that's what counted.

Sebring is part of the Hendricks Army Airfield, a featureless strip of concrete in 1950 which was turned into a temporary race track, marked by cones. Jack Brabham famously pushed his out-of-gas Cooper Climax across the line in 1959 to finish fourth in the US Grand Prix, clinching his first-ever world championship. It's so lacking in camber or points of interest that in the early days it was possible, like Macau, to lose your way there but for an entirely different reason. Turn 17, a long bumpy right-hander onto the start–finish straight, can handle three cars abreast.

Sebring has had several changes in format over the years. The 8-kilometre track on which I would be racing was the second go at getting it right—the first one abandoned after five people were killed in two separate crashes at one race meeting.

I was the only one of the team not to boast F1 experience. BMW used Redman and Stuck, winners between them of the Targa Florio in Sicily, and the Spa and Nürburgring long-distance races, to qualify. They held back Sam, with whom I'd raced in

Trans Am, and myself to do the race-tuning laps—an entirely different prospect.

In qualifying, you go for broke. Doing race-tuning laps, you're working out tyre mileages and how the car handles on full fuel tanks. It's important work, but not exactly at the glamour end of the business.

So quick were the cars that, even in our race set-up mode, we were close to the previous race's pole times.

The BMWs were dominant. The first two hours were spent dealing with the leading Porsche that was taken out by a lapped car. After that it was us: 1–2, Stuck and Posey in front, and Redman and myself behind. I took my first two-hour stint at the four-hour mark, reaching 280 km/h on the bumpy back straight and being awfully careful of lapped traffic. BMW had limited us to passing only on the straight. With amateurs around us, there was to be no risk taking. I had one spin, avoiding a back-marker, and that was most embarrassing, but I did no damage and recovered quickly.

The race average was looking like being more than 160 km/h—or the magic ton in imperial measure.

Then Stuck blew up the lead car, and they transferred him to mine. They were terribly polite about it but you could understand that they would want their lead driver to guide the car home. It's what Brock did at Bathurst.

It didn't matter to me, not really.

I got to see from the inside how one of the most accomplished teams in world touring-car racing worked. And at 11 p.m. that night I was crowned winner of the Sebring 12 Hour along with Brian and Hans. Now that looks good on your record.

If only I'd left it there.

We were standing by the car in the darkened pits when two grid girls walked by. We decided that was a photo opportunity if ever we'd seen one, so Brian and I invited them to sit with us on the bonnet of the car. A better picture, of course, would be on the roof, so we clambered up there, oblivious of the girls' high heels.

Jochen Neerpasch was the team manager. He had considerable credibility, having won the Daytona 24 Hour race outright in a fearsome Porsche 907. I recall him going past me in the Trans Am car on several occasions in the 1968 race. He also ran a very tight ship, of which I was most envious. It was very precise, very Germanic.

'What are you doing there, putting holes in my roof?' he demanded. It was an uncomfortable moment and I learned a lot from it. I didn't receive an invitation to drive for the team again.

Most times, international opportunity is linked to factory alignment. My two Daytona 24 Hour assaults for Mazda and our magic fourteenth outright at Le Mans for the same make, when it became the first Japanese car ever to finish the race, are testament to how being part of a bigger effort is always important.

Ford took Fred Gibson and me to the Philippines in the early 1970s to showcase their brand in the area. It was a three-hour race on a circuit owned and operated by Pocholo Ramirez, a seriously good competitor who'd come third to me in the 1973 Macau touring-car race.

Ford was keen to push its small 1.6-litre Escort in the region and they'd brought a stove-hot version of the car to Australia for me to drive in 1970, alongside the Falcon GTHO and my own Mustang.

It had been built by the Alan Mann team, with whom I'd had my love–hate relationship in the States, and a similar car had carried Australia's Frank Gardner to the British Saloon Car Championship in 1968.

'My' car had at first been sent to the United States but, when Ford's plans shifted up a gear to go Trans Am racing, it had sat in a corner of the workshop of Holman and Moody, one of Ford's racing teams. Al Turner knew it was there and brought it to Australia for me to race in what was the predecessor of the Australian Sports Sedan Championship. They called the category: Sports Racing Closed.

Straight off the boat it went to Calder Raceway, still in its blue-and-white Ford racing livery, and I won two races that weekend, taking on the likes of Peter Brock in a Torana GTR. Ultimately I'd even race it successfully against Bob Jane's mighty 4.4-litre Repco Torana sports sedan, virtually a front-engine open wheeler with a body.

By the second race meeting Ford had painted the Escort in Coca-Cola red and it had Coke signage. They got it slightly wrong. The signwriter spelled my name incorrectly and it stayed like that on the flank for some time. This was all a bit extraordinary. I had no equity in this car—but it looked like mine. It never came to my workshop, but when I turned up at a track, there it was, waiting for me to drive it. I was never really in love with it.

Globally it had become Ford's weapon of choice. Whether on track, in rallies or in rallycross, which was big in those days, the Escort was everywhere.

It was quick for its size, light and responsive but by then my heart lay with faster cars. I was happy to drive it, though.

Ford used it across Asia as a promotional tool not only for the brand but also for their parts division. At the time there were a number of us travelling, and some of those early race meetings were eye-openers.

You'd turn up in the pits and do your sponsorship deal on the spot. The oil company representatives would enter into a bargaining duel to get their sticker on your car. It wasn't a lot of cash, but there was still, in total, a fair amount of money changing hands. I was immune from it as a works driver. But it was interesting to watch the deals being done—just like in a bazaar.

You had to be cautious. Because of the tropical weather, there were sometimes huge drainage ditches running alongside the tracks and it really paid to walk the circuit first to know what lay to the sides. Spectator control was also a bit *laissez-faire*, and it was best not to use a photographer post as a braking marker because it might move, along with the photographer.

They were wild times. In the Philippines three-hour race the Ford drivers were sharing a pit with a local team whose pit-stop technique was extraordinary. Their driver, keen to get their attention, pulled a gun on them, forcefully imploring them to work faster.

Firearm control was instituted by President Ferdinand Marcos only in 1972, in response to a lot of civil unrest and insurgencies, but for us, this was more than a bit like being in the Wild West. We were careful not to accept invitations to some of the after-parties.

I couldn't wait for the Escort era to end. I was keen to swap to another Ford that was far faster.

I'd won at Macau in 1973 in the Bob Harper Cologne Capri RS2600 and now there was a better and faster 3.4-litre version in place, called the RS3100 after its initial engine capacity. It was built at Ford's Cologne factory in Germany—hence its name, although, confusingly the engine was made by Cosworth in Great Britain . . .

The world energy crisis, triggered by the Arab–Israeli War, had changed the face of the motor industry, and of motor racing. Factories were drawing back from big-budget commitments.

Ford had sent two RS3100s to South Africa for the Kyalami Nine Hour, and I was aware of them sitting there, gathering dust. I contacted my old 'pal' Bill Bourke, now with Ford in Europe, and he said I was welcome to one of them.

Cars of that pedigree don't come with a recommended retail price. Their value is negotiated between the factory and the team on the basis of what one can do for the other. My Trans Am Mustang came to me FOC (free of charge), which was extraordinary. The Capri cost a little more. For the first time, I can reveal it was $30,000, paid for by Ford Australia and owned by me until it came time to sell it. And that's exactly what I stupidly sold it for a few years later. In today's market, it's worth millions.

My goal with the Capri was to enter it into sports-sedan races in Australia. Although it had been a homologated touring car in Europe, the upcoming Australian Sports Sedan Championship, and the various regional series that preceded and surrounded it, were lucrative sources of income for me.

I had absolutely determined not to desecrate the Mustang by cutting and shutting it for use as a sports sedan, so the Capri was the logical choice.

The Capri and I won at our first outing at Sandown 1975, but the car came with rear tyres so wide that, when you looked underneath it, you were hard pressed to see air between the left- and right-hand sides. It looked like a steamroller. Each tyre was 16 inches (40.6 centimetres) wide and the rules limited us to 10 inches (25.4 centimetres).

Naturally the regulators were unimpressed and they forced us to accept the narrower tyre width, and that effectively nobbled us. It was still a delight to drive, especially when I secured purpose-built sprint tyres from Goodyear, but when so many of Australia's top operators were building V8-powered Neanderthals of sports sedans, effectively hot-rods, it just couldn't keep up.

This was a golden age in Australian motor racing. Races for sports sedans were drawing big crowds and prize purses were comparatively huge. Calder was hosting the $10,000 Marlboro Sports Sedan Series. That was a huge incentive to be inventive.

There were Chevrolet-engined VWs, Holden Monaros with Repco engines and a Chrysler Charger with a F5000 engine mounted alongside the driver. It was Rafferty's rules and if you're being positive about it, an opportunity for engineering skill and ingenuity to triumph. Alongside these cars my allegedly oversize tyres looked like a paltry sin. I found myself dicing with the back of the front pack instead of being at the front.

Even as my RS3100 was settling in, in Australia a very— and I mean *very*—wealthy Greek shipping owner, Harry Theodoracopulos, known as Harry T for obvious reasons, asked me to co-drive his upgraded RS3100 at the 1975 Riverside Six Hour International Motor Sports Association race in California against the very same BMW team of which I'd been a member.

It wasn't a full works car, but he'd spent a lot of money on the upgrade and it was virtually indistinguishable. My old adversary Horst Kwech had done the work and he ran the pit that weekend.

The BMWs were quicker, but this RS with its extra horsepower was a weapon. I was able to stay in sight of Redman and Stuck and, after an early pace-car intervention, close right up on them.

Riverside was an amazing track, super fast in places. You take the first turn flat in fifth, accelerating like crazy. Then through the esses you were flat in fourth, trying not to feather the throttle.

On the re-start the BMWs used their incredible torque to move away from me and the race was on as I used lapped traffic to help me get back up to them. I passed Redman and had closed right onto Stuck's tail when my engine blew.

There was no suggestion I over-revved it. We had the tacho-meter's telltale set at 8800 rpm, 200 revs less than it could handle.

A valve seat had become detached in an engine that had been troublesome all weekend and that was that.

Two things arose. A permanent drive was on offer if I wanted it, and my love for the RS3100 had been even further confirmed.

I reluctantly declined the drive, because I had too much happening in Australia, but if ever I'd needed a pick-me-up to give me a positive outlook for the upcoming inaugural Sports Sedan Championship in the 1976 season, this weekend provided the incentive.

It was time to do something amazing.

In 1972 I had discussed with Horst and my old buddy Lee Dykstra the prospect of building a tube-framed Falcon. It was to be the ultimate sports sedan, intended to replace the Mustang. Both Horst and Lee were working at Kar Kraft at the time and, while they moved the project along quietly, it never really hit its straps and I ran out of funding.

Two years later the pair left Kar Kraft and formed DeKon Engineering. They took the idea with them, but in response to an opportunity for a one-design series in the USA called All American Grand Touring, the Falcon had become a Chevrolet Monza.

Chevrolet invested a lot of money into the DeKon Monza project. It was the first race car ever built using CAD/CAM technology, provided by the giant General Motors organisation. Computer-aided design (CAD) has become the industry standard for building cars and race cars, but at the time it was totally leading edge. It was indicative of how serious General Motors was.

Chev wanted to enter the International Motor Sports Association series. The high-profile year-long championship was being dominated by European makes—particularly Porsche and BMW—and it had the potential to cost them sales.

For all Chev's high-tech investment, the Monza, in truth, was still a bit of a bitzer. It had Ford steering, a Ford rear end and a Ford wiring loom, all carry-overs from my original idea.

The first car rolled out of DeKon's Libertyville, Illinois, workshop in mid-1975 and they invited me to the States to co-drive it with Horst in an 800-kilometre event at Road Atlanta. Horst qualified well, but crashed before I got to drive.

At the Daytona 250, the last race of the hard-fought International Motor Sports Association series, I qualified the Monza third in a field of 70 cars, but the engine broke early in the race. The Daytona race is held on the in-field road course but even there I went faster than I'd ever been in a race car to that point—204 miles per hour (326 km/h).

I signed up on the spot to buy the Monza for the Australian Sports Sedan Championship.

In total, DeKon built seventeen Monzas. They've been so successful they've become iconic, and very expensive to buy even now as historic racers. At the time they were selling for $38,000, still a lot of money in those days.

One of the first owners was Harry T. He crashed the car in a private practice and DeKon installed an additional protective bar in the roll cage in anticipation of him crashing again. It became known forever more as Harry's Bar, a play on the name of Ernest Hemingway's favourite drinking haunt in Venice.

A lot of people have speculated that I brought the Monza to Australia just to needle Ford into sponsoring me. I wish I could say I was that smart, or that brave. The truth was a lot simpler. I didn't have Ford's backing—in fact I owed them money for the Capri—and I needed a car that could help me lift a fair percentage of the sports-sedan prize purses on offer around Australia. I wasn't going to win the Sports Sedan Championship with the Capri. It was as straightforward as that.

I took the Monza to New Zealand for their 1976 summer series while I was still running it in and it scored two wins, three seconds and a third. It felt good to be back at the sharp end of the field.

In Australia the Monza caused Bob Jane apoplexy. He owned Calder, which had run the country's richest sports-sedan series, and he also owned what was arguably the country's fastest sports sedan. I blew him away. Bob refused to pay me my prize purse—a massive $5000, claiming my car was illegal.

Then he refused to run his car against mine at the next race meeting at Sandown in 1976—a very unorthodox protest.

I served Jane with a summons. He responded not directly to me but with a Supreme Court writ against three officers of the regulator CAMS for having issued the Monza with a permit that allowed it to go racing. In those days CAMS was unincorporated so its officials were, theoretically, liable for their own actions.

CAMS withdrew Bob's track licence and sent me a cheque for $5000, intending to recover it from Bob. I determined never to race at Calder again.

By the time the inaugural Australian Sports Sedan Championship got underway in 1976, it had all been sorted. The Monza was legal and ready to race.

There were seven rounds and the first, held over two heats at Surfers Paradise, resulted in two wins for the Monza. I'd taken both the Monza and the Capri to the track, and the Chevy was far faster. It was a pretty hollow victory, though. I'd taken first and third positions on the grid, one with each car, sandwiching Jane's Monaro. But he failed to front on the day, citing a back injury he'd sustained.

The second round was at Sandown and again, no Jane. The Monza was decked out like a fourth of July flag. It was the celebration of the American Bicentenary and the American consul asked me to run a US flag on the roof and the racing number 200. It was my pleasure.

I won the first heat. In the second heat, Pete Geoghegan and I staged a race better than our 1972 Bathurst battle. Our finishing times were identical, according to the officials, but they gave the win to Pete.

Round three at Oran Park saw a new contender arrive. Australian international Frank Gardner had built the most radical sports sedan of all—a Chevy Corvair, low slung and challenging the technical scrutineers in just about every area of its construction. It gave Bob something new to hate.

CAMS allowed it to race at Oran Park only on the proviso that it started from the back of the grid, didn't earn series points and would be black-flagged (disqualified) if it interfered with the racing. Talk about ridiculous. I was all for it being there. Competition improves the breed.

There was a lot happening in my life.

The unintended consequence of my racing, and winning, in the Monza was that it was, after all, getting in the way of my relationship with Ford. Through another channel they'd re-engaged me for what would prove to be my sensational two years of Falcon dominance. It's wrong to suggest I'd applied needle—my motives were pure. But Blind Freddie could see it would be politic for the Monza to take a holiday.

I arrived at round four in Perth with only the Capri to take a win and a second and add to my points lead. In Adelaide, I took both cars but the Monza caught fire and I raced the Capri into a points-scoring third place over two heats.

I simply didn't turn up at the last two rounds. There was a theoretical possibility someone could score sufficient points to beat me, but Frank Gardner, who hadn't contested the earlier rounds, was my spoiler. He won the last two rounds, blocking out anyone from the teams that were contesting the whole series.

And that's how I used two cars to win one title—and why I parked them both, out of sight, as I concentrated on my best-ever touring-car season: 1977.

The Cologne Capri left my ownership during that year after I'd run it once more, regrettably without success, at Surfers Paradise. I accepted a ridiculously small amount of money for it and repaid Ford.

The Monza stayed under a dust cover until 1979, by which time in the great cycle of sponsorship, Ford had again disappeared, this time for good. I was able to bring the Monza out in new sponsorship colours. It won one race, too, at Sandown but it was obvious that development had passed it by and at this level it was uncompetitive. I sold it to an enthusiastic amateur in 1980.

It's not like I had a lot to do in 1980.

Ford had abandoned me and I was hanging on by my finger-tips just to run at Bathurst. The Mazda deal was still in gestation. But a good colleague came to my aid—another guardian angel.

The Porsche concessionaire Alan Hamilton had been part of my Bathurst-winning team in 1977. I was surprised, and delighted, when he rang me in 1980, at what you'd have to say was one of my lowest ebbs, and asked me to drive for him in the Australian Sports Car Championship.

Alan and I respected rather than liked each other. There was no dislike, but we weren't close. We just lived in different worlds.

I was surprised when Ford nominated him for my winning Bathurst team, but I wasn't opposed to the concept. We'd shared my very first Falcon GTHO drive at Bathurst in 1969 when we came fourth.

In 1977 he did exactly the job that was asked of him and never once complained about the enforced 1–2 finishing order. He was paid by Ford, received his cheque ten days after the event, and was completely satisfied with the outcome. 'It was Allan's team and he had every right to impose team orders, even though I could have won with Colin Bond,' Hamilton said. 'It was a totally professional thing to do.'

Alan was one of the most accomplished sports-car drivers of his time, and certainly a leading exponent of Porsches. He'd won the title himself in the year we won Bathurst, but after a major open-wheeler race crash at Sandown in 1978, he'd become an insulin-dependent diabetic and, at the time, that made him ineligible for a CAMS racing licence.

The Sports Car Championship was essentially a series for wealthy amateurs but, as the head of Porsche in Australia, Alan felt a duty to fly the flag with a works car. He was an avid collector of special Porsches and he'd laid his hands on a 934, which was an improved production version of the turbo-charged 930 customer car known widely as the 911 Turbo.

The 930 served as a foundation for a number of increasingly powerful variants built for racing series around the world. The so-called Group 4 category car—the 934—allowed for modifications that boosted performance from around 300 hp to 480 hp. Group 5, the 935 car they used at Le Mans, was up around 740 hp.

There was a 936 Group 6 car as well but that was held by the factory and never sold to customers.

That year, in 1980, I'd drive both the 934 and the 935.

Alan's offer was the epitome of a gun-for-hire drive. I had to do no work on the car, bring no money to the deal, and do virtually no testing. All I had to do was turn up at the race track, pull on my gloves, ask which way the circuit went and enquire what the lap record was.

I'd never experienced that before in a series, and I never would again.

Porsche had won the sports-car series for the past five years, but a red-hot competitor had turned up in the shape of filmmaker Peter Hopwood. Although he was driving a Lotus Elan only half the cubic capacity of the Porsches, he had a big chance to roll the amateurs and seize the title, an untenable situation for Porsche.

There were five rounds of the series. By round four, I'd done my job and claimed the 1980 title.

Hopwood scored three heat wins; it would have been four but he broke a throttle cable at Amaroo Park while leading me. I didn't have to contest the last round. The final points score was me 48, Hopwood 43 with the next best Porsche, third on 35. Alan Hamilton had made a good decision and a wise investment.

I enjoyed that car, but frankly, I could have done with more time in it to extract more from it. The turbo unit was troublesome. In its first iteration it suffered from major turbo-lag, a huge hesitation that meant when you got off the throttle the turbo took a long time to spool up again. When you went into a corner you had to anticipate the delay and hit the gas for a long time before you wanted the power. If you got it right, you looked like a genius. If you got it wrong, you either had no power to pull out of the corner or too much power too soon, which tested your reflexes to the limit.

The car Alan gave me was a 934-and-a-half version that had been modified to slightly ease the problem but it meant that, in the heat of battle, if you took it to the rev limit, the car would automatically cut out and the turbo would still spool down. Starts were equally as troublesome and on more than one occasion I had to come from behind after being swamped on the line.

All this was good practice for what was to be my ultimate challenge: Le Mans.

In 1979, my Falcon was sponsored by Federation Insurance, a legacy of Ford's withdrawal. Federation's chairman, Lindsay Keating, was truly enthusiastic about the role motor sport could play in boosting his company's growth in the motor vehicle market.

My co-driver at Bathurst was John Fitzpatrick, winner with Bob Morris in 1976 and an international gun for hire.

Also at the circuit was a gun hirer. His name was Dick Barbour, an American who sold cars very successfully through a number of dealerships, so he could afford to race cars around the world. Motor racing was his passion.

Dick's first Bathurst that year was unfortunate. He was sharing a Chev Camaro that didn't qualify, started from the rear of the grid and lasted only sixteen laps before failing.

But Dick, ever-smiling, Fitz, Lindsay and I got together to talk opportunity and, specifically, Le Mans.

Fitz had signed with Dick to race his Porsches in the 1980 International Motor Sports Association series in the States. Dick asked me on the spot if I'd join Fitz for the long-distance races at Daytona and Sebring, but at the time I was courting both CAMS and Mazda to field the RX7 in the ATCC and I reluctantly declined—a dopey decision as it turned out, as the Mazda opportunity was postponed for another year.

But we did talk Le Mans and Lindsay, especially, was very excited.

The upshot was that Dick's two-car Porsche 935 team would run with Federation support.

In 1980 I went to the States to have my first Porsche 935 drive at Riverside, in practice for the international association race that Dick and Fitz won. In fact, that year they would win seven of the fourteen rounds of the title and emerge champions.

The 935 was exceptional. It put out more horsepower than anything I'd ever driven and it demanded more of its driver than any other car of its time. You didn't just point it, you engineered it on the run, altering boost pressures and aerodynamic wing angles as well as brake bias and balance—many of the things race drivers of today take for granted as part of their in-cabin job.

I didn't drive it flat out at Riverside. It had a race to win the next day, but the practice session was good enough for me to understand, at least in part, why this wasn't just a race drive at Le Mans. This was a chance to win outright.

The extent of the investment was enormous. Each car was worth $250,000. Each engine, and there were many, was worth above $30,000. The whole assault had to be worth seven figures—not what Federation was paying by a long shot, but I guess even millionaires appreciate a bit of help along the way.

Dick and Fitz took one of the cars to the Nürburgring 1000 just prior to Le Mans as a bit of a trial and scored a healthy second on debut. Things were looking good.

Le Mans is the Olympic Games of world motor sport. South of Paris in la Sarthe, it has been used since 1923 as the ultimate proving ground for the motor industry. It is where reputations are made. In 1980 the circuit was 13.6 kilometres around, of which 6 kilometres were the awesome Mulsanne Straight, intact before regulations demanded it be cut by chicanes into three two-kilometre lengths. Le Mans had created legend and tragedy. In 1955, at least 80 people were killed when Pierre Levegh's Mercedes flew into the crowd opposite the pits, the most horrendous motor-racing crash of all time. In 1967 Dan Gurney created a motor-sport legend when he sprayed the crowd with champagne from the victory dais. It was a spontaneous gesture and now everybody does it.

Le Mans is a fast race. The target is always close to 5000 kilometres, which is an average speed of around 200 km/h. But it depends on the weather. And in 1980 it was horrible.

The start was so wet and foggy that Jacky Ickx sat in his car and cruised until he could see where he was going. Then he got motoring and made up enough ground to lead the event before ultimately coming second after a last-hour mechanical failure.

Ickx was driving the only Porsche 936 in the race. The 936s were factory cars, not available to the public, and Porsche had promised its private entrants, like Dick Barbour, that they'd stay away to give their customers a chance to win in their 935s. Jacky's car was rebadged a 908, another Porsche nomenclature. But it was subterfuge. Just like Alan Hamilton's entry in the Australian Sports Car Championship, the factory was hedging its bets.

I was in a three-driver crew, which is normal at Le Mans. I was with Bobby Rahal, a 27-year-old up-and-comer who had already raced Formula One and who would go on to win the Indy 500 and the American CART series. The third member couldn't have been better. It was Bob Garretson, who was in charge of technical matters for the team. In a long-distance race like Le Mans, mechanical empathy is worth at least as much as speed, if not more.

Rahal, the rising star, took the start and was in seventh place when he handed the car to me. I brought it up to fifth, just behind Ickx. The two Federation Barbour cars were by far the most dominant of the fifteen Porsche 935s that started.

It took some delicate work to keep them intact. They were scary things. My first lap in practice—in the dark, in rain—was punctuated by sighting not only the kink on Mulsanne Straight but also the braking area at its end. I arrived hard on the brakes only to have the night sky light up behind me with a tremendous explosion. *Good god*, I thought. *Somebody has crashed.*

But it was the overrun from fuel in the Porsche's twin turbos. The combustion explosion when you backed off created its very own massive fireworks show, and keeping those turbo-chargers intact was an art form. The team instructed us all that, each lap down Mulsanne, we needed to lift off, just for a fraction, to allow a squirt of oil to find its way into the turbo-chargers. It was a dire warning. 'Don't do that and on the long straight you will blow up.'

It wasn't like we were being asked to give up the race lead—just to momentarily lift.

At 2 a.m., after my second two-hour stint in the car, I handed it over and went for a rest. And it was then that the motor blew. One of my co-drivers, Rahal, had disobeyed the order.

Dick, Fitz and Brian Redman brought the second team car home in fifth, the first customer Porsche to finish. We all made promises to do it again the next year, but my Mazda program got the green light and I was next at Le Mans in the Mazda team.

15

OBSESSION AND SUCCESS

'ON THURSDAY MOFFAT SET OFF ON A FEW LAST LAPS OF THE MOUNTAIN in each of his immaculate white Sierras. As nobody else realised the significance of this occasion, he was left alone to his reflections and memories.

'It was a quiet, unheralded conclusion to a magnificently obsessional and successful driving career.'

That was the only epitaph ever written about my retirement. The words were those of Bill Tuckey, the now-deceased doyen of gonzo motoring journalism in his coverage of the 1990 Bathurst 1000.

I couldn't have asked for more.

As Bill said, my career had been both obsessional and successful, and on that day at Bathurst, driving my cars for the last time, I never felt more alone nor more at peace. I had spent my career in a turmoil of trying. Every move I made, every decision I took, seemed like life or death depended on it. I was never satisfied with what I achieved, and my striving to do more bordered on desperation.

Once I had made the decision to stop driving, I felt I was at least halfway towards some sort of personal resolution. But I was still deeply addicted to my calling. My love for car racing and my dedication to it were both so indelibly ingrained that I could not simply step away. I was moving, as I saw it, to my next phase—that of team owner.

After the Fuji retirement decision, armed with both Will Bailey's imprimatur and the still-enthusiastic support of Rudi Eggenberger and his team, I determined that I would make one race my goal. There would be no touring-car championship contested, no Sandown 500—just Bathurst.

One roll of the dice. Bet it all on the black.

I ran Klaus Niedzwiedz and Frank Biela in the lead car and Pierre Dieudonné and Gregg Hansford in the second. Although I had no intention of competing, I cross-entered myself in both cars.

On the Thursday I suited up and took both cars for a sighting lap. No one knew my intention, not even Rudi. I remember it as surreal, an out-of-body experience. At the time it was just another lap: total concentration, feeling out the car, looking for strengths and weaknesses, always respecting the track, knowing that this was Thursday and it was too early to take a risk.

That night, alone, I played the laps back in my head. It was like I was hovering above each car, critiquing my own performance. I knew I'd driven Bathurst for the last time in a race car, and I was okay with that. Better to go out when you're near the top than to emerge bloodied and bruised from a career in decline. There's still, though, an emptiness in your gut.

Two days later Klaus put the ANZ Sierra on pole with a spectacularly brave and forceful lap. When it came to a hot lap in a Sierra, you couldn't be smooth and sympathetic. Brutality was the only requisite. At 39 years of age and on top of his game, Klaus delivered. His teammates were eighth.

The next day, from pole position and with the boost turned right up and blowing black smoke, Klaus jumped the start and incurred a minute's penalty. After a flat tyre and a long stop to replace a blown differential, he still finished the race second on the road just five seconds behind the winning Holden Commodore, dropping to tenth with the penalty. Gregg and Pierre retired in the third quarter of the race, also with a blown diff.

Three years of campaigning the Sierras had resulted in just two second places, one of which was denied. It was frustrating.

But worse was to come. The ANZ bank was haemorrhaging profits. It was not a good time to be a banker. The financial industry was experiencing its toughest downturn in a century, and my sponsor was about to make a significant proportion of its staff redundant.

Will explained that, along with the benefits enjoyed by his C-suite—all the executives whose titles started with chief—high-profile sponsorships would need to be relinquished.

You couldn't lose 3000 people and keep racing a car. Like everything Will did, the cessation of my contract was performed with dignity and a degree of sensitivity that I'd not previously experienced. He met his obligations on every front, including paying me an agreed bonus that I honestly felt I did not deserve.

Then he took me aside and implored me to retire from motor racing. We'd spoken passionately in the past about the value of a large corporation like his to a small business like mine. We'd agreed that my taking on anything smaller in the way of a sponsor—a start-up business, for example—was fraught with financial risk and that I could be left holding the baby.

'You've achieved so much,' he told me. 'Quit while you're ahead.'

But I couldn't. The decision to retire from driving was comparatively easy. But to walk away from the only thing I knew—and might I say my only source of income? It was all too hard.

Against the best advice from a man and mentor whose wisdom was undisputed, I set out to learn the lesson myself, the hard way. It took five years before I graduated.

'Moffat's unique Bathurst preparation was to keep the cars in the shed and bring them out once a year,' Bill Tuckey mockingly commented.

Well, I was not in a position to do much more than that.

Cenovis Vitamins came on board and stayed with me for the duration. They were a good and enthusiastic sponsor, but not blessed with ANZ-type funds. Along with Dunlop, who were prepared to pay money as well as provide tyres, I was able to field a locally based two-car Sierra team in 1991, but without Rudi and therefore without his works drivers.

The cars were being prepared by Ian Walburn, who was also spannering for Queenslander Charlie O'Brien, once a member of the Holden Dealer Team. At the time Charlie was contesting Bob Jane's NASCAR series at the Calder Park Thunderdome—a giant $28 million flawed investment in bringing America's favourite speedway pastime to Australia. I asked Charlie to be one of my drivers and that's how his NASCAR Thunderbird ended up in my 711 workshop. It was a horrible piece of rubbish beside the Sierras. I wasn't happy—but a deal is a deal.

Alongside Charlie I'd secured Gianfranco Brancatelli, the European and Italian touring-car champion, winner of the Spa 24 Hour and the Macau touring-car race and a so-far three times Bathurst competitor whose best finish at the Mountain had been seventh in 1997. It was his personal goal to do better, but he was surprised and dismayed when he arrived to find Rudi wasn't there.

I'd not misled him but he'd expected to be driving not just an Eggenberger car, but directly for Rudi. It was all I could do to persuade him not to go home before the first practice started.

I'd secured two of Jack Brabham's three sons for the other car—elder brother Geoff and middle brother Gary, but Geoff was badly injured in an American sports-car-testing crash just before Bathurst. Four broken ribs and two compressed vertebrae kept him away.

At the last minute I secured New Zealand all-rounder Steve Millen to replace him. Steve and Charlie O'Brien had raced each other in the 1970s and he came with Charlie's strong recommendation.

Brabham and Millen were in sixth place and charging when the turbo blew. O'Brien and Brancatelli stroked it along all day and came in fourth behind two of Fred Gibson's new works Nissan GT-Rs, appropriately nicknamed Godzilla, and Win Percy's Holden.

Then, when we went to scrutineering, we were disqualified.

As a privateer team we'd cut corners wherever possible. The previous year our works differentials had both failed. This year we had replacements, but I'd bought them on the open market and they were branded Richmond, not Ford. They were exactly the same component and even our competitors came to our defence with supporting evidence. But we were out.

For the following year, 1992, there was only one choice. Rudi had to come back—and he had to bring Klaus with him. Ka-ching. The cash register rang out again. There was money only for Rudi and Klaus, not the others.

Gregg Hansford had gone with another team the previous year but I enticed him back with promises of the second seat alongside Klaus.

Charlie and Gary Brabham would take the second car. At the time, you entered a second car not as an equal contender but almost as a Plan B, a spare if anything went wrong with the lead vehicle. Our second car wasn't to get much attention. Charlie was concerned that 'Gary hadn't learned a lot in the past twelve months', and they spent the weekend being frustrated with each other. It was to be Gary's last drive at Bathurst.

Klaus was, as usual, magnificent. He didn't get pole, but he put a car that had not turned a wheel for a year onto third place on the grid behind one of the all-conquering Nissans and the works Holden Commodore. This was to be the last year of the Sierra. In 1993 the Great Race would become an all V8 affair—Commodore versus Falcon—with a smattering of BMWs under licence in the transition period and, of course, the small classes still included.

In one respect I couldn't wait to get back into a V8 assault on Bathurst, even if only as a team owner. On the other hand this was my last chance to turn my Sierra into a winner.

Once more it didn't work. In the worst, most dismal Bathurst ever, we again suffered differential failure, and Klaus and Gregg finished nineteenth when the race was called off in driving rain after Jim Richards crashed the winning Nissan twenty laps before the chequered flag.

Jim was given the win on a lap countback, denying Dick Johnson a victory some thought he deserved. The baying pack at the bottom of the victory dais was in uproar at the local car being denied.

'You're all a pack of assholes,' Jim told the booing crowd from the victory podium, an outburst that shocked the nation and caused him to apologise the next day.

If only people had known. Early in the race, New Zealand's only F1 world champion Denny Hulme had suffered a heart attack and died at the wheel of his BMW after neatly parking it at the side of the road, his last act of concern for others. The news had been kept from Jim, his good friend, until just before Jim went to the victory balcony.

Sometimes life can be just too cruel.

I thanked Rudi and Klaus for their service, put the Sierras on the market and embarked on a quest to go back to the future.

If the Great Race was going V8, then I would get aboard a Ford.

The problem was Ford was not interested. I'd long since passed out of their field of vision. Fred Gibson, who'd proved how good his Nissan team had been in the past three years, was also denied access. Maybe understandably, they went with contemporary teams. Glenn Seton, son of Bathurst winner Bo, won the touring-car title for them that year and Dick Johnson was still the favoured son.

There wasn't a lot of enthusiasm from Ford even for those guys, and it would be several years before the Blue Oval would come back to racing with its own team.

Fred Gibson determined to run Holdens, using his substantial tobacco sponsorship to back him.

I chose to take my small vitamin company and build what I truly thought could be a race winner. You wouldn't make the effort if you didn't think you could win.

It would have been so nice to have real money behind me. Everything Will had said to me was unfolding before my eyes.

I couldn't knock Cenovis. They were keen, supportive and in growth, but even though their annual turnover was expanding, neither their bottom line nor their marketing budget were anywhere near enough to warrant the sort of investment I needed.

Nonetheless we built what to this day is still regarded as the best Falcon rolling chassis of the era. Ian Walburn built it on my surface plate—the secret weapon that separated me from every other team in Australia. Its primary surface provided accuracy to the thousandth of a millimetre, so any jigging or tooling you did was totally precise.

When we took the car to Calder Park for its first hit out we had to change not a thing—not one hole on the sway bar needed to be moved. The car was absolutely perfect.

This was going to be good.

I went to my friends in the States.

Lee Dykstra would come out to run the pit and help develop the car. He also brought with him a special gift—a carbon-fibre briefcase to replace the leather one I'd been using for years. I'm known for travelling with my office at my side and Lee's gift in 1993 was as modern as it gets.

Holman and Moody, the best V8 engine builders of the Trans Am period, were commissioned to build an engine that would be bulletproof for 1000 kilometres. Then I went to my spare-parts stock and took down the best Hollinger gearbox I had left over from the Sierra program. Those were my two mistakes.

As good as they were, the engine builders were simply not as up with fuel-injected technology as we were in Australia. They sent an engine fitted with a Holley carburettor. It may as well have come from the ark. In itself it wasn't a problem but it was symptomatic of the challenges we faced.

It was Australia that was leading the arms race when it came to extracting maximum, usually reliable, horsepower from a race V8.

When we got to Bathurst we were the fastest car in the corners, thanks to the chassis, but the slowest on the straights. We estimated we could have been anywhere up to 60 hp off the pace.

Gregg Hansford had left me, again, and I was so pleased for him that alongside Larry Perkins he finally won the Bathurst 1000 that year in the most sensational manner, just 10 seconds clear of Jim Richards. He became the only person to win Bathurst on two and four wheels.

I had Charlie O'Brien, again, and he brought in another former Holden Dealer Team driver, Andrew Miedecke, a very successful Port Macquarie car dealer who raced for the love of it and not necessarily for the promise of great riches. I needed that.

Charlie and Andrew were a great pair, seniors both of them, and both very content and secure with their own lot in life. They brought a new team dynamic. I'm always the most uptight person at a race meeting; I want no interruptions, no distractions. I thought when I turned team manager I might mellow, but I was discovering I was the same whether I was driving or team managing.

The boys loved a joke.

I'd hide away in our team area at the back of the pits, and someone would come to the pit and ask Charlie if he could get me to come forward to sign an autograph. Charlie knew what my answer would be so he'd lie to me.

He'd tell me, for example, it was an old friend, out from the States, and could I spare a minute. I'd go out, reluctantly, to find a sea of autograph hunters and there'd be no escaping.

Don't get me wrong—I have nothing but respect for the fans, but I was breaking the habits of a lifetime and all Charlie could do was laugh.

It was the same with my rule about No Women. Klaus had turned up with his wife the previous year, defying my longstanding dictate that you're there to go motor racing. Klaus's wife was the talk of the pits—some said a former Miss Germany—and besides, it was Klaus and different rules applied.

So Charlie brought his wife Anne, unknown to me. I walked into his room one night to discover them in bed—I have to say quite properly sitting up watching television. I breathed fire: 'I thought I told you "no women".' All they could do was laugh. I guess I left it pretty late in my career to learn a little about humanity and, for that matter, humility.

It was such a shame our grand effort lasted just 41 laps—one-quarter of race distance. Andrew was at the wheel of the car across the top of the mountain when he found a gearbox full of neutrals. He simply couldn't select a gear. The gear linkage had broken.

There's a lesson I learned years before from Rudi Eggenberger, one of the most demanding of team bosses.

He took the gear knob off his shift lever and sent his drivers out to learn how to drive gingerly, changing gears on the sharply exposed end of the gear stick without hurting their hands or the gearbox. Smooth, precise and sympathetic changes beat gorilla tactics any time.

I wasn't in the car. I couldn't blame Andrew, and he was to be with me for two more years, so we both looked on this as an investment in our future.

I took the Falcon home, put a dust cover over it, and started to plan 1994.

•

There's a lot of time to fill between Bathursts. You can't just sit around waiting.

In the Northern Territory, Chief Minister Marshall Perron, a car enthusiast and an incredibly inspirational political leader, had determined he wanted to put the Territory on the map by running Australia's version of the Cannonball Run.

In the United States, the Cannonball Baker Sea-to-Shining-Sea run was an underground, highly illegal event, held just five times on public roads in the 1970s before it was discovered and banned.

The highest-profile winner was Le Mans 24 Hour victor Dan Gurney, the man who invented the champagne spray, who was famously quoted on the Cannonball as saying his Ferrari Daytona 'at no time exceeded 175 mph [280 km/h]'—this on public roads in a race without rules, named after a guy who set 143 long-distance road speed records, most of them under the radar.

I visited Chief Minister Perron in his office in Darwin. He'd been approached by the executive officer of the Darwin Motor Sports Council, Bruce Lindsay, who'd suggested that since the Northern Territory had no speed limits perhaps it might be possible to run a Cannonball recreation, but with a lot more control.

Chief Minister Perron spoke to Bob Jane, who responded, according to Perron, by asking for an upfront fee of $500,000, non-refundable, to run the event. 'This was unacceptable and I rejected it,' Perron said in a later statement.

Along with a Channel Seven employee and friend, Graham McVean, I conducted a feasibility study and, in early 1993, even as I was preparing for the first Falcon run at Bathurst, we started organising the Cannonball on behalf of the Northern Territory government.

It was uplifting to be in Chief Minister Perron's office. He was a man with a big vision for the Northern Territory. There was a huge map on his wall showing not Australia but Darwin at the base of the South-East Asian countries north of it: his view of where the economic future of the region lay.

The Cannonball would run from Darwin to Uluru via Alice Springs and back again, a distance of just on 4000 kilometres. There was a determination from everyone involved that this would be a well-organised, safe celebration of car performance. It was not a race but a run.

'Deep down all motoring enthusiasts are Cannonballers at heart,' I said in the opening prospectus.

We involved all the relevant authorities, both in the Northern Territory and from CAMS, and obtained the right permits. I did the recces, noted areas of concern and appointed a whole raft of marshals to place in areas of safety control.

Just under 120 enthusiastic competitors entered, along with another 90 media. They came in everything from turbo-charged Porsches to vintage Mini Minors. It was quite a coup for a first-up event. It started on 22 May 1994.

But on day three, on a stage from Alice Springs to Stuarts Well, en route to Uluru, two Japanese participants in the fastest car of all, an F40 Ferrari, lost control, hit two marshals and they all died.

I was one of the first on the scene. At first I didn't see the marshals—only one of the Ferrari crew lying beside the vehicle, and the other still inside. No one was seeing to the obvious shutdown mechanisms of the car. In motor racing we use an electrical cut-off switch to prevent fire. Cars in the Cannonball weren't required to have them so my first thought was to go straight to the battery and disconnect it, securing the scene.

When I turned back, what I saw was shocking. The person beside the car, whom I'd believed to be lying down, catching his breath, was dead. By now there were others, police and rescue people, dealing with everyone else. My shock was absolute. I'd been in motor racing many years. I'd known the dangers and even known death. But not like this.

Today there is a monument at the scene. It recognises the Ferrari crew Akihiro Kabe and Takeshi Okano and the marshals Tim Linklater and Keith Pritchard. The dedication says: 'They died participating in the sport they loved.'

The event continued at the request of competitors, although, understandably, some pulled out.

After consultation with Marshall Perron, we imposed a maximum speed limit for the remainder of the event at 180 km/h. Today that seems high. Then, and in those conditions, it wasn't.

Coronial enquiries, debriefs and long discussions as to how the deaths could have been prevented were a necessary part of the aftermath.

My major contribution was that of driver training. In motor sport there is a defined path to competition. You need to be trained and assessed, and then you work your way through several grades of competition licence before, for example, you can race at Bathurst.

I had instituted a prologue day at Darwin's Hidden Valley race track as a means of letting the participants ease into the event, and also so I could observe them. On the basis of what I had seen, I had spoken to some and urged caution.

I wished I'd done more, but the mechanism wasn't there at the time, as it is now.

No one comes out of an incident like that unscathed. Not the families and friends of those who lost their lives. Not the people who were on the scene at the time. Not the organisers.

Inevitably the Cannonball never ran again.

The Northern Territory Government continues to vacillate about speed limits, seemingly depending on which political party is in power at the time.

My preparation for Bathurst 1994 was naturally subdued. Charlie O'Brien had moved on to another team and was to come fourth. Andrew Miedecke had enjoyed his time, although brief, with me in the first year and he stayed on.

Gregg Hansford, understandably, was staying with Larry Perkins to defend their win, so I looked for someone who could do the job and gain us that edge in publicity. My solution lay in another international who had unfinished business with Mount Panorama.

Englishman Jeff Allam was a safe pair of hands who had raced at Bathurst six times previously, winning the inaugural Group A class in 1984 and claiming second outright in 1990 in Dick Johnson's second car.

Truth be told it was unlikely my car was going to deliver him a win—but you have to start positive.

We leased and installed a locally made fuel-injected V8 engine and it was Miedecke, not the star import, who qualified it sixteenth, outside the top ten for the second successive year. It was something of a minor miracle then, when, at just on one-quarter distance, we'd worked our way up to third outright.

It couldn't last—a steam train of much faster cars mowed us down and we finished eighth, four laps off the winners Dick Johnson and John Bowe.

The race had been tragic. In practice, Victorian truck company owner Don Watson had gone straight ahead at the Conrod Straight Chase and hit a tyre barrier. He was the sixth driver to die at Mount Panorama, all of them on Conrod.

Could it get much worse? I wondered.

It did.

On 5 March 1995, Gregg Hansford was driving a Ford Mondeo in a Super Tourers race at Phillip Island when he slid off, hit a tyre wall and bounced back onto the race track into the path of an oncoming Peugeot. He died instantly.

I get annoyed about it to this day, really steamed up. It was such a waste of a talent, the loss of a really superb human being. I wasn't there, I can't say what could or might have been done. But surely a T-bone is avoidable.

Gregg achieved so much in his life—his international bike-racing career, his successful transition to four wheels, his wins at Bathurst—both in V8s and in production cars—and his Sandown win with me. His sons race now and I only hope they've inherited their father's skills. There was never a smoother driver, a result, surely, of his bike-riding days.

In 1995 Ford released a new model Falcon, an EL, and everyone racing at Bathurst had one, except me.

Budget dictated that I stayed with the EB and, despite suggestions that I should bring back Jeff Allam, there just wasn't the money to do it.

Instead I took on a nineteen-year-old, a youngster called Mark Noske. His father Tony had done three Bathursts before stepping down to get on with running his vastly expanding trucking empire, and he was spending his money wisely on supporting his son's career.

Young Mark had already raced Formula Ford 2000 in the States and he was being widely put about as the next big thing. Like so many careers that fall short, it didn't happen for him, but he was a talent.

Many people asked at the time: why did I take him on? Was it for his dad's money? The answer, truthfully, was partially.

But I could have found another way.

I guess I'd finally conceded that a win wasn't on. So I'd have one of the youngest drivers in the race paired with one of the oldest and most experienced, Andrew Miedecke.

If my team couldn't win, I reasoned, at least I might be able to help foster a career.

'Driving for Allan Moffat was surreal,' Mark said later. 'I'd met Peter Brock when Dad was working for him, but here I was, nineteen, and driving for another icon of the sport. Allan was really good, very patient. He knew I was green and he made me feel very comfortable.'

So why did Andrew Miedecke stay? 'I used to dislike Allan,' he said. 'When he was racing the Sierras he was brusque, rude and difficult. But when you were inside his team, you were made welcome. That gruff exterior is just a self-defence mechanism.'

Andrew never paid to drive for me. But neither, as it turns out, did I pay him.

'We had an agreement, but I didn't mind,' Andrew said. 'I was making enough money through my business interests. It was just a pleasure to drive in his team.'

CAMS had devised a parity system that was meant to promote close racing between Holden and Ford so, with some aerodynamic aids that transformed the old car, Andrew qualified it faster than it had ever been before. But we were still sixteenth on the grid. It was also to last just sixteen laps before the engine blew.

Mark Noske never got a race drive, but his career didn't suffer. He went on to join Holden and become a member of their Young Lions team.

There was a lot happening behind the scenes. A firebrand called Tony Cochrane had turned up in the sport and he was promising drivers he could get them a better deal. It was music to everybody's ears. In September 1996 he arrived in the pits at the Sandown 500 and announced the formation of V8 Supercars, commencing the following year.

It was a strange name—a showbiz name—and it was initially hard to get used to. But Tony was from the world of show business and, more than any of us, he understood the value of the performers and how they should be treated.

I couldn't have been more pleased. Cochrane's consortium included TEGA, the entrants' group I'd helped to start, and finally it seemed there was to be some form of equitable treatment for all involved in the business of motor racing. For too long drivers and teams had been the unwitting supplicants to the ambitions of others, particularly but not exclusively the promoters.

Cochrane was an outspoken and uncompromising character and his new deal was not to come without blood-letting.

The Australian Racing Drivers' Club, promoters of Bathurst, were committed to Channel Seven and both, in the first instance, were committed to an alternative form of racing, the 2-litre Australian Super Touring Championship, a title based very much on the British concept rather than our out-and-out V8s.

That meant that in 1997 there were to be two Great Races at Bathurst—one for Super Tourers, held on the traditional New South Wales October long weekend telecast by Channel Seven, and then two weeks later Cochrane's group would run the inaugural V8 Supercar race at the same track, telecast by Network Ten.

Bathurst would be a battlefield for the next three years until Super Tourers just could not sustain the financial pressure any longer. They became defunct and V8 Supercars took the ascendancy.

For me, it was getting too hard. I felt as if the world was passing me by.

In four years I'd gone from being one of the leading teams— backed by a bank, supported by Ford's European works team—to being among the ranks of the privateers, almost among the also-rans. Amazingly, I still had my reputation. People still sat up and took notice when I spoke, and there was a lot of goodwill shown to me. I knew, also, I still had the ability to run a strong team.

But I'd allowed the world to move on. You cannot live on hope alone. The fewer results I got, the less attractive I was becoming to potential commercial partners.

Cenovis had been sold to Fauldings, a larger conglomerate, and for 1996 they spread their investment, putting Cenovis down the flank of the car and another of their brands, Banana Boat, across the bonnet. To all intents and purposes it looked like I was gaining support. But it wasn't the case.

I brought Klaus back for a last hit out. I was asking one of the best touring-car drivers in the world to step into a car that was now four years past its build date and at least two years past its use-by. It was a credit to the man that he said yes. Lauda Air, Niki's airline company, appeared on the front bumper to pay for his airfare.

The engine was built by Victorian Ken Douglas, one of the acknowledged early experts on engine-management systems and a noted production car driver. As payment he would co-drive with Klaus, and it was to be his first and only Bathurst 1000.

It was a measure of the lack of competitiveness of the car that it qualified only twenty-fifth, even in the hands of Klaus Niedzwiedz.

The race started wet and Klaus was simply superb. As cars spun and caught fire around him, he drove in the wet on dry-weather slick tyres and he moved us all the way up to fourth.

'It was,' he said, 'the greatest experience in my life to be at Bathurst on slicks in the wet.'

According to media, that drive cemented Klaus's reputation as the greatest driver never to win Bathurst.

We had our problems. Ken Douglas spun in the Dipper but miraculously kept the car off the walls. Then the exhaust headers came loose, and the floor became too hot to bear and the cabin filled with smoke. By race's end our grand old car had fallen back to finish tenth. But this old nail, this dinosaur, was still in the Top Ten of Australia's Great Race.

There would have been a time I'd be so distressed by that result it would be unbearable.

But that night I allowed myself a small smile of satisfaction. My team had achieved something amazing and, if it had to be, it was not a bad way to draw a line under the career of both the car and its team owner.

There was to be no 1997 for Allan Moffat Racing.

That year Peter Brock sat in the pits, sipping from a mug of tea as Mark Skaife brought their Holden Dealer Team Commodore to a halt at the top of the Mountain. Peter didn't say a thing—just stared serenely at the television monitor. He'd announced this would be his last race. Of course he was tempted back, but on that day, for that moment, a curtain closed on a great era of Australian touring-car racing, ironically but perhaps not coincidentally as another, fuelled by V8 Supercar, opened.

If ever there was a changing of the guard it happened in those two years.

16

REAR VISION

I AM THE PROUD FATHER OF TWO SUCCESSFUL SONS, BORN TO DIFFERENT mothers.

James, son of Sue McCure, my partner of more than three decades, is in the family business. He is a professional racing driver and currently the only member of the Australian Supercar brigade to have raced four different makes: Holden, Ford, Nissan and Volvo.

Andrew, Pauline's son, is the vice principal of one of Melbourne's most progressive schools.

Sue has been my rock as my career has evolved, loving, immensely supportive, spirited and defensive when she feels the situation deserves it.

I reckon I've come out of my life way ahead of expectation.

Sue came into it as a young girl.

When Al Turner arrived in Australia to run Ford's performance activities, he bought a house in North Balwyn from Sue's dad, Bill, a prominent real estate agent in the area.

Bill was a motor-racing enthusiast. Sue says he should have had three sons, not three daughters, because his weekends were spent taking the girls to the football on Saturday and motor racing on Sunday. He was a mad keen South Melbourne supporter—the team destined to become the Sydney Swans.

Al gave pit passes to the McCure family for the April 1969 Sandown meeting, my debut appearance in the Trans Am Mustang.

I took three wins for three starts, a promising beginning. The middle of the three McCure sisters, Sue, and her older sister Lizzie, decided they liked motor racing, and they had someone they were interested in watching and supporting—me.

Bill, Lizzie, Sue and the youngest sister, Caroline, came to many of my races for a lot of years after that.

Sadly, the girls' mum passed away in October 1970, and Sue and Lizzie became something of a surrogate mother to Caroline.

Bill was away most weekends selling real estate interstate, so I guess the sisters missed out on some of those important years, being children and teenagers without much parenting.

I got to know Sue very well because she came to so many races.

When she was seventeen and still at school, Pauline and I asked if she would be interested in compiling all my press clippings in one book. In those pre-computer days, it was very important to have a 'boast' book properly put together.

Sue worked part time after school and in her holidays for a chain of retail jeans stores, and Bill would happily drop her at 711 every couple of weekends so she could deliver the clippings she'd collated and scrapbooked, and be loaded up with the next lot. Just before she was nineteen, we asked her to become full-time secretary to the race team. By then she was secretary to the managing director of the jeans-store chain. It was a very good position but she enthusiastically jumped at our offer.

A year later we were together.

Pauline insisted on marriage counselling. We saw the counsellor just once. She reported that my infatuation with a woman I described as being a mixture of Miss World and Mother Teresa was immense. It seemed I was hooked.

It was a very difficult time for all of us and certainly nothing that either Sue or I ever intentionally planned. It just happened.

Sue went back to work for the jeans-store boss, then in 1986 started a job in the investment banking industry, first in Melbourne and then eighteen months later in North America. She moved there with our young son James, working as executive assistant to the managing director of one of North America's largest distribution companies.

It was in the late 1980s that she returned to Australia, needing the support of family and friends and especially not wanting to raise James alone on the other side of the world.

We weren't initially together when they returned, but our love was too great for us to remain apart.

Years after we separated, Pauline met up with a mutual friend, my long-term car builder and crew chief Lee Dykstra. They married and now live in Indianapolis where she is director of the Indyfringe Festival, a showcase for developing artists.

Sue works in the prestige motor industry. She has held senior sales, customer relations and marketing related positions over almost 30 years, most of them with BMW Group Australia.

For the boys, motor racing became a common denominator, Andrew initially driving under a pseudonym, Andrew Andrews, and me entering the pits in a disguise topped by massive aviator glasses so I wouldn't embarrass him. Andrew was a good driver, too, very smooth—a bit like his Dad, but his interests evolved elsewhere: tennis, skiing and hockey, where he reached state league level. His real forte is in music and education. He's been a member of the Australian Chamber Choir. He has a beautiful bass baritone voice and is a gifted trombonist. Most importantly he works so hard to give back to the community through mentoring programs.

James took a more traditional path, at least for someone with the name Moffat. Like me he was a late starter. He started karting at thirteen—really late by today's standards, but he enjoyed success. His first year in cars was spent in the Lotus series where he was runner-up and crowned Rookie of the Year.

The rookie title was a recurring theme. He won it again in the V8 Ute series, then in Formula Ford, the Porsche Carrera Cup and in his debut in the V8 Supercars development series. Each time he was front-runner, third in Formula Ford, fifth in the Carrera Cup and second in the V8 development series.

When he scored his first supercar victory at Winton in 2013, I cried. I did so again in 2014 when he stood on the podium of

Australia's Great Race—my race—after he had scored a great second for Nissan just four seconds behind the winner.

Like Andrew, James has been responsible for his own success. Throughout his childhood, all he wanted to be was a V8 Supercar driver. He has worked very hard to be where he is today. It's hard for people to grasp but in most cases the name 'Moffat' has been a hindrance rather than a help. There's a weight of expectation that is unfair. But he's been persistent and determined and his work has paid off.

Strangely it's another family member who's been the most help to him. His uncle Andrew Reid, married to Sue's younger sister, Caroline, has been with him throughout his career. Not bad if you consider that when we first met, Andrew was a one-eyed Brock fan.

Now James and his wife Leah, together for ten years and married in 2015, have made Sue and me grandparents for the first time.

Leah reminds me a lot of Sue—both James's rock and his spirited protector. She's a very dedicated intensive-care specialist nurse at Melbourne's Royal Children's Hospital and we couldn't be more proud of her. She's also a former kart-racer, which helps.

James and Leah's baby, Max, has brought another dimension to our lives.

We live in a bright, spacious apartment in the middle of Moffat Central, or what some people call Toorak. It's a 700-metre walk to my all-time favourite cafes, where some even hang one or two old motor-racing photos of me.

Until two years ago, I used to pack my briefcase each morning and go to work at 711. I'd rented the front half of the workshop to a Porsche repair workshop, but the rear was mine—full of the equipment I'd gathered over a whole career and the trophies that came with success.

When I first entered the non-competitive part of my life, I promised myself a toy. I responded to an advertisement for a Hummer for sale—not the panty-waist look-alikes that General Motors was selling to civilians before the brand went bankrupt, but the genuine military-version Humvee, complete with camouflage. I drove up to Dubbo in New South Wales and bought it on the spot.

I don't drive it much but it was sitting happily in the workshop when a property developer walked in and made me an offer that I wanted to refuse, not for the Hummer, but for the business premises.

Malvern Road had been my life for just under half a century, the one constant in an ever-changing environment of cars and people. It was old, there were cracks in the walls, and there was even a bit of asbestos in it, but it was where I came every day to conduct the business of Allan Moffat Enterprises. I told him no.

The developer's offer went up in equal proportion to my resolve coming down, and ultimately the deal was done.

Before I moved out we held a two-day garage sale. I wasn't as selective as I should have been in retaining things that mattered, but those that I did retain are now in our basement, to Sue's horror.

I stood there for two days as people came in and took away my life, piece by piece, or so it felt. It was gratifying in a way.

Most everyone was an enthusiast and many seemed to have a greater detailed knowledge of my life than I'd retained.

The building came down overnight. Today, 711, a prime piece of real estate, is yet another block of pleasant condominiums, a stone's throw from the first high-rise that I bought off the plan, and it's unlikely anyone living in either place will ever know what we did in all those midnight hours that so enraged our neighbours.

We've just built a man cave in the basement of our apartment. It's not big enough for the Hummer but it does hold a substantial number of trophies and it's a good place to visit from time to time.

Not that there's a lot of time to spend there. The life of a retired racing driver is increasingly busy.

When I first pulled the pin on my racing career, I was pretty much immediately picked up by television to become an expert commentator. These days that's nothing unusual in any sport. Participation in sport has become almost just another career step on the pathway to becoming an on-air personality. Back then, I was a pioneer.

Mike Raymond, the executive producer of Channel Seven's motor-sports coverage, saw potential in me as someone who could help put his viewers in the driver's seat. Seven's technical genius Geoff Healy had already introduced Race Cam to the world of motor-racing broadcasts, transforming external vision of cars rushing around a race track into compelling, almost interactive, television.

Early Race Cam came with some teething troubles. Who will ever forget the voice-activated microphone in Bob Morris's helmet at Bathurst that failed to work all day until Bob screamed at a lapped car with the use of a very forceful expletive, loud enough for the microphone to transmit? And who could help but admire commentator Garry Wilkinson's lightning-fast reflexes when he informed a national television audience that they'd just heard, for a historic first time, the voice of Bob Morris instructing a slower competitor to 'Back off'?

Mike Raymond figured I might offer a safer path, not in a car but in a studio.

He flew to Melbourne twice to put the proposition to me. The first time I said no. A bit like Tom Walkinshaw—who refused a Race Cam in his car because 'I'm too busy trying to win a motor race'—I was so fixated on my job of preparing and driving a car that I doubted my ability to be able to verbalise the experience.

The second time down, Mike had a surprise. He'd spoken to the other teams, against whom I was now not competing, and they'd offered to let me track-test their race cars during race week. It was an extraordinary show of faith in me and one that I would never have reciprocated. I would never have turned the driver's seat over to a non-essential activity in the lead up to a race but that's what they did.

I was nervous, but I also got my reports down in one take. In television-land that's regarded not only as good form but also as cost efficient. You don't want to be stumbling around with multiple attempts to explain a single subject. It would be difficult if you were talking about a sport you don't know, but motor racing is second nature to me, and the grabs came easily.

Mike equipped me with a red jacket and a tie, the company uniform, and I became the network's first expert commentator. People seemed to like me. After years of being somewhat unapproachable at race meetings, this leopard was not going to be easily able to change its spots, so my commentary was inevitably, occasionally, caustic. The viewers seemed to like that too.

Mike and I struck up a commentary partnership that lasted for many years, and he was kind enough to recommend me, and even insist upon me, when he was offered new race-calling opportunities. He taught me a lot. After years of being used to the role of captain of my own race battleship, with mine being the only undisputed voice, it was difficult to adapt to the concept of sharing. My opinion was no longer the only one, and a bit of disagreement in the commentary box enhanced the product.

Mike and I shared the booth on more than one occasion with Murray Walker, the rapid-fire F1 commentator who was both universally loved and derided for his 'Murrayisms'—those malapropisms that grated on your ear but you couldn't wait to hear again. Whole books have been written about Murray's gaffes and yet for more than twenty years he was the benchmark for F1 commentary, his voice rising to a V12 pitch as exciting as the cars.

Murray had been in Melbourne for the motor show and we had invited him into the Sandown 500 commentary booth for an interview. 'Instead,' he said, 'can I call the race?'

What do you say to a legend? We handed him a headset.

First thing he did was draw the on-air monitor to himself. Murray's eye-sight isn't what it used to be, so we had to peer around him at the screen.

And then he called 'Jim Johnson and Dick Richards'—Mike and I glanced at each other over Murray's head and wondered what we'd gotten ourselves into. But he was Murray, after all, and it was an honour to be on the same team.

Mike was a stickler for accuracy. 'It's okay for an expert commentator to have an opinion, but it has to be based on fact.'

In my racing career, it's fair to say that, like most teams and drivers, I wasn't always forthcoming to the media with the full and complete story.

But I never lied.

There's no law that says you have to spill the beans on television, especially as you could well be telling your competitors something they didn't know.

Espionage can win or lose motor races, and you always have to be careful not to accidentally show your hand. A clipboard left lying around with vital facts on it is all it takes for your opposition to be onto you. Race cars left in an open pit with exclusive parts exposed are just screaming out to be photographed by your rivals.

Computer screens contain so much data that they are an open invitation to theft.

But when it comes to PR, the other face of the information equation, when you're asked a leading question by a journalist or pit reporter, it's up to you to have ready a credible answer good enough to 'feed the chooks', as Queensland Premier Joh Bjelke-Petersen used to say, without revealing your secrets.

As a driver I used to understand that and play the game. As a television reporter, it drove me mad. I could handle the half-truths but the blatant brush-off or, worse still, the implausible lie, used to infuriate me. Which is why my commentary tended to cut through, even if it occasionally offended.

Television coverage these days is as good as it gets. It takes the sport seriously with a mass of information and explanations that interpret the mystique of motor racing into something the average viewer can understand.

There's still room for fun; indeed, the banter between commentators is one of my criticisms, because it is occasionally so in-club that I wonder why I'm not a member. But it's so much better than the formative days of television. I was on the grid at Oran Park: front row, pole position. Alongside me was Peter Brock. When the one-minute board came up, a signal to clear the grid, a television reporter doing a live cross rushed forward and put a microphone in Peter's face. 'Who will be first to the first corner?' he asked, perhaps the most inane question imaginable.

Peter was perplexed but, because he was a PR master, he mumbled something suitable. Around came the interviewer to me. Thirty seconds to go and this clown was surely inciting a start-delay. I looked down at his microphone, not up at him, leaned in close and gave him the Bob Morris expletive. It went live, and that time without Garry Wilkinson to smooth it away.

Next morning the ramifications from everyone, from the Australian Broadcasting Control Board to CAMS, were immense. At least they never tried that little number on again.

In 1995 Mike Raymond was hosting a valedictory dinner for Larry Perkins at the Melbourne Grand Hyatt when he had a heart attack. He was fortunate that there were two medics already on site attending to another incident. Both of them were motor-sport officials and they gave Mike tremendous care. He spent quite some time in hospital and I visited him regularly. 'Allan was the only member of the motor-sport community to come and see me,' Mike said. 'It says a lot about his character.'

I don't know. It's just what you do for a mate.

Commercial endorsements followed on from active motor sport.

Ford Performance Vehicles hired me as an ambassador. They needed someone to promote the brand and they weren't looking for a cricketer. They wanted a car guy, and someone with commitment.

They remembered very well the Ford-versus-Holden television commercials of the 1970s when Peter Brock punched a radial-tuned suspension Holden through a series of witch's hats to promote Holden's new-found handling capability—and therefore vehicle safety—and our Ford response in which, with a bit of tongue in cheek, we turned our factory race drivers into human pylons and drove among them.

I recommended to Ford that they bring Edsel Ford out to be the pylon nearest the camera. The reply from Ford management was a huge laugh, so I did it myself.

Fred Gibson drove the XC Falcon and I felt my pants rustle as he skimmed by them. That's commitment.

I took another ambassador role with GT Radial tyres— they sold really good tyres at a reasonable price point—and for many years I assisted them not only as an advertising presence but also with direct dealer engagement, helping to open new stores.

Both were things I wouldn't have had time to do as an active competitor, and it taught me a lesson far too late in my career.

If only I'd taken a more holistic view of myself, I could have done so much more. Look at some more contemporary sports superstars. They've become brands in their own right, well managed and increasingly potent in whatever marketplace their minders arrange for them to enter.

By and large, I never had a manager. Those who tried, failed. When I look back on it, perhaps there was contributory negligence. It's too late to think 'if only', but it's something I hope I'm passing on to James in his supercar career. There's a lot more to the commercial side of the sport than simply knowing how to spell the sponsors' names correctly.

These days I'm regarded as a legend. It's definitely not how I see myself, but it is a huge honour to have been made an inaugural member of the Hall of Fame of both V8 Supercars and the Confederation of Australian Motor Sport. The CAMS award embraces all motor-sport disciplines so it is particularly pleasing to be recognised among a select group of people, including world champions. In both cases it was doubly an honour to be in the first induction.

There is a growing trend to protect and preserve the past.

Historic racing has become a big part of the sport. International events like the Goodwood Festival of Speed and the Monterey Motorsports Reunion attract huge crowds, massive sponsorship and presumably make someone a lot of money. As a celebration of the contribution so many people made to the development of the sport, they are without peer. And yet it's important that none of us, the individual contributors, give too much of ourselves away.

I have just become a trademark.

I've done so not to cash in on my success, but to prevent other people from doing so.

The trade in memorabilia has become an epidemic.

At historic motor-race meetings people queue to get drivers' autographs on everything from T-shirts to posters to model cars. Most people are legitimate enthusiasts, some of them fanatically so. You see them at race meeting after race meeting and they kind of become friends, certainly nodding acquaintances.

But others, you know, are traders and you feel like saying: 'Should I dedicate this autograph to eBay?'

The problem is that the resellers devalue the market. They can take a genuine memento that has a strong emotional value to a collector, and turn it into nothing more than a commodity. Then they flood the market and the value plunges.

It's unfair to me and my equally ageing colleagues but, more importantly, it's unfair to the genuine fans who regard the time they spend with us as something special.

It's a disease that affects the current drivers too, but I suspect they already have mechanisms in place to protect themselves.

There are unethical people who will steal your persona and replicate it without thought to your reputation or your rights to protect it.

It would have been more than twenty years ago that I began to work with one of the most ethical people I knew in the memorabilia market. Western Australian Trevor Young, a builder, developer and car dealer, saw a real opportunity in quality model cars. He began working with a Chinese factory to design and construct scale models as large as 1:18 in size. His first huge success was the Ford Falcon GTHO Phase 3, and that led pretty naturally to a reproduction of the 1971 Bathurst 1000 race winner—my car.

I guess Trevor could have just gone ahead and done it, but instead he approached me and we struck a royalty deal that paid me quite handsomely for each model he sold with my name on it. He subsequently produced more than 30 Allan Moffat model cars, encompassing everything from my Coke Mustang to my ANZ Sierras. An example of each is in my trophy cabinet.

The cars are exquisite. Each cost somewhere between $100,000 and $250,000 to tool up for series production. They are intricately detailed and worth hundreds of dollars. Make a mistake, however, and they could be worth thousands. Trevor once produced a Falcon GTHO and accidentally left off a side mirror. Rather than it being rejected by the market, it became highly sought, like a poorly minted coin, and the few that were made before the error was rectified now sell well into the four figures.

Trevor and I had a contract and even after his untimely death in 2006, it has always been honoured by his company, Biante.

But there are other model makers, even now, trying to make a quick buck. They're the ones who steal your name and your image, and hang up on you when you call to discuss the matter.

The same goes for the internet. There are at least three direct Facebook pages in my name, only one of them official—and I created that not because I felt the need to be online but so I could give my fan base a legitimate point of connection.

It amazes me how that fan base continues to renew itself. Just as emotional attachment to cars like Falcons and Commodores is passed down from parent to child, so, too, it seems that people have a generational connection with drivers.

I would have honestly thought that, with the passing of time, the number of people who have followed my career would start to diminish in size. But it's not true. If anything the autograph queues get not only longer but younger.

It's incredibly humbling and also perplexing. If I'm honest with myself, without false modesty, I did some pretty spectacular things in my time and enjoyed them all immensely. But I didn't think I'd done anything that amounted to a legacy.

That's something I thought rested with other folk. But such is the craving by people to stay in touch with the past that it's become almost obsessional.

If only I'd kept a few of the old race cars! Once they'd passed their use-by date, they were pretty much disposable. Now they are collector's items, worth far more than you'd ever have imagined.

The number of historic festivals seems to grow, almost in proportion with those of us who are no longer around to attend them. Was it only in the blink of an eye that we lost Sir Jack Brabham, Leo Geoghegan, Harry Firth, Frank Matich—all of them stars and all of them gone to natural causes? And Peter Brock, unnaturally taken.

I've been on both sides of the fence. I've been invited to historic meetings and special functions where I am, for want of a better description, an attraction. But I've also gone to events as nothing more than a spectator, eager to catch up with people I've admired.

I was until recently a director of the Australian Racing Drivers' Club, promoters of Sydney Motor Sport Park. They run a special Father's Day event called Muscle Car Masters, which brings together the best of the touring cars of all eras and the people who drove them. It's a marvellous way to stay in touch with your contemporaries, but I prefer not to spend too much time in the Legends' enclosure. I'm happiest with the fans.

It is, I know, a role reversal. For so many years, out of shyness or a dedicated work ethic or both, I did my best to avoid fan contact or at least to limit it. Now it's something I enjoy immensely.

The retro-revolution has taken me happily around the world. When Waterford Hills, the tiny race track outside Detroit, celebrated its 50th anniversary, they invited me over as guest of honour, picked me up in a Mustang at the airport and feted me throughout their race weekend. At the celebratory dinner, I was guest speaker and the room went uncannily quiet. I had to talk up over the sound of pins dropping. It was a huge show of respect and after I'd finished I went around and shook as many hands as I could.

Peter Quenet, my Ford guardian angel, was there as a special guest and my weekend could not have been more complete.

Then they put me in a red Lotus Cortina to do a few laps, and it spluttered and coughed its way around the track. It was one of the ex-Alan Mann cars so I understood why.

I paid my own way to the Monterey Motorsports Reunion at the Laguna Seca track in California. I'm an enthusiast and I wanted to celebrate the Ford GT40, their feature car, as much as the next person.

As I walked through the pits I was hugged and kissed, in the European way, by Jacky Ickx. It had been just under 40 years since we'd last met.

Then Edsel Ford excused himself from a conversation and hugged me too. Pretty soon I was in the Rolex tent and receiving invitations to attend exclusive showings of car collections as a featured guest.

I saw Jacky again in January 2017 at the New Zealand Grand Prix. The Manfeild track on the North Island had been renamed in honour of New Zealand's favourite motor-sport son, the late Chris Amon, and Jacky, who had been Chris's Ferrari F1 team-mate in 1968, came out to inaugurate it. I was asked up on stage, not for a long time because it was the Amon family's special night, but it was nice to be recognised.

Just the same, I try to keep a low profile at race meetings where James is competing. It's his time now, not mine. At the last Bathurst 1000 I was in the Brock Hotel on Conrod Straight as ambassador for GT Radials and I ventured over to the pits in a quiet time for a chat with my son. Suddenly there was a text message from Sue at home, saying be careful of what you say—you're on national television. I turned to find a camera in my face.

The last race I ever competed in wasn't, in fact, the 1989 Fuji 500. It was two weeks later at Macau and promoter Teddy Yip had assembled sixteen name drivers from throughout the world to compete in a single-make hit-and-giggle event in Mazda MX5 Miatas.

I was faced with a brace of Unsers, American motor sport's first family, and a host of other IndyCar specialists. In total they'd won ten Indianapolis 500s between them. There were two F1 world champions, Alan Jones and Denny Hulme, American sports-car champion and soon to be Le Mans winner Geoff Brabham and two true legends of the sport, Roy Salvadori and Innes Ireland.

Not one of us had driven anything quite so lacking in power since the start of our careers but we made up for it with wilful determination.

When the mayhem was complete, I coasted across the line third behind Big Al Unser and went up on the podium.

As I shook the champagne, there was a look of contemplation on my face, unusual because normally I can happily spray bubbly with the best.

All my life I'd not had heroes but people whose successes I'd aspired to emulate. I knew it would be the last time I'd stand on a podium with any of them, and the last time I'd race, especially against such illustrious competition.

But the great truth was there before me. Against amazing odds I'd realised my dream, and I think, maybe, I was satisfied.

I'd spent my life in the impossible pursuit of perfection, and on reflection I'd done pretty well.

Within the twists and turns of a campaign waged on four continents, I'd competed and won on a level that I'd always known I could, and in that respect I'd met my own expectations. There was satisfaction in that.

I'd worked with, driven alongside, employed and competed against some of the greats of motor sport on the best tracks in the world. The mere fact that I was there, with them, didn't seem extraordinary then, but on reflection it was pretty personally outstanding. Satisfying.

Motor racing gave me the opportunity to go places and to have access to people who inspired me.

One was Australia's Prime Minister Malcolm Fraser. In 1976 we raced around Sandown in my Falcon coupe, in helmets labelled AM and PM, and I became his performance-driving coach.

Fraser's famous phrase was: 'Life wasn't meant to be easy'.

Maybe, but sometimes, also, you don't realise how lucky you are.

My counter to the Fraser line is the acronym Champion— Courage, Heart, Ambition, Motivation, Perseverance, Intuition, Optimism and Nous. All are necessary components of success.

Of all of those component words, one of the most important to me is ambition. Not some vague desire along the lines of 'I'd like to', 'I want to' or 'wouldn't it be nice to'. I'm talking about the absolute, bone-crushing determination for the achievement of a special goal.

Nothing in the world can ever be allowed to stand in your way. In my career, I guess, I ruthlessly pursued my targets.

On my tombstone I want another of the words, the one that means the most to me: perseverance.

Some said it was a character flaw, this inability of mine to ever give up, but to me it was the driving force in a life that otherwise could have stumbled to a halt at any one of its many obstacles.

There may have been people with more money, better support, and, yes, I admit it, greater talent. But no one had a greater, unrelenting, driving dedication to achieving his goals.

The greatest man ever in the car industry, the innovator, motivator and dominator who raced his own cars on Sunday so he could sell them on Monday—Henry Ford I—said it all: 'Perseverance is at the heart of all progress.'

For me everything else is just an alibi.

ACKNOWLEDGEMENTS

THIS BOOK IS FAR MORE THAN THE RECORDING OF ONE MAN'S LIFE STORY.
It is a celebration of the people and events that have made motor
racing one of the most compelling sports on the planet and,
we hope, provides insight for the first time into some of the
moves, motivations and machinations that have helped shape
Australian motor sport. Many of the stories have never been told
before and, while we admit they are presented from a singular
perspective, it's our hope they'll add to the accurate history of
the development of both the sport and the Australian motor
industry over half a century.

There was a time—the Golden Age—when the sport and
the industry were inexorably linked, one totally dependent on
the other. In Australia and in the United States, Ford versus
General Motors, with a big input from Chrysler, was the story of
an entire industry's success, both on the track and on the road.
Whole tribes of one-eyed fans and followers were born, loyal

only to one marque, and it was our good fortune to be there at the peak of the evolution.

Compiling this book has revived a lot of memories and provided the opportunity to renew many friendships and acquaintances. We spoke in depth to more than 30 old friends and in passing to many more to check our facts and recollections, in some cases gleaning new takes on old perceptions. To each and every person who so willingly co-operated, and even to those who didn't—sometimes providing their reasons in no uncertain terms—thanks for not only your input now but also your contribution to one man's career and our sport's development.

It is not possible to name everyone to whom we've spoken, but we would like to acknowledge those who generously contributed in detailed interviews and recollections: Will Bailey AO, Colin Bond OAM, Philip Christensen, Lori Dietze, Lee and Pauline Dykstra, Fred Gibson, Bill Gibson, Harvey Grennan, Alan Hamilton, John Harvey, Allan Horsley, Bob Jennings, Ray Kennedy, Andrew Miedecke, Bob Morris, Barry Nelson, Charlie O'Brien, Sue Ransom, Mike Raymond OAM, Tim Schenken OAM, Vern Schuppan AM, Al Turner and Peter Thorn.

In addition, we relied on the collected works of Bryan Hanrahan, David Hassall, David McKay and Bill Tuckey, and appreciated the accuracy of their reporting. We're particularly thankful to Ray Berghouse for his generosity in making more than 60 years of motor-sport data and pictures available from his extensive collection, and to his colleagues Steve Normoyle, Chris Currie and Luke West for their willing co-operation.

Allan appreciated the support of friends, among them Rod Barrett, Peter Boylan, Phil Grant, Peter Lyall, Perry Scarfe, Daryl West and Larry Perkins.

Allan wants to mention those people with whom he's renewed friendships in his travels to Classic events in the United States, New Zealand and Australia and, while every conversation has contributed to his recollections, it's important to recognise Edsel Ford, Lee Holman, David Hobbs, Jacky Ickx, Ray Parsons, Peter Quenet and Brian Redman, among many others.

And then there are our families, without whose love and support we would never have survived long enough to get the words down. For Allan it's long-time partner Sue McCure, sons Andrew and James, with Leah and of course baby Max. For John it's Jenny, Kate, Andrew with Karen, Cameron and Matilda, and cousin Ian Heads, who provided inspiration and encouragement.

We both want to thank Allen & Unwin, particularly publishing director Tom Gilliatt, senior editor Sarah Baker, copy editor Susan Keogh and cover designer Deb Parry. It's been an amazing experience, made all the more enjoyable by their professionalism.

And finally thanks to our mutual old mate Peter Carpenter, who brought us together for lunch at Romeos in the hope that we'd both realise this book was not only possible but also necessary.

Allan Moffat and John Smailes

INDEX

13B engine 271–2, 275, 278
221 Fordor (Ford) 30
711 Malvern Road workshop 67–8, 92,
    116–18, 201–3, 215, 222, 285, 312,
    402–3

A
Aaltonen, Rauno 59
Adelaide International Raceway 131,
    231, 267
Alan Mann Racing 79, 80, 83, 84, 86,
    91, 94, 351
    Cortina tyres 160
Alfa Romeo 47, 59, 81, 82, 86, 91, 93,
    194
    GTA 79
    TZ 52, 54
All American Grand Touring 356
Allam, Jeff 387, 389
Allan Moffat Racing 67, 215, 251
    Mazda deal 258
    memorabilia 411
Alonso, Fernando 297
Amaroo 223, 277, 363
Amon, Chris 414
Ampol Around Australia Trial 85
ANZ Bank 312, 321, 326–7, 375
    Esanda 322–3
apartheid 31
Armstrong 500 35, 85

Australian Automotive Research Centre
    259
Australian Endurance Championship
    251, 265–7, 275, 277–8
Australian Grand Prix 103, 134
    1956 318
    Corporation 304
Australian Motor Sports Club 37
Australian Racing Drivers' Club 157,
    191, 326, 391, 413
Australian Rally Championship 140, 236
Australian Sports Car Championship
    361–2, 366
Australian Sports Sedan Championship
    351, 357
Australian Super Touring Championship
    391
Australian Touring Car Championship
    (ATCC) 6, 55, 56, 69, 103, 113,
    189, 192, 230, 251, 263, 284, 291,
    322
    1970 125, 173–4
    1973 133, 184, 224
    1974 194, 224, 347
    1975 228–9
    1976 230–1, 235
    1977 238
    1978 242
    1979 243–4
    1983 269

1989 332
Mustang, and 122–4, 149, 183

B

B52 221–2, 224–3, 229, 232
  fire 231–2
Babich, Mike 6, 80–1, 212
Bagshaw, John 141, 150, 207, 240, 241
Bailey, Will 318–19, 321, 323, 330–1,
  336, 374–5, 380
Baillie, Sir Gawaine 59, 62
Barbagallo Raceway 186
Barbour, Dick 364–5, 368
Bartlett, Kevin 190, 227, 279, 347
Bathurst 263, 288
  Mount Panorama *see* Mount Panorama
Bathurst 12 Hour 304
Bathurst 500 59, 85, 139, 141–2, 284
Bathurst 1000 149, 155, 191, 277, 284,
  315, 373–4
  1969 5, 13
  1970 13
  1971 5, 344
  1972 183
  1973 191–2
  1977 3–6, 8, 9–17, 290
  1986 299–301
  1987 303, 320
  1991 376–8
  1992 378–9
  1993 379–83
  1994 387
Baxter, Ray 254
Beatles, the 23–4
Beckwith, Mike 53
Beechey, Norm 40, 55, 67, 70, 78, 92,
  119, 124–5, 127, 149, 150
  Holden Monaro GTS350 174, 175,
  176, 177
Behra, Jean 318
Bell, Derek 260, 261, 264
Bennett, Anne 36–7, 39–40
Biante 412
Biela, Frank 333, 334, 335, 374
Bingham, Gordon 35, 41, 215, 249, 348
Bingham, June 215
BMW 249–50, 251, 260, 261, 269, 271,
  313–15, 317, 321–2, 347–9, 355,
  357
  factory team 283
Boeing B52 Stratofortress 221
Bond, Colin 4, 6–15, 154, 155, 157,
  163, 190, 268, 361

Allan Moffat racing team 235–7,
  240–3
  ATCC 1975 230, 232
  Holden Dealer Team 227–8, 236
  rallying 237
Bond, Robyn 236
Bourke, Bill 15, 146, 148, 154–5, 159,
  178, 353
  Super Falcon program 174, 175
Bowden, David 134
Bowe, John 335–6, 388
Bowin Designs 183
BP 206–7, 211
Brabham BT15 open wheeler 98
Brabham Climax 69
Brabham, Gary 377
Brabham, Geoff 264, 377, 415
Brabham, Sir Jack 8, 22, 38, 114, 147,
  180, 234, 250, 348, 377, 413
Brancatelli, Gianfranco 377
Brauer, Chris 125
Brickyard (at Indianapolis) 22
British Motor Corporation 59
British Saloon Car Championship 351
BRM Competitions UK 83
BRM engine 73, 74, 84
Brock, Bev 300, 304
Brock, Peter 3, 4, 9, 11, 76, 121, 146,
  149, 155, 158, 162, 163–4, 190,
  193, 239, 266, 304, 317, 321, 334,
  346, 349, 351, 408
  anti-smoking 292–3
  ATCC 224, 242
  Bathurst 1000 167, 190–2, 284, 320
  BMW 322
  Brock-and-Moffat show 284–6
  business empire 287–8
  character 284, 287–9, 291, 300, 407
  Commodore 285, 287
  death 305–6, 413
  Donington 295–6
  energy polariser 289, 293–5, 299,
  302–3
  fire sale 311–12
  friendship with 303–4
  General Motors, and 294–5, 299–302,
  311
  Holden Dealer Team 224, 226, 227,
  240, 283, 285–7, 291, 327
  King of Moomba 292, 303
  memorial service for 306
  Mobil, sponsorship of 292–3, 303
  retirement, and 304, 393

Brock, Peter *continued*
    rivalry with 184–5, 186, 188–9, 223,
        234, 235–6, 244, 260, 270,
        273–4, 275, 278, 284–6, 288–9
    Spa 24 Hour race 297–8
    Special Vehicles division 288, 293,
        299, 302
    sportsmanship 257
    Surfers Paradise 300 261–2
    working relationship with 288–290,
        293–5, 303
Brock, Phil 273
Brooks, Jack 75
Brown, Bill 153, 163–4
Brown, Warwick 276
Brut 33 133, 222, 225, 227–8, 347
Bucknum, Ronnie 101, 102
Burgmann, Mike 301
Bussinello, Roberto 59, 63

C

Calder Raceway 37, 92, 124–6, 185,
    223, 263, 269, 315, 320, 351, 354,
    358, 377, 381
Canadian Grand Prix 57, 58
CanAm series 47, 75
Cannonball Baker Sea-to-Shining-Sea
    384
    Australian 384–7
Carr, Greg 237
Carroll Shelby team 47, 91, 101, 112
Carter, Murray 40, 162, 187–8, 192, 223
Casey, Paul 211–12
Castrol International Rally 237
catering 205–6
Causeway (Sandown) 61
Cenovis Vitamins 376, 380, 392
Central Division (CENDIV) Touring Car
    series 77, 79, 80, 81–2, 86
Cesario, Lucio 268–9
Chambers, Greg 298
Chaparral 2 47
Chapman, Colin 22, 48, 49, 51, 52, 53,
    72, 183
Chapman struts 49
Chesterfield 250 190
Chevrolet
    Camaro 96, 97, 126, 364
    Chevy Corvair 359
    Monza *see* Monza
Chivas, Doug 167, 191
Christie, Jack 45–6, 57, 58
Chrysler

Charger 156, 163, 165, 167, 355
    Pacer 156
Circuit de la Sarthe 265
Clark, Jimmy 22, 23–4, 38, 47, 50, 51,
    72, 77
    death 296
Cleveland engine 156, 158, 162
Coca-Cola 115, 123, 133, 209–11, 351
Cochrane, Tony 209, 390–1
Co-driver, role of 9–10
Collins, Sid 22–3
Commodore 299, 313, 317, 322, 362,
    375, 378
    Brock, Peter 260, 285, 311
    Falcon, versus 379
    Grice, Allan 299, 301
    HDT 287, 393
Computer-aided design (CAD) 356
Confederation of Australian Motor Sport
    (CAMS) 37, 76, 150, 225, 230,
        239, 316, 321, 325
    Australian Cannonball 385
    Hall of Fame 409
    Mazda, and 251–2, 255–6, 259, 272
    Moffat relationship with 207–8
    rule changes 165–6, 184, 188–9,
        271–2, 390
    timekeepers 71
Conrod Straight 4, 5, 129, 130, 154,
    162, 191, 205, 234, 273, 301, 388,
    415
Cool-suits 10
Cooper Bristol 114
Cooper Climax 348
Cooper-Offy 22
Cortina
    GT 35, 48, 49, 55, 63, 174
    Lotus *see* Lotus Cortina
Costin, Mike 48
Cosworth 48–9
Cowan, Andrew 144
Craven Filter International Trophy for
    Formula Libre Cars 38
Crichton, Neville 317
Cumstey, Harry 223
Cutting, the 3, 154, 245

D

D'Abrera, Robin 70
Daigh, Chuck 38
Daiichi Banking 336
Davison, Lex 59, 61, 62, 69, 70
Dawson-Damer, John 122

Daytona International Speedway 93, 263, 264, 364
  3 Hour race 91
  24 Hour race 101–2, 256, 262–3, 279, 350
  250 357
DeTomaso Pantera 102
de Villiers, Jimmy 33
Dean, Pauline *see* Moffat, Pauline
Dearborn Proving Ground 99–100, 148
DeKon Engineering 222, 224, 225, 356, 357
Detroit 24, 52, 73, 98, 103
Detroit Auto Locker differential 152
Deveson, Ivan 318
Dieudonné, Pierre 333–4, 374–5
Dipper 328
Dix, Bill 241
Donington 295–6
Donohue, Mark 'Captain Nice' 96, 98, 102, 225
Douglas, Ken 392–3
Dowker, Eric 292–3, 298
drug testing 132
Duckworth, Keith 48
Dunlop 41, 376
Dykstra, Lee 100, 222, 226, 356, 381, 399

E
Eau Rouge 297
Ed Sullivan Show 24
Eggenberger, Rudi 317, 319–20, 324–5, 327, 330–1, 333–5, 374, 376–8, 383
  Ford Sierras 303, 321–3
Eichstaedt, Don 73
Elfin 400 sports car 104

F
Fanning, Bill 104
Federation Insurance 364
Ferrari 58, 79, 270, 414
  Australian Cannonball race 385–6
  Fiorano course 99, 100
  takeover bid for 47–8
Ferrari, Enzo 47–8, 99
FIA touring car title (1986) 288
Firth, Harry 11, 40, 85, 86, 139–48, 155, 165, 239, 413
  B52, protest over 225–6
  CAMS chief scrutineer 188

Holden Dealer Team 156, 224, 228, 236, 240
Fisher, Stu 256
Fittipaldi, Emerson 347
Fitzpatrick, John 59, 243, 286, 364–5, 368
Focus 8, 21
Foley, Brian 59, 63
FoMoCo 48, 51, 91
Ford 178–9, 252, 254, 380, 389
  221 Fordor (Ford) 30
  351 Windsor V8 151
  Anglia 94
  Broadmeadows plant 146
  Capri 346, 353–6, 360
  Cortina *see* Cortina
  Cosworth DFV 49
  Escort 351–3
  European car division in Detroit 24
  factory team 283
  Fairlane 1/2 318
  Falcon *see* Ford Falcon
  Ferrari, takeover bid for 47–8
  Flathead V8 29–30, 32
  German team 346
  Galaxie 59, 61, 62
  GT40 7, 12, 48, 99, 414
  Holden, rivalry with 3, 97, 139, 141, 240–1, 408
  Lincoln-Mercury *see* Lincoln-Mercury
  Lotus 34 Ford 23
  Mercury division 97
  motor sport, and 16, 47–8, 194–5, 242
  Motorcraft division 229–30
  Mustang *see* Ford Mustang
  Sierra *see* Ford Sierra
  work team 283
  Zephyr 51
Ford Advanced Vehicles 99, 100
Ford America 113, 146
Ford Asia Pacific (FasPac) 159
Ford Australia 69, 113, 161
Ford, Cynthia 242
Ford Dealer Team 14, 230
Ford, Edsel 213–14, 241–2, 243, 245, 344, 408, 414
Ford Europe 160
Ford Falcon 3, 71, 174–80, 245, 322
  EB 389
  EL 389
  GT 140, 143, 146, 148, 318
  GTHO *see* GTHO

Ford Falcon *continued*
  Number One 8, 16
  Superbird 6, 184, 189–90, 193
  XA 184, 187, 189–90
  XC 7, 242, 409
  XD 244
Ford, Henry I 99, 213, 417
Ford, Henry II 71, 99, 100, 110, 112,
  144, 146, 213, 242
Ford Mustang 70, 78, 82, 97, 98, 100–3,
  110, 114, 206, 351, 354
  Boss 302 100, 103, 109, 112–14,
    115–28, 131–4, 147
  Boss 429 100
  Mustang Mach2 102
  Super Falcon program 173–81
  Trans Am Mustang 175, 199, 222,
    353
Ford Performance Vehicles 408
Ford Sierra 313, 319–24, 329, 330, 373,
  375–6, 379, 381
  RS500 317, 319, 322
Form 1–2 finish 12–15, 240, 242, 349,
  361
Forrest's Elbow 4, 273
Fosters 326
Fox, Lindsay 319
Fraser, Malcolm 14–15, 416
French, John 150, 152, 163, 167, 181,
  190
Fuji Intertec 500 336–8
Fuji Raceway 337
Funny Car 151
Fury, George 269

G
Gardner, Frank 68, 79, 83, 86, 250, 351,
  359
Garretson, Bobby 367
Gasoline Alley 22, 72
gearbox, Toploader 120
General Motors (GM) 97, 143 *see also*
  Holden
General Smuts High School 29, 30, 33–4
Geoghegan, Ian 'Pete' 55, 68, 70, 114,
  120, 122, 125, 127–31, 140, 149,
  150, 154, 181, 359
  Bathurst 1000 190–2
  Super Falcon program 173–5, 182–3
Geoghegan, Leo 140, 163, 192, 413
Gerber, Dan 80
Gibb, Don 114
Gibson, Bill 214

Gibson, Christine 261
Gibson, Fred 140, 145–6, 150, 152,
  156–8, 163, 167, 189–91, 214, 224,
  243, 350, 380, 409
Glemser, Dieter 225, 346, 347
Goodwood 39, 234
  Festival of Speed 122, 410
Goodwood Revival meeting 305
Goodyear 6, 80–1, 95, 96, 153, 155,
  160, 164, 212, 222, 354
Goss, John 189–90, 191, 227, 231–3
Gough, Malcolm 254
Gowland, John 147, 154, 155
Grand Central Racetrack, South Africa
  32–3
Gransden, Max 16, 241, 242
Great Race 3
Green, Evan 14, 165
Green Valley Raceway 85, 95
Greenwood Roadway 50, 52
Gregg, Peter 93
Grennan, Harvey 165
Grice, Allan 229, 260, 261, 262, 264,
  266–7, 272, 295, 296
  Bathurst 1000, 1986 301
  King's Cup team trophy 298
  Sandown 500, 1986 299
GT Radial tyres 409, 415
GTHO 126, 129, 131, 139, 151, 153–9,
  161, 162, 189, 201, 212, 313, 330,
  345, 351
  Phase 2 156, 158
  Phase 3 159, 161–2, 164, 167, 184,
    411
  Phase 4 164–5, 168, 190
Gurney, Dan 22, 79, 83, 366, 384

H
Hall, Jim 47
Hall of Fame 409
Hamilton, Alan 4, 6, 7, 10–12, 14, 155,
  361–2, 366
Hamilton, Norman 103
handling options 148
Hanenberger, Peter 149
Hansford, Gregg 6, 268, 273, 275–9,
  323–5, 327, 329–35, 374–5, 378–9,
  382, 387
  death 388
Hardie-Ferodo 14, 162, 192
Hardie's Heroes 244, 272–3, 277
Harding, David 276
Harper, Bob 346

Harvey, John 103–4, 244, 273–4, 278, 286, 288–90, 292, 298, 301, 303, 313–16
  Bathurst 1000, 1986 301
  fire sale, Peter Brock 311–12
Hasemi, Masahiro 337
Hawke, Bob 274
Hawkins, Paul 68
Hayes, Walter 49
Healy, Geoff 261, 403
Hegbourne, Tony 53
Hernandez, Fran 97
Hibbard, George 192
Hill, Graham 74
Hillman Hunter 144
Hobbs, David 261
Hockenheim 296
Hodgson, Ron 314
Holden 252, 254, 256, 300
  bolts, flywheel 93
  Commodore see Commodore
  Director 299
  Ford, rivalry with 3, 97, 139, 141, 240–1, 408
  Monaro 124, 139, 140–4, 148, 150, 174, 355
  racing driver wages 236–7
  Torana see Torana
  Young Lions team 390
Holden Dealer Team 6, 141–2, 230, 240, 273, 278, 291–2, 301, 393
  Director 299
  Moffat relationship with 224, 226, 227, 285
  tobacco sponsorship 223
  Walkinshaw, Tom 296
Holman and Moody 134, 351, 381
Hopkirk, Paddy 59
Hopwood, Peter 363
Horner, Keith 141, 150, 159, 192, 194–5
  friendship 178–80, 213, 241
  Super Falcon program 173–5, 178–81
Horsley, Allan 121
  Mazda 255, 257, 265–6, 268, 270, 275, 279
Hoshino, Kazuyoshi 337
Howard, Ron 337
Hulme, Denny 379, 415
Hume Weir 76
Hummer 402, 403
Hunt, James 337

I
Iacocca, Lee 110, 160
Ickx, Jacky 6–8, 10–12, 14, 79, 243, 260, 264, 290, 414
  Le Mans 1980 366
Indianapolis 500 (Indy) 21–2, 24, 59, 69, 72, 224, 415
IndyCar 8, 51, 415
Inglis, Sir Brian 14, 16, 159, 164, 242
innovations, race team 204–5
intellectual property 285
International Harvester 229, 259
International Motor Sports Association series 347, 357, 364
Ireland, Innes 415

J
Jacobi, Doug 229–30
Jaguar 55, 103, 174, 278
  D-type 33
James Hardie Industries 326
Jane, Bob 35, 40–1, 67–8, 122, 126–9, 131–2, 149, 185
  Calder 263, 269, 358, 377
  Cannonball, Australian 384
  Ford Mustang 70, 114
  Jaguar 55
  legal action 358–9
  Lotus Cortina 59, 63
  Moffat, relationship with 103, 104, 110, 120
  motor-racing division 103
  Repco Torana sports sedan 351
Janson, Peter 4
Japanese Grand Prix 337
Jeffrey, Peter 158
Johnson, Amos 256, 324–5
Johnson, Dick 76, 152, 235, 245, 261–2, 264, 273, 275, 277, 322–3, 327, 329, 334–5, 388
Jones, Alan 103, 346, 415
Jones, Stan 103
Joyce, John 183

K
Kabe, Akihiro 386
Kar Kraft 99, 100, 102, 111, 112, 117–18, 148, 175, 222, 356
Karmann Ghia 50, 57
Katayama, Yoshimi 263, 267–8, 269, 273
Keating, Lindsay 364
Keeffe, John 261
King's Cup team trophy 298

Kirksey, George 95–6, 97
Knudsen, Bunkie 144, 146
Kojima F1 337
Kranefuss, Mike 160
Kwech, Horst 81, 82, 85–6, 93, 101, 102, 222, 355–7
Kyalami Nine Hour 353

L
Laguna Seca 414
Lakeside 55, 125, 127, 182, 264, 271, 272
Lauda, Niki 337
Le Mans 30, 33, 46, 48, 233, 259, 260, 264–5, 271, 333, 338, 350, 365–6
  24 Hour 6, 7, 48, 79, 99, 262, 343–4
  1966 12–13, 112, 238
  1979 364
  1980 365–7
Leighton, Jon 40, 60, 61, 84, 86
Levegh, Pierre 366
Light Car Club of Australia 285
Lincoln-Mercury
  aerodynamicists 151
  Cougar 97, 98
  division 56, 102
  drag-racing program 145
Lindsay, Bruce 384
Linklater, Tim 386
Lisboa Hotel 345
Longhurst, Tony 330, 334
Lot Six 146–7, 150–1, 156, 160, 174–6, 182–3, 189, 213
Lotus Cars 51
Lotus 18 F1 51
Lotus 30 sports-car program 51
Lotus 34 Ford 23
Lotus 38 Ford 72
Lotus 39 Coventry Climax 77, 78
Lotus Cortina 7, 47–52, 57, 59, 61, 67–8, 70, 72–3, 78, 80, 91, 92, 94, 104, 414
Lotus Cortina team see Team Lotus
Lotus Elan 48
Lotus Elite 46
Lotus F2 296
Lovely, Pete 54
Lowe, Neal 290, 298, 301
Lowndes, Craig 316
Lowndes, Frank 316
Ludwig, Klaus 319
Lukey bridge, Sandown 60
Lunn, Roy 99

M
Macau 346, 415
  Grand Prix 214, 225, 344–6, 348, 353
Maserati 250F 318
McCall, Allan 74, 75
McCure, Bill 397–8
McCure, Caroline 398, 401
McCure, Lizzie 398
McCure, Sue 397–9, 401, 402, 415
MacDonald, Dave 22
McKay, David 140, 141–4
McKay, H.V. 34
McKeown, Jim 35, 55, 70, 78, 92–3, 94, 178
McLaren, Bruce 38
McLaren team 74, 75
McLeod, Max 231
McLeod, Peter 262, 275, 279
MacPherson strut 49
McPhee, Bruce 12, 142–3, 155, 158
McPhillamy Park 299
McVean, Graham 384
Mäkinen, Timo 59
Mallala 121, 122, 123, 127, 181
Mallia, Lou 175
Mann, Alan 80, 83 see also Alan Mann Racing
Manton, Peter 59, 63
Manufacturers' Championship 91, 168, 184, 189, 192, 194, 227, 230
Maranello 99, 100
Marlboro 52, 59, 73, 84, 223, 258, 273, 275, 278, 292, 354
Marlboro 12 Hour 52, 59, 73, 84
Marsden, Howard 80–1, 160, 161, 164, 167, 182, 184, 192
  Nissan 267
  Superbird 189, 193
Massey, Daniel 25
Massey Ferguson 28–9, 34, 56
Massey-Harris 25–6, 28, 34
Matich, Frank 68, 413
Matich A53 F5000 231, 233
Maxwell, David 115, 123
Mazda 194, 251–2, 257, 259, 275, 278, 283, 284, 286–7, 292, 312, 319, 323, 350, 361, 368
  929 project 275, 277
  Bathurst 1982 267–9
  crash, 1984 288
  international racing 262–3
  rotary engine technology 252–4, 271
  RX7 252–6, 259, 260, 261, 263, 364

memorabilia 410–12
Michelin 142
  XAS 155
Mid-America Raceway 80, 81
Miedecke, Andrew 382–3, 388, 389–90
Miles, Ken 47
Millen, Steve 377
Mini Cooper S 59, 63, 70
Mobil 292–3, 303
model cars 411–12
Moffat, Allan
  40th birthday 249–50
  50th birthday 338
  Allan Moffat Racing see Allan Moffat
    Racing
  ambition 21, 344, 416–17
  appearance money 199–200
  Australian citizenship 304
  career path, dual 344
  character 291, 373, 416–17
  childhood 26–8
  competition 332, 416
  concentration 163–4, 256
  crashes 288, 299–300
  driver training 386
  eyesight 28
  fame 409–12
  focus and dedication 8, 21, 54, 109,
    289, 374, 416
  'forceful' driving 76
  gambling 346–7
  gun for hire 343–68
  Holden Dealer Team 285, 291
  losing 69
  marriage 126, 399
  mechanical knowledge 30
  public relations 406–8
  retirement 303, 304, 338, 373–6
  salesman, career as 21, 22, 45–6
  school years 28, 30–2
  television commentator 403–6
  testing, repetitive 150
  university studies 34–5, 41
  winning 69, 82, 332
  women at the racetrack 382–3
  work ethic 289, 416–17
Moffat, Andrew 203, 305, 397, 400–1
Moffat, Arthur Wilfred 25–29, 34, 36,
  56, 82, 126, 185–6
Moffat, Evelyn Anne 25, 26–7, 29, 82,
  126, 185, 304
Moffat, Gordon 27, 29

Moffat, James 397, 399, 400–1, 409,
  414–15
Moffat, Leah 401
Moffat, Max 401
Moffat, Pauline (nee Dean) 14, 109, 115,
  125–6, 173, 178–80, 201–4, 249,
  258, 268, 397–400
Moffat, Terry 27
Molloy, Peter 232, 234
Monk, Maurie 37
Monterey Motorsports Reunion 410, 414
Monza 294–5, 312–14 , 318, 336, 347,
  356–61
Moore, Bud 97, 98, 112, 113, 115,
  120–1, 175
Morris, Bob 244, 261, 314, 364, 404
Morris, Milton 165–6
Moss, Stirling 38–9, 163, 234, 318
motorcycle Grand Prix 267–8
Mount Fuji Raceway 336
Mount Panorama 3, 7, 157, 260, 297,
  315, 320, 387, 315, 320
  anti-clockwise circuit 267
  experience at 330
  long-distance races 52
  rhythm and pace at 12
Mountain Straight 158, 273
Mueller, Lee 263
Muir, Brian 'Yogi' 70
Mulholland, Barry 142
Mulvihill, Tony 316
Murray's Corner 5, 263
Muscle Car Masters 413
Mustang see Ford Mustang

N
Nalder, Wes 40
NASCAR 93, 95, 112, 120, 225, 320,
  336
Nasser, Jac 161
Neerspasch, Jochen 350
Nelson, Barry 78–9, 80, 94–5, 98, 119
New Zealand 289, 301, 414
  Pukekohe track 290, 301
  Wellington 500 290
Newbold, Max 60
Nichols, Mel 162
Niedzwiedz, Klaus 319, 325, 327–30,
  333–7, 374–5, 378–9, 382–3
  Bathurst 1997 392–3
Nissan 267, 269, 272, 380
  GT-R 318, 378
  Skyline 299, 337

Noske, Mark 389–90
Noske, Tony 389
Nürburgring 365

O
O'Brien, Anne 383
O'Brien, Bill 245
O'Brien, Charlie 376–7, 382, 387
Okano, Takeshi 386
open-wheeler racing 231–2
Oran Park 121, 122, 124, 127, 132–3,
    156, 165, 183, 188, 224, 264, 265,
    271, 277, 323, 359, 407
Order of the British Empire (OBE)
    242–3

P
Palmer, Jim 59, 74–5, 77–8
Pan Am 211
Parsons, Ray 49–50, 54, 77, 84, 85, 86
Passino, Jacque 101, 110–12, 120, 121
Patrick, Scooter 54
Patterson, Bill 38, 141
Penske Chevrolet 96, 102
Penske, Roger 96–7
Percy, Win 378
Perkins, Larry 4, 277, 278, 289, 322,
    382, 408
Perron, Marshall 384–5, 386
Peters Corner, Sandown 62, 63
Peterson, Ronnie 40, 347, 348
Peugeot 264, 388
Philippines 350, 352–3
Phillip Island 35, 104, 140, 192, 227,
    240, 388
Porsche 47, 94, 233, 259, 264, 305, 343,
    349, 357, 361–8
  904 52, 54
  907 350
  911 91, 93, 178
  930 362
  934 362–3
  935 362, 364–5, 366, 367
  936 362, 366
Posey, Sam 347, 348–9
Powell, Les 71, 92
Pritchard, Keith 386
Prodrive 237
production cars, racing 165–6
Pryce, John 206–8, 209

Q
Quenet, Peter 63, 68, 69, 72–3, 77,
    83–5, 91–4, 97, 99, 414

R
Race Cam 403–4
Racing Car News 39–40, 127–8
Raeburn, John 63
Rahal, Bobby 366
rallying 237, 265–6
Ramirez, Pocholo 350–1
Raymond, Mike 403–6, 408
ReDEX 114
Redman, Brian 347, 348–50, 355, 368
Reid, Andrew 401
Repco-Brabham engineering works 147
Repco Round Australia Trial (1979) 305
Reventlow, Lance 38
Reynolds, George 35, 41, 59, 144
Richards, Dave 237
Richards, Jim 133, 269, 379, 382
Rindt, Jochen 79
River Rouge plant 99
Riverside International Raceway (RIR)
    86, 91, 365
Riverside Six Hour International Motor
    Sports Association 355
Road America 500 54
Road Atlanta 357
Roberts, Tony 155
Rodríguez, Pedro 57
rotary engine technology 252–4, 265,
    271
Rothmans 258, 259, 263, 279, 312, 315,
    316
Rothmans Tasman Series 233
Rouse, Andy 317, 319–21, 324
Rover factory team 283
Rude, Kathy 263
Rush 337
Russell, Geoff 63

S
Sachs, Eddie 22–3
Salvadori, Roy 415
San Enduro 332–3
Sandown 250 190–1
Sandown 400 224, 232, 259–60, 265–7,
    269
Sandown 500 239, 284, 285–6, 390
  1986 299
  1988 324–5

Sandown Raceway 8, 12, 38, 39, 41, 131, 185, 223, 243, 272, 275
CAMS Australian Gold Star Drivers championship 104
Craven Filter International Trophy for Formula Libre Cars 38
memorial service for Peter Brock 306
Six Hour Touring Car race 55, 57, 59, 61–3, 74, 157
Three Hour race 152
Saskatchewan 25
Saskatoon 25
Sawyer, John 103
Schenken, Tim 40, 68
Schuppan, Vern 233–5, 264
Sebring race track 348
4 Hour 79
12 Hour 50, 101, 102, 249, 347, 350
Sekiya, Masanori 337–8
Seton, Bo (Barry) 150, 154, 157, 158, 380
Seton, Glenn 380
Sharpeville Massacre 31
Shelby, Carol 175
Shelby Cobra 190, 242
Sheppard, John 240
Sime Darby 346
Skaife, Mark 306, 393
Skyline
    Mount Panorama Circuit 4, 153, 260
    Nissan see Nissan
Smith, Carroll 6, 10, 12, 13, 238
South Australian Touring Car Championship 78
Spa 24 Hour race 297–8, 312, 315, 319, 320, 377
Spartanburg 112, 115
Spence, Mike 24, 46, 47
Spirit of Goodwood Trophy 305
sponsorship 41, 114–15, 206–7, 209–12, 215, 228–9, 258, 315, 318, 326, 352, 360, 364, 375, 392
    commercial endorsements post-racing career 408–9
    tobacco 223, 238, 258, 380
Sports Car Club of America 47, 77
Sports Sedan Championship 354, 356
Stewart, Jackie 53, 59, 63
Stibbard, Ivan 191, 261
Stillwell, Bib 187
Stoddard, Chuck 54
Stuck, Hans-Joachim 347, 348–50, 355
Studebaker Lark 59

Stuyvesant, Peter 258, 275, 292
Sunday Telegraph 149
Super Falcon GTHO see GTHO
Super Falcon program 175–82
Supercars Australia 209
Surfers Paradise 127, 132, 141, 181, 186, 192, 199–200, 261, 264, 267, 276, 278
    Mazda crash, 1984 288
Surfers Paradise 300 229, 235, 261
Surtees, John 38
Suzuka circuit 337
Sydney Motor Sport Park 413
Symmons Plains 126, 177, 180, 184, 223, 276, 330

T
Targa Florio 59, 348
Targa Tasmania 305
Targa West 306
Tasman Series 76–7, 156
Tassin, Thierry 319
Tate, Ian 145
Taylor, Henry 50–1
Team Lotus 7, 21, 24, 46, 47, 49, 51, 53–4, 58, 69, 72, 73, 78, 238
Team Neptune 70, 78
tennis 202–3
Terada, Yojiro 264, 265
theft of race car 187–8
Theodoracopulos, Harry 355, 357
Theodore Racing 346
Thompson, Bryan 120
Thompson, Jerry 73
Thomson, Donald 207–8, 209
Thorn, Peter 95, 98, 116, 118, 119, 134, 151
Titus, Jerry 91, 101, 102
Toby Lee Series 156
Tooheys 326
Toploader 128–9
Torana 139, 156, 157, 162, 164, 167, 229
    A9X 8, 239
    L34 234
    XU1 156, 184, 345
Torino 159
Touring Car Entrants Group (TEGA) 209, 391
Toyo Kogyo 251
Toyota 256
    Supra 337

Trans Am series 77, 79, 81, 82, 84, 91–2, 94, 97, 98, 101, 110, 347, 351
  1968 350
  1969 112
  Mustang 353, 398
Trans-Canada Yellowhead Highway 25
Tresise, Rocky 69–70
Triumph TR2 33
Triumph TR3A 36, 37, 41, 49, 203, 348
Truesdale, Larry 96, 212
Tsuchiya, Keiichi 338
Tuckey, Bill 74, 163, 373, 376
Tullius, Bob 73–5
Turner, Al 12, 145–8, 150–6, 158–61, 164, 212, 221, 351, 397–8
  Super Falcon program 173–4, 177, 182

U
Unser, Al 415
US Grand Prix 348
US Road Racing Championship (USRRC) 21, 47, 51–2, 53, 77

V
V8 29–30, 91, 151, 165, 259, 264, 269, 379, 381
  Ford 70, 156, 194, 345, 380
  Holden 164, 167, 224, 313
  RX7 comparison 252, 255
  Supercars 390–1, 393, 400–1, 409
Vatanen, Ari 237
Vereeniging 29, 31
Victorian Short Circuit Championship 69, 76
Vietnam War 75–6, 221
Villeneuve, Gilles 337
Volkswagen Australia 34–5

W
Walburn, Ian 376, 380
Walker, Murray 405–6
Walkinshaw, Tom 278, 296, 298, 327, 404
Wanneroo 186, 263, 270, 276, 323

Ward, Max 166, 210
Ward, Rodger 59
Warwick Farm 125, 131, 189–90
Waterford Hills 73, 74, 84, 98, 413–14
Watkins Glen 21, 24, 46–7, 50, 53, 96, 97
Watson, Don 388
Webb, Mick 270, 297
Weber, Mark 250
Wellington 500 290
West, Des 155
Wheels 74
Whitmore, Sir John 24, 46, 50, 53, 73, 79
Wilkinson, Garry 404, 407
Williamson, Peter 262
Willing, Warren 268
Willmington, Garry 276
Wilson, Andrew 215
Wilson, Ben 215
Wilson, Max 141
windscreen
  Plexiglas® 61
  'safety' 61
Windsor engine 156, 158
Winton Raceway 305, 400
Woelders, Jan 141
Woodfield, Vince 78–9, 80, 94
World F1 Championship 72
World Touring Car Championship (WTCC) 287, 301, 312–15, 316, 321, 326
  1987 283–4, 288
Wright, Jerry 255, 256

Y
Yamamoto, Kenichi 255, 258, 259
Yip, Teddy 346, 415
Yorino, Takashi 264, 265
You Yangs test track 71, 150, 156
Youl, Gavin 177
Youl, John 177
Young, Trevor 411–12
Yunick, Smokey 112